INHIBITED

INHIBITED

Unmasking Yourself and Owning Who You Are

FORGIVENESS
PROMISES
VALUES
CONFIDENCE
ON MY OWN ACCORD

Leaving behind my self-un-consciousness, stepping into my self-assurances, regaining my self-reliance, claiming back my self-worth; not just walking into it but owning it!

PAMELA L STAPLES

XULON PRESS

Xulon Press
2301 Lucien Way #415
Maitland, FL 32751
407.339.4217
www.xulonpress.com

© 2023 by Pamela L Staples

All rights reserved solely by the author. The author guarantees all contents are original and do not infringe upon the legal rights of any other person or work. No part of this book may be reproduced in any form without the permission of the author.

Due to the changing nature of the Internet, if there are any web addresses, links, or URLs included in this manuscript, these may have been altered and may no longer be accessible. The views and opinions shared in this book belong solely to the author and do not necessarily reflect those of the publisher. The publisher therefore disclaims responsibility for the views or opinions expressed within the work.

Unless otherwise indicated, Scripture quotations taken from the King James Version (KJV)–*public domain*. Scripture quotations taken from the Holy Bible, New International Version (NIV). Copyright © 1973, 1978, 1984, 2011 by Biblica, Inc.™. Used by permission. All rights reserved. Scripture quotations taken from the English Standard Version (ESV). Copyright © 2001 by Crossway, a publishing ministry of Good News Publishers. Used by permission. All rights reserved. Scripture quotations taken from the Amplified Bible (AMP). Copyright © 1954, 1958, 1962, 1964, 1965, 1987 by The Lockman Foundation. Used by permission. All rights reserved.

Paperback ISBN-13: 978-1-66286-896-2
Ebook ISBN-13: 978-1-66286-897-9

I am anew

Inhibited

Unmasking Yourself and Owning Who You Are

The Beginning of Our Walk Toward Self-Fulfillment!

All Scripture is breathed out by God and profitable for teaching, for reproof, for correction, and for training in righteousness, so that the servant of God may be thoroughly equipped for every good work. (2 Timothy 3:16)

Staples Treasures

Inhibited!

Inhibited, unable to act in a relaxed and natural way because of self-consciousness or mental restraint. To prohibit from doing something. To hold in check. To shy away from.

My actions now have reaction: With Christ I am no longer inhibited!
It's time for change! Unmask yourself and own who you are!

A Time for Everything

There is a time for everything,
and a season for every activity under the heavens:
a time to be born and a time to die,
a time to plant and a time to uproot,
a time to kill and a time to heal,
a time to tear down and a time to build,
a time to weep and a time to laugh,
a time to mourn and a time to dance,
a time to scatter stones and a time to gather them,
a time to embrace and a time to refrain from embracing,
a time to search and a time to give up,
a time to keep and a time to throw away,
a time to tear and a time to mend,
a time to be silent and a time to speak,
a time to love and a time to hate,
a time for war and a time for peace.

(Ecclesiastes 3:3–8)

Inhibited!

It's time to break out of my mental detainment, gaining control of the encumbrance of my spirit.

When your spirit feels burdened, hindered, or inoperable, it's time for a change? For an unmasking!

Table of Contents

Preamble..xiii

A. Caricaturist Characteristics—Godly Attributes............. 1
    I.   A Corruptible Spirit—Jezebel Spirit................. 17
    II.   Reflections of Jealousy—Hagar Spirits............... 31
    III. Mental Seduction—12-Step Program 40
    IV.   Extravagantly Rare—Virtuous Women—Ruth Spirits... 157

B. Integrated Integrity—Does Your Reputation Precede You?.. 165
    I.   Betrayer—Judas 166
    II.   Negative—Esau 186
    III. Judgmental—The Pharisees............................190
    IV.   Bitterness—Saul.....................................202

C. Pleasingly Powerful—The Fruit of the Spirit............. 209
    I.   Love—Love Ourselves as Christ Loves Us 210
    II.   Joy—Happiness Within Ourselves.................217
    III. Peace—Mind and Body, Spirit and Soul...........220
    IV.   Longsuffering—Health and Wellness 225
    V.   Gentleness—Patience (Family time) 231
    VI.   Goodness—Reach Out and Lean On One Another ...235
    VII. Faith—Trusting One Another 239
    VIII. Meekness—Power Under Control 244
    IX.   Temperance—Self-Restraint ... Forgiveness 248

TRIBUTES

To my loving children: Keith, Darius, Jasmine. To my stepchildren: Curtis Jr., Cornelius, Christina, and my precious grandchildren: Ariya, Kura, Kynnedi, Aleena, Kayden, Kaliyah, Elijah, Curtis III, Laila, K'Torah, Londyn and Chase. . To my belated parents: Ellis and Virgie (RIP), my sisters: Aliesa (RIP), Patrice, Crystal, and Rayvetta; my brothers: Joseph, Harry, and Hubert. To my belated grandparents: Ben and Lizzie (RIP), Ellis Sr. and Josie (RIP), and Ivory and Thelma Cobbs (RIP). to my daughters-in-law: Jamila, Jocelyn, and Taylor and my son-in-law Benjamin. To my aunts, uncles, nieces, nephews, cousins, stepparents, stepbrothers, stepsisters, and all my spiritual family and supporters: I love you all.

Thank you all for being my inspiration. You all challenged me in some way, shape, form, or fashion to want to change my life for the better and gain more patience and love in my heart. You've helped me to learn that my faith and trust in God was necessary in every area of my life—family, friends, finances, and career—in everything! I love you all very much. God granted me grace and unmerited favor and I am truly grateful! He deserves the glory, not me!

To my husband Curtis Sr., thank you for not being selfish with our love and allowing me time with the Lord to write His will. You've supported me in owning and operating a business for over thirty years. You have allowed God to show you how to become not only my husband, but my pastor, my friend, and my perpetual love. You've directed and steered our family professionally and spiritually; through the good and bad we still sought your lead, all while nurturing our thirty-one years of marital bliss you gave us your greatest moments.

God united us not only as partners in marriage and business, but He inspired us to found The Call Worship Center Church together. Through the obedience, trust, and faith in our Lord God and His Word we are walking in our calling on one accord. I am so proud of the man God has made you, though I know I sometime take the credit for that! God knows my heart and to Him we owe it all! You have helped me to become more Christ-centered by setting the example inside and outside of our home. It wasn't always a vibrant or steady walk, but we stayed rooted and grounded in the love of Jesus who taught us how to exhibit His same agape love. I love, respect, and cherish you very much. To God be the glory for all He has done! Amen!

I would also like to thank my family and friends of The Call Worship Center Church for trusting me with your spiritual needs and allowing God to speak through me into your spirits. His Word is the only one that truly matters!

I'm extremely grateful for my friends and family at New Mission Missionary Baptist Church for helping mem and my family to grow up in the Word through extensive training and biblical preparation.

I'm grateful to our first pastor, Dr. Robert Smith Jr., who joined me and my husband as a married couple over thirty years ago and for all his words of wisdom, and to Pastor Tracy E. Ventus, our second pastor, who spiritually fed our family for fifteen years. You continue to spiritually feed into our family unto this day. You have poured more into our family, than any pastoral duties require, and we will forever be grateful for you and your love for our family! Thank you from the bottom of my heart!

Preamble

Forgiving yourself and others is crucial in gaining your truths.

People who are searching for their own truth have to begin by acknowledging the sinful nature of man. We have to search for an understanding of what sin is, where it comes from, who sins, what the consequences of sin are, and what the solution for sin is. Sin is about more than the bad things that we do; it is also about those things that we should be doing that we don't do. It's what we think and the attitudes that we have that are against God's will.

Sin is doing what I want to do, my own way, whenever I want to do it, rather than doing what God would have me to do and doing it His way. In other words, sin is when we act like we're our own god instead of letting God be our God and His Word be our guide. Sin has us believing that when we make bad decisions or have bad thoughts, we don't have to do what we're supposed to do to correct it. Although we fully understand what it means to sin, we choose to still partake in its gratification.

When will we come to the knowledge that sin is real, that sin is more than an issue of immoral behavior, that it is an act of disobedience against God? It's essential that we get this revelation and accept that we have inadequacies, in order to prevent its reoccurrences. Our behaviors cause us to curse, mistrust, abuse, lie, reject, and betray one another.

Sin reflects the things we allow to touch our hearts and we fall in tune with it being good and acceptable when it truly isn't! Our behaviors cannot be corrected without correcting our sin problem, which means that we need to repent about some things. True repentance is less about our specific actions and more about our heart attitude that gives rise to our actions causing us to become sinful. If we don't seek God for correction, we will not overcome.

There are things that our actions will reveal about what's in our hearts. If you stop speaking to someone just because someone else said so, and allow bad things about them to be fed to you, are you committing sin?

What about our outward actions, our eruptions, they are not so much the sin, as much the underlying heart attitude is, but the issue is our reactions, our expressions that gives rise to the situations. Whatever is in your heart that causes an unwarranted up rise out of you is your sin source. The actions associated to your sins are what follow! One's sinful nature causes one to be sinful! We need forgiveness, repentance, and to be restored back to the origin God has purposed for us!

Foundations must be set in balance that we are able to work at overcoming our heart issues, taming our outward actions, and controlling our heart's attitude. It starts with our obedience to God the Father, our earthly fathers, our mothers, our grandmothers, our grandfathers, our teachers, and other adult authorities. Having no integrity or respect for authority separates us from God, who commands us to honor our parents that our days may be long. A level of appreciation for authority is imperative to inhibited lives. We must get past a stunted emotional life setting to reveal what is embedded in our hearts, so that we can set proper foundational healing.

God loves us, but He hates our sin. He seeks our faithfulness to give us better lives. He wants us to follow His ways, relinquish our own authority, to obey His command and His rules which lead to a more fulfilling future. Healing will occur once we understand that we carry filth in our hearts. The Holy Bible says. *"Ask, and it shall be given you, seek, and ye shall find, knock, and it shall be opened unto you: For every one that asketh, receiveth; and he that seeketh, findeth; and to him that knocketh it shall be opened"* (Matt. 7:7–8 KJV). But until then we have to make ourselves available to be spiritually poured into. Seeds can't grow if there's no planting, watering, or nurturing!

Our sincerity about changing our sinful nature starts by asking a question, and the answer to our question is the measure of our faithfulness. Do we want to be better equipped? Are you planting bad seeds that won't produce a harvest or good seeds planted in good soil? *Do not be deceived: God cannot be mocked. A man reaps what he sows"* (Gal. 6:7 NIV). Do we believe that there's nothing too hard for God? Where we plant will show if we're mature in spirit or are merely babes still on milk.

We can ask God to heal us, restore us, remove anything that is not of Him, to make us whole. We can even ask for forgiveness for ourselves and others if we so choose. Then we can work at taming our outward expressions targeted at others when we have a momentary relapse.

Once we understand this concept, God's forgiveness of ourselves and others can start to transpire and materialize in our lives! God wants to shape our faith and help start the healing process. Sometimes all we need to say is

Lord forgive me of my sins and my trespasses, I was wrong, I repent and ask for your forgiveness. I believe you are God, and your son is Jesus who died for my sins and rose with all power to someday return for me.

Lord, please grant me the strength to forgive myself and others, help me to do so willingly in love, that my trespasses shall be forgiven of you. I need help in this area of my life, so I ask of you Lord, that I may receive and find what I am seeking through you and Lord now that I have knocked and partitioned unto you for your divine guidance, please open my eyes to see your vision and not my own sight, open my heart to feel your love and my ears to hear your voice when you reply. Amen.

How can you forgive others if you feel no forgiveness toward yourself? When you forgive yourself, you'll be able to forgive others for their transgressions against you. apostle Paul wrote, *"Be kind and compassionate to one another, forgiving each other, just as in Christ God forgave you"* (Eph. 4:32 NIV). In the Old Testament, the psalmist says, *"You are forgiving and good, O Lord, abounding in love to all who call to you"* (Ps. 86:5 NIV). And Luke's gospels say this, *"Judge not, and ye shall not be judged: condemn not, and ye shall not be condemned: forgive, and ye shall be forgiven"* (Luke 6:37 KJV).

If healing is what we desire, then it can only come through the power of forgiveness! It is imperative that we forgive one another and ourselves. This is a hard pill to swallow especially considering how harshly some crimes were committed against us and to us, but we must understand that forgiving others is for our personal growth (through forgiveness, we are gaining back our power). Our accusers, nor our abusers, no longer can control our responses unless we allow them.

Tell yourself: I have been delivered. I forgive you, because I am forgiven. My forgiving doesn't mean I have forgotten; it just means that I have chosen to forgive without the initial investment of anger, bitterness, resentfulness, or revenge. I am freeing up myself by forgiving. One of Les Brown inspired life quotes says "it frees up your power, heals your body, mind and spirit. Forgiveness opens up a pathway to a new place of peace where you can persist despite what happened to you."

Now, I am ready to start focusing on redirecting my pain, anger, bitterness, and my guilt. By forgiving myself I am acknowledging it wasn't all my fault, I had no control over some of the mishaps in my life. I am sorry I allowed them to control me and caused me to act out emotionally. I have been forgiven and I forgive you! This is for your own benefit and no one else's, that you may mature in Christ and live peacefully. No one can hold you bound to your mistakes and chain you to your circumstances once you have been cleansed by the blood of Jesus.

In many cases, incidents in our lives are embedded in our subconscious and Satan will take every opportunity to use our unforgiveness to keep us heavy ladened. These events are always on our mind, we can't get past them, they affect our homes, careers, even day. We can't function without it overtaking our thinking. ...en we allow Satan to live in our conscious space, he tries to claim our mental freedom.

Claim it back singing: I am free, free, free there's nothing holding me, because with Jesus I am free, free, free—Satan, you can't have me—I have been set free! Again, the Bible says, *"But now that you have been set free from sin and have become slaves of God, the benefit you reap leads to holiness, and the result is eternal life. For the wages of sin is death, but the gift of God is eternal life in Christ Jesus our Lord"* (Rom. 6:22–23 NIV).

Sometimes forgiveness must start with sitting down and seeking the counsel of professionals, laying back on a couch in discussion, or even being temporarily admitted into recovery. God can bring you out of your pain and heal you of all offenses if you will release them, but sometimes other avenues might be necessary as well to help you manage your discomfort! Don't be ashamed to seek expert guidance when necessary!

Ask God to direct you and help you to recover so that you can forgive yourself to grow toward forgiveness of others! With Christ all things are possible! One of my former employees, Ms. Camille King, mentioned in an Instagram post "My affirmation today is that there is nothing about me that is inadequate. I am whole. I am enough. I am adequate in every area." This is coming from a woman who endured pain her entire life, underwent several bypass surgeries, and then finally her healing and transformation came! I was blessed to be a witness to how God brought her out and I couldn't leave her out of *Inhibited,* because she was never a quitter, even in her battle for life. I am amazed at how she overcame and the example of greatness in women like her.

SESSION ONE
A. CARICATURIST CHARACTERISTICS

Are you demonstrating the attributes of God?

I remember hearing Priscilla Shirer speaking on her network and she said something that summarized what we're breaking down in *Inhibited*; she said

You are not your behavior, you are not your struggle, you are not your worst mistake, you are not your past, you are not what has been done to you; those things might be what you have experienced, but that's not who you are. . . . [A]ll of us have to realize that there is a difference between where you've been, and what you've done, and what has happened to you, and who you are. Your significance is not rooted in those things. Your significance, and value has already been established, by God. You are who your Father says you are, no matter what has happened to you.

Sometimes, our characters become distorted, we forget who we are or maybe we're struggling with learning about the person we never knew! A Caricaturist Character is a distortion of the character of who we truly are. In terms of our relationship to Christ, our caricature shows defects, or peculiarities, in us: a trait, a manner, a characteristic, or a habit that is odd or unusual in our walk with Christ. We must not focus on these things or they might become exaggerated by us or others in the midst of our struggles.

When someone doesn't understand you, they will try to portray your Christianity as a joke, as a picture of ridiculous character flaws, even if they don't agree with your views; you shouldn't follow suit just to get alone. If you find yourself joking around about things concerning your father God that should be taken to heart seriously, remember He already established your significance in Him; nothing outweighs that. Don't downplay your role as a Christian, it will magnify the flaws to your image. Demonstrate godly attributes at all times.

Some godly people display many outward functions of distortion, especially when they live in darkness. Consider this scripture, *"But you are a chosen people, a royal priesthood, a holy nation, God's special possession, that you may declare the praises of him who called you out of darkness into his wonderful light"* (1 Peter 2:9 NIV). You can be holy and sanctified and still be in a dark place. Our distortions occur when we go dim—when our spirits are disrupted by the many negative life choices we encounter that have not been rectified with God—so we find ourselves moving closer to our darkness, rather than to our lights.

Not all of the negative choices you have encountered are by choice, so the moment you have a way out, make sure you take it. The darkness formed in life could become so familiar that adapting to its surroundings is easy. Keeping on our lights, is like having on the bright lights in your car; you know the road is dark, the streets aren't clear, it's slippery, so you point yourself toward His wonderful light, and that drives you away from some of those dark places. When they start feeling comfortable it's because you're choosing more of them, and less of who has called you out of them! Be the light!

Something in your life has happened or may have been done to or possibly said about you that has made you feel insignificant! Like at some point in your life you'd dimmed, chipped, or cracked your bulb and you were ready to pop; instead, you gathered yourself together, and replaced the broken pieces, so that you wouldn't get stuck in your darkness! Up until then you were bound to it, therefore the decision you made to rid yourself of the people, places, and things that had blinded you, that had held you in bondage with their magnetic vibes that once were hindering how you were operating as the salt of the earth, changed.

Salt adds favor to whatever it is added to. Therefore, it's up to you to add the favor to everything you touch. You are the extra kick needed in order for the places you were put in, to become the perfect seasoning! The perfect touch! You are the perfection of your surroundings! Jesus is the light of the world and light and dark cannot dwell in the same place. We have been called out of darkness into His marvelous light, you can't have both! The Holy Bible encourages us to choose for yourselves this day whom you will serve in Joshua 24:15 (NIV). If not protected, the light beaming inside of us will first give off flickers just like a lightbulb right before it goes out. The flickering is warning us that it's about to blow out or even pop, and if we don't give attention to the threat, it might be too late. You might not be able to just put in a new bulb and turn the light back on; the lamp might be broken to the point where it can never be fixed, just replaced.

When we've been in darkness too long, we start to function like people roaming within the night, just living in a dark place! We don't operate like who we are; we are not our behaviors, not our struggles, not our worst mistake, not our past, not even what has happened to us. Are we going to allow our circumstances to put us in a category unpleasing to God? We tend to forget that we are not our experiences, so we will start to act like nightlife type of people, people who are willing to let themselves be nighttime pieces, but never a daytime mate. We shouldn't get offended, that's why God wants us shining in the light, because some of us love the acts of darkness.

If you don't trust yourself to live with value and significance, then you might need to discontinue in some of your night activities. Having a Caricaturist Character is a distortion of the character who we truly are to Christ, and it can sometimes cause us to live recklessly, instead of remaining calm and orderly; even some orderly people are reckless too! I am talking about those of us whose distorted functioning have become regular accepted habits.

When we have tolerated way too much of our own mess and now, we have begun to believe, it's the norm! Our standards have lowered, our expectations are minimal, because the company we keep isn't always with the people who have our best interest, and our lights will become dimmer as a result of our choices! Dimmer switches are put in place to either turn up our lights are to turn them down, but they don't intermingle! Be careful who you allow in your circle! Do they add light or so they keep dimming yours?

> *The character of Jesus from the beginning was of pure love for He was serving, aiding and providing; proving that His character didn't go dim, but it manifested into teaching, preaching, and restoring. He became everything that He expects us to rise up and mature into as well. The love He gave before long, became safeguarding, rectifying, and disciplining for His people, nothing was ever compromised!*

What will you do with your light?

We are the people Jesus came to correct, restore, and save from extinction. We are the people Jesus came to save from darkness. We are the people Jesus loved before we ever knew what love was. We are the people Jesus knew couldn't make it in their weaken state. We are His chosen-elect! He purposely healed us in our weakened state. He purposely restored us to His own although our stubborn characters still rebuked His correction. He purposely gave us restoration and life transformation. We cannot negotiate with our darkness over His light! It's Satan or Jesus; no other way! I pray that you will choose Jesus!

Jesus's infinite love will begin to transition your characters, recreating His people to be the light of the world; restoring them whole; rectifying them back to Himself by making them His disciples with the ability to walk upright, speak profoundly, and assume a new identity in him. Satan can only create the havoc, cause more distortion, and keep you as a partaker in his scheme. It's up to you to break the cycle.

T.D. Jakes, said in a message on Facebook, "Satan cannot create, he can only imitate." He can only imitate the things in our lives that we are seeking after, making our way appear to be a better choice. He imitates the beauty of Christ with the tackiness of himself. He will put a pretty picture of the desires of our hearts and dangle the words "available" all over it, hoping you're seeking after self-fulfillment and buy into it. He'll put everything we're chasing after right in front of us with a pretty bow on top.

All the things he has plotted to kill, steal, and destroy you with suddenly will look like gold! He makes it appealing to the eye gates and ear waves hoping for a catch. Now, what you see and hear looks realistic! Don't let him reel you in! Don't take the bait. Declare your liberation in every area of your weaknesses, before it becomes your god (small *g*). Be fishermen for Jesus, not bait for the devil's use.

Declare and decree,

I am taking back all that the devil stole from me; my love, my marriage, my health, my career, my dignity, my children, my healthy relationships, my grandchildren, my finances, my emotional being; and I cancel every plot, scheme, or plan of attack devised against me. I speak life into every dead situation and prophetically claim the blessings of Abraham into everything and everyone attached to my life. I have been redeemed by the blood of the lamb and I declare and decree that my life will never be the same again.

Say to the Lord,

Let your perfect will be done and proclaimed in my heart that I may line up according to your will as I come to recognize your moves of glory on my life. May I clearly see your desires and petitions granted in my spiritual maturing. Give me a fresh revelation that's designed just for me to rack up all the goodness of who you are that I may live my life as though I've already been given a concrete revelation of the details of my life's circumstances and I have prevailed!

When you find His truths, make the essential rectifications to seal the cracks and watch God open the doors He has allowed to close in your lives! Sometimes, God allows doors to close for our own good. Some of them we are not ready to have opened just yet. Some doors slam shut, while others sway back and forth. When they sway, it allows us time to push out and bring in! Some people need to go and some new people have to come in that we may evolve.

When a door sits open too long anything might come in that you want to stay out, so let God open and close the ones He chooses. In some cases, there are people who are not ready for the swaying, because they keep trying to prop the door open when God keeps trying to shut it!

Some of us can handle simple instructions, but there are times when we need some tougher, firmer ones, otherwise we won't listen! Being stubborn can block blessings! We need to be planted in the house of God, so that we can grow. When we expand our relationship with Christ, we develop thicker skin.

Correction mandates our decision to be women of faith and not emotionally unavailable in character, to be a willing vessel, a queen installed upon the throne by her savior, not an unpredictable or unstable person. Align your character with God's, before you speak against His will and follow pagan gods over Yahweh!

When your character goes into feeling mode, being emotionally unstable, having unhealthy moment-by-moment plays of your life, that's when you are liable to do, say, or act any way you feel at that moment. You ought to hunger and thirst after God, so that you can concur and tame your desire to be always in control of everything and everybody. Emotional people are people who respond before they consider the effects of their response to the reaction.

Some of us need the two-second rule that drivers follow in traffic to maintain a safe trailing distance at any speed: they follow two cars distance to be able to have time to break in an emergency. If your mouth flares off instantly you need to stay at a safe distance to maintain how you trail people. Count "one," "two," and then speak! Michael Johnson said, "Prayer routinely manages to move mountains, so imagine what kind of damages they can do to that little storm that you are currently going through!" Pray your way through and trust that prayer works!

It's extremely important that we maintain a conscious awareness of times when we are in our "feelings" mode, because our feelings can have an emotional connection to a situation, person, place, or thing that will misrepresent the God in us. We cannot be on an emotional roller coaster and expect God to bless our mouths nor our behavior.

Recognizing your spiritual challenge, before your emotions carry you away will save you many repeat offenses, from the occurrences. Think before you respond. When you respond, then think, that's when people tend to believe you are what you preach good or bad! Don't be counted out because you abruptly blurted out an emotionally charged response! Tamara Jenkins a known comedian said in one of her acts, "[D]on't let nobody count you out, if they counted you out, they can't count." You are the one that counts!

When you're in an emotional state and feel out of control regain your power by walking away, petition God in prayer, seek a prayer partner to hold you accountable until you're able to remain faithful, as a humble servant, without having repercussions. Start to get direction in understanding why you are in this uncomfortable way and slowly work your way back out of it, the goal is always to get back on the course! As long as you reclaim your control over all the situations coming up against who you are, you're learning the difference between where you've been and what you've done and what has happened to you and who you really are in Christ. These circumstances are God's way of getting you where He needs you to get to, so He can help you spiritually mature by correcting your natural views and aligning you to His spiritual ones.

When assessing your character traits, you must ask yourself "What kind of person am I?" Seek self-awareness of who you really are and work at becoming who you want to be. It can happen if you put the conscience effort into gaining an understanding of who am I and ask yourself,

"Am I... of a corruptible spirit, like Jezebel?"

"Am I... envious, like Hagar?"

"Am I... seductive, like Potiphar's wife?" or

"Am I... virtuous, like Ruth?"

This is a victorious moment when you are willing to ask, seek, and knock your way to finding the answers to your dark questions, all while encountering the reasons why you have so many open doors. There are many answers to our questions found in God's Word.

The answer to the question "Who am I?" should remind you, that you are a Christ-produced product. Regardless of your past, that is who you are! By processing the events of your "flesh," you are curing your soul of what's inoperative like a cancer to the spirit. That process will produce larger scar tissue in a person's heart by making them believe they are less than who God says that they are in their spirits. He said I am fearfully and wonderfully made, but have I processed that in my spirit?

When God heals us of the battles of our minds and our lingering scars, just let them deteriorate! Let them diminish! Instead of battling with evil, Give thanks! Show gratitude! Be grateful! Focus your attention on the measure of your faith that you have received; for you survived, you persevered, you're healed, and there's no looking back. The enemy would have us focused on the scars instead of the healing that took place. Psalm 9:9 (NLT) says, **"The LORD is a shelter for the oppressed, a refuge in times of trouble".** *He will protect you when you're under attack.*

You see, your battles are now in the hands of the Lord, and in His hands all things are made new! The hand of God is upon you and you are never going to be who you once were with the Lord touching your life. His Word says, **Therefore I say to you, whatever things you ask when you pray, believe that you receive** *them,* **and you will have** *them. (Mark 11:24 NKJV)* In believing, your change is coming, the scars of your past cannot control how you feel any longer; you might still have scar tissue, but you've been healed! You are no longer inhibited to your past! You are no longer inhibited to your behavior! You are no longer inhibited to your mistakes! You are no longer inhibited by your struggles! You are no longer inhibited by the things you have done!

We are a forever-changing, socially accepted, well-crafted, beautifully created being, all mixed up together, and our characters will become reflections of a fake imitation of life if we don't believe in who we are in the Lord. Some of us live lives without consequences, lives without understanding, instead of living by Christ's design, because we're not sure where we fit. God designed us for a specific purpose that He would want us to walk in and be anchored into. *This I say then, Walk in the Spirit, and ye shall not fulfil the lust of the flesh"* (Gal. 5:16 KJV).

Your soul must be anchored in the Lord and by faith you must choose to live responsibly together as one soul united to Christ. When you don't really know what you're called to do you should continue going to God and seeking for answers. We must release the clouds of mistakes and negativity that's hovering over our existence and impeding and distorting our characters and regain the use of the power of Christ that lies within us. When you keep on pressing through with Christ, your cloudy days will soon fade away and you will eventually realize that by creating you God has given you value, and He adds all the significance your life will ever need.

Your mistakes that have become a problem will become less and your faith will grow stronger as a result of you overcoming your predicaments. Every situation will not fade away, but you'll be able to cope much better than before.

Bishop Hilliard said in one of his sermons on YouTube that there are four facts every believer needs to know about problems. "Your attitude toward your problem defines your level of success, solving your problems defines the limitations of your potential, your problems uncover your flaws, in a plan that might lead to failure, and your problems are a wake-up call to your Divine creativity." We all have problems, but our problems shouldn't have us!

Our characters should never reflect a drive-by-night presence that demonstrates a lack of morals or dignity for others or ourselves. Our characters should show that we have made an investment in our self-worth and our self-esteem as people who are walking as men and women of faith living out the blessings of God as He intended.

In this walk with Christ, it's crucial to talk to Him daily through our prayers, asking Jim to reveal to us our strengths and weaknesses, that we may see who we are, and work toward earnestly walking in His grace to become models of His goodness. Models of Christ will seek only Him for approval not the approval from others. In Him your character will be revealed. It's all for His love and for His divine glory. The affirmation of God is what allows us to put aside our limitations and grab ahold of His glorification and propel ourselves ahead by faith.

Isolating with Christ can reveal something about yourself that needs work. How do you treat people, your family, your friends? When you isolate even if just for a little while, that's where God can begin to reveal! In your fasting phase God is made alive. That's the place where He can reveal the real you! He can reveal the necessities of a weary soul! He can reveal His desires and even His concerns. If you don't like the revelation, if what you see causes you to wonder about some things in your life, then how do you think God feels about it? Does He wonder, how can that person in the shadow change? It's time to take your prayers into your prayer closet and ask the Lord for revelation.

How does your season of isolation become a season of revelation? First, you can start by repenting! Confess your faults and flaws! Next, you must turn away from the people, places, and things the man in the mirror craves, surrender your distractions to Christ. Then, believe! God promises us that He will make us new men and women and now that the distractions are gone, He can!

Now that the distractions at work are gone, now that the clubs and sports bars are unattractive, the bad relationships are over, the gambling is under submission, the family quarreling has ceased, now you can put your sights on God. Now you can stop playing with God and give Him the stuff that's holding you hostage so you can be set free. God sometimes must slow us down, so we can see Him, and to help us see ourselves as we really are! Even, saved, sanctified, Holy Ghost filled folks get distracted and must repent! Then a change in you can take place!

Change takes place when we put our focus on pleasing God and doing our best to love ourselves as He does! How we appear to others is only partially important. We reflect God's love for us when we have a greater love for ourselves and respect for how Christ sees us. That's the love we want others to see, His godly appearance in us. But don't trust what they see, their sight might be distorted too. God gives us His vision to rely on. People don't see you as Christ does, because they can't see themselves as He does, so why should you expect them to see you clearly.

We want man to see the goodness of Jesus and His character of love shinning in us, but the sincerity God sees in our hearts is what's relevant. Reveal how important God is in your life, not because you need anyone to approve the God in your life, but because you want them to see how He has changed your life.

Everyone should ask themselves, "Do I have godly morals, a Christlike attitude, a warm loving personality?" "Am I filled with the joy of the Lord or am I just another version of me where it doesn't matter what kind of attitude or lifestyle I may or may not have?" No one should ever want to remain the same when there's room for growth. Your change is for you and must come forth, so that you can grow closer to God. Are you pleased with what you see? If you said no, then ask, seek, and petition God into your life. He's waiting on you! We all have room for improvement!

Morality and ethics must match your confessed level of Christianity. If I profess Christ, am I wearing Christ? What's my makeup, how many masks cover my confession? Am I evenly covered or showing imperfections? Do I have a radiant glow, a clean fresh look of confidence in the Lord? Don't just ask yourself these questions without seeking God to find out the answers for yourself! Get to know your own character traits! You should continually ask self-seeking, self-improving questions in order to evaluate areas in your lives that need improvement and to seek fundamental growth in your development. Smears are on us all, but what are we all going to do about it?

When you ask "What makes me different from all the rest; what makes me stand out, sets me apart from everybody else?" God will answer. When you ask questions, always be sure you're keeping in mind that we are all of the same body with different members, and if God answers one, He'll answer the other. God designed us to fit together in the body of Christ with our differences.

We all need to understand our own makeup and why our masks are so much heavier or lighter than others. Individually, we need to know why we are showing blemishes, open sores, even why we are bleeding out. How do I get cleansed of my character flaws? Everyone has their own cross to bear, so go to God for His help with your own!

People sometimes pretend they have it all together, but deep down, do they? Is there a negative, lonely, insecure, isolated me deep inside just waiting to erupt? You need to find out what's behind the masks and understand that this really is you!

Somebody has to say, I'm a person whose love for herself has an impersonal, dead and useless appeal, until it has been revealed and dealt with; it's killing you from the inside out. When I learned how to personally seek God's face and allowed Him to reveal Himself to me, that was the moment when He placed this song in my heart, and I penned it to His glory.

My Esteemed / My Redeemed

Chorus:

Since you went away, I am always seeking

Searching my soul, Looking for my love

Just to find your face, Since you've gone away

Gone away . . . from me

I search for you, For more of thee

Just to hear your voice, Is all I Need

I know someday we'll meet again

That's why I can forever say . . . you are my esteemed . . . yes you are, you are my redeemed

Verse 1:

    My life has changed

    My Esteemed Love has been declared . . . My Redeemed

    There's no more pain

    No greater love

    No Savior more worthy than my Lord Jesus

    No other above thee . . . You are My Savior, My God

    You are My Esteemed . . . You are My Redeemed

[Repeat Chorus]

Verse 2:

    I am wonderfully made

    Exquisitely changed

    Totally free

    The essence of your love . . . Empowers Me

    You searched my heart

    Made It To be . . . More Like Thee

    You Warmed my Spirit

And Your Unfailing Love

Has captured me

You CALLED and I ANSWERED... YES, MY, LORD

My Soul has been . . . Esteemed . . . Oh . . . My Soul has been . . . Redeemed!

My Savior, My-Esteemed, My Savior, My-Redeemed (repeat)

[Repeat Chorus]

Vamp

You Are . . . Oh...You are

You Are . . . My Esteemed

YES, YOU ARE . . . OH . . . YES YOU ARE!

You Are . . . My Redeemed

Yes . . . You Are . . . Oh . . . Yes You Are

You Are . . . My Esteemed

Yes YOU ARE . . . Oh . . . Yes YOU ARE

You Are . . . My Redeemed

Inhibited

Oh How ... Oh How ... Oh, How I love thee

I'm Declaring ... It ... I'm Proclaiming ... It

Yes ... You Are ... Oh ... Yes ... You Are

You are ... My Esteemed / My Redeemed

YES, YOU ARE ... OH ... YES YOU ARE

You are ... My Esteemed, My Redeemed

OH ... YES YOU ARE! Written by Pamela L. Staples

I

A CORRUPTIBLE SPIRIT– JEZEBEL SPIRIT

When you're alone what does your spirit really say about others?

Many of you might know someone who's hard to be friendly with, because of how they treat people. You're not used to being spoken to loudly, abruptly, forcefully, and they tend to make you want to step out of character!

Not all people have the capability to stand down when they're being attacked verbally and their enemy stands within feet of them. Standing down in the face of criticism coming at you when you're trying your best to flee it, isn't an easy thing for most people to do, let alone deal with it without retaliation. When you have a Jezebel spirit, you are a complicated human being and, in most cases, you already know your personalities. This type of person enjoys being with people of like-minded character who love being complicated as well!

Although the Bible doesn't use the term Jezebel spirit as we do, it does mention a lot about the queen named Jezebel and her traits. Many people who have volunteered their opinions about what contributes to having a Jezebel spirit. It's been said that having a Jezebel spirit can be anything and everything from sexual looseness in a woman to the teaching of false doctrine. In this session we're going to discuss a version of the Jezebel spirit a woman can!

In the Holy Bible, it teaches who Jezebel was and what kind of spirit she displayed. Here's a little background summary. You know spiders spin webs that catch prey so they can suck the life out of it, sometimes while it's still alive. Well, let's talk about the web of Jezebel. "This was a woman born as the daughter of Ethbaal who was king of Tyre/Sidon, and also priest of the cult Baal." Stay with me, it gets worse. Ethbaal was a repulsive false god, rich and filled of cruelty, whose worship involved sexual depredation and insalubriousness. Ahab, king of Israel, married Jezebel and led the nation into Baal worship. Together they reigned over Israel and this was one of the saddest chapters in the history of God's people. Jezebel was now in charge, and she showed no mercy when she wanted it done her way!

The Bible states, **"Can two walk together, except they be agreed?"** *(Amos 3:3 KJV) How can two people walk together except they be in agreement; on one accord?* This was the first mistake Ahab made, marrying someone he was unequally yoked to, for they served separate gods! This woman made people serve her and partake in her corruption. She was a disruption to her husband Ahab's spiritual growth and challenged him on every level in it!

Have you ever been in a bad relationship that you thought you should get out of, but it was so toxic, yet it was so appealing, that you stayed thinking it was love? Jezebel was toxic, she even turned Ahab away from the God of Israel's people to her false gods. And she expected her husband to do as she willed, to follow after her command, then called him weak when he didn't! She made herself ruler above all others, even God! She put herself above God!

Some churches today are still dealing with Jezebel spirits. There are people coming to church just to talk negative, disrupt the preaching, contradict the teaching, lie on the people, carry grudges, and even rob God in their offerings. When you're at odds with structure, authority, and anyone or anything that you don't agree with disruptively, then it's time to check what has infiltrated your spirit.

When we see a Jezebel spirit manifesting inside the church, we must immediately tackle this defiant spirit, go against it in spiritual warfare, and cast it out of the church immediately, through the laying on of hands, preaching, teaching, and giving instructions of the Word of God with all power. In some cases, these disruptive spirits have to go before they taint the whole house! No one with a Jezebel spirit should be allowed to bring fuel into God's house and light a match of confusion, disruption, or separation to cause anyone to turn away from the truth and to follow false prophets. Everything a Jezebel touches she purposely corrupts!

Can you imagine dealing with someone who doesn't want what you want, like how you look or how you carry yourself so properly, so they plot against everything that matters to you? They put a price on your head for no apparent reason all just because it's you!

As women we have to be careful how we treat other women. Some of us are mad that others have a man and we don't . . . let that resonate! Some of us hate men because they have more power; when really, they don't! Some of us won't give a man authority over us because we believe that we must give up our natures and stop being who we are for them. Some of these spirits won't even claim having a man, because they want others. The Jezebel spirit attacks, dominates, or manipulates, especially male authority, in some cases, all authority!

We cannot be women who treat men we love like our dependents, acting domineering, bossy, competitive, depriving them of intimacy, speaking with harsh voices, publicly criticizing or humiliating them or even making decisions without their input, all because we believe we should. If you date or marry a man, let him be the man of the house. It doesn't mean you're submitting your thoughts, opinions, nor yourself, but you're trusting that the one you're with is reliable enough to be included and responsible enough to lead you and his family. Too often, we make them feel unloved, unappreciated, insignificant, low in spirit, and then we swear that we can't understand why they have stopped talking to us, relying on us, including us, trusting us, or they're fed up enough to just leave us! When your character is flawed it's easy to say farewell; that goes both ways.

When your boys see their moms emasculating men, especially their fathers, their masculinity sets up a threat against us, as women. They want to show us that they are the alpha dog, and their aggression becomes overbearing and sometimes violent toward women of power, because they think to themselves, *I won't allow that to happen to me too!*

Some men even use our distorted behaviors as an excuse to live double lives with other women or even other men. Men who stray already have their tendencies, don't allow them to use you as their reason! We are not always the cause for their behavior, but of our behavior toward them can give them unwarranted justification! Not all men are this way and definitely not all women fall victim to this personality. We're still defining a Jezebel spirit and how someone operates with this kind of aggression.

This can definitely go both ways. Men, there's a book coming out just for you all real soon; in the meantime, let's break more barriers together for the women. Ladies, when you curse out or yell at the one you love and never let them know you appreciate and need their opinion, they take it as you don't need them. When you are disrespectful without cause—yes, most of the time it has been building up—this is a Jezebel spirit we're talking about: one without cause, acting out just because you feel like it.

If this personality applies to you, please don't close the book, there's so much more ahead. If it doesn't, we have more personalities to uncover until you find yours. All of us have one, or maybe two, we need help identifying!

In most cases no man wants a woman he can't trust with his heart and vice versa. He doesn't want a Jezebel! He wants someone he can leave the world behind and have companionship with, make love to mentally as well as physically, and relax in the comfort of her arms . . . well at least most men do! When a man gravitates toward you, if he puts down his armor, and rests upon your bosom, he is saying "I am content even if only for the moment!" What he has found in you is so comforting he can let go of all apprehensions, for his spirit has connected to your righteous spirit! Don't cause him to start to see you as he does his attackers!

We are to be the peace, the integrity, the humbled heart they need, not someone who makes them feel inferior. Our spiritual maturity will influence our Jezebel rebellion, not to just insinuate a change, but to truly make one. Wisdom comes when we are in the right frame of mind to maintain our dignity!

Let's discuss more about the lifestyle and who Jezebel was as mentioned in the Holy Bible. Jezebel's life is characterized and defined as a woman exhibiting traits of what is meant by having a Jezebel spirit. She was a queen who exhibited a trait of being obsessively passionate for domineering and controlling others, especially in the spiritual realm. She forced men to accomplish her goals with torture.

When she became queen, she began a relentless crusade to rid Israel of all evidence of Yahweh worship and forced the people by threat of death to worship her gods. She enforced her beliefs upon everyone requiring them to worship the false god of Baal or die. She even ordered the execution of all the prophets of the Lord and replaced their altars with those of Baal. She had a spirit of seduction, disruption, destruction, and disturbance to everyone she ruled over. Of course, she's an atheist in nature, for everything she'd said and done was against the will of God! Jezebel's strongest enemy was the prophet Elijah, who loved God. She hated him because he knew who he was in God, and she couldn't intimidate him with her nonsense.

When you put your faith and trust in God you will surrender to His will. God will always win over anything and anyone we choose to worship or put above Him. Nothing should ever separate us from the love of God! A woman is a very good thing given to man and her loyalty to God shows in her loyalty to her mate. Do you feel the need to challenge everyone who doesn't agree with you just to gain power over them? Why would you want someone you can control?

It's very important that we choose men who know who they are in Christ, or we will wind up with men who allow women to run over them and become their Jezebel! No real man wants a Jezebel spirit in his house cooking his meals and causing his spirit to be corruptible, so don't allow yourself to become one! Don't flatter yourself by believing they like being controlled, or they appreciate you for who you are in your Jezebel spirit! Don't be someone who's being kept, because he feels there's no way out!

A Jezebel spirit is an ungodly spirit! We're unveiling how to recognize what kind of a spirit that might be attached to you, and God wants you to see it's not the Holy Spirit you're operating under if you have to force it!

When I was twenty years old, I had a friend in the military who was being abused, controlled, and disrespected by a woman who forced him to be with her! Yeah, I said it, she forced him to sleep with her, he couldn't even look or speak to any other woman or she would literally punch him in the face in front of everybody, then grab him and force him to go home. She moved herself into his apartment and became his abuser!

Many people might say, "Why would he allow himself to be put in such a position?" Well, not all women are gentle in spirit, small in stature, or beyond forcing others to get what they want. Clearly, this is an example of someone with a Jezebel spirit.

When we find ourselves putting other people or things in place of God, remember it is said God is a jealous God; instead of waiting for defeat, surrender and repent for the Lord our God is wonderful, almighty, powerful and He is able to do exceedingly abundantly above all we ask or think.

The Lord Himself referenced to the church of Thyatira with a warning against having a dishonorable spirit filled with sexual immorality, idol worship, refusal to repent, and false teachings. As Jezebel demonstrated to Israel, it is not to be tolerated He stated. We are given grace, but God will not tolerate our disobedience! That's why repentance is so important!

Should we have to wait for God to mention our refusal and dishonor of His word? Do we want to jeopardize our eternal lives for eternal damnation? God will not tolerate any man or woman in the church or anywhere else who has influenced others not to believe in Him but who walks in this same manner of wickedness as Jezebel did.

God will not tolerate anyone who tries to persuade others to worship themselves and puts things above the God of Israel. People who will not repent of their sins, and whose sexual orientations are immoral, God will not stand for your defiling His name. Be careful not to get caught up in the corruption of this world and the things thereof. Watch who you receive your counsel from! Everyone doesn't have your best interest at heart! Let's continue on because God needs us to open our eyes to His warnings.

Perhaps the best way to define the Jezebel spirit is to say it characterizes anyone who acts in the same manner as Jezebel did, engaging in immorality, idolatry, false teaching and corruption, betrayal, and unrepentant sin. God will not have any unwillingness to repent, to love or a lack of disobedience in His presence.

We are unrighteous in ourselves and in daily need of repentance and forgiveness. Dr. Johnnie Blount spoke these words of wisdom in an inspirational email he sent to me, he said, "my friends, what love the Father has for us; His children." In the Bible, Jesus says this about the Father, He will send "the Helper (Comforter, Advocate, Intercessor—Counselor, Strengthener, Standby), the Holy Spirit" (John 14:26 AMP).

This is the same power or Spirit that empowered Jesus Christ the Son of the Living God. The Word tells us the same Spirit that raised Christ from the dead lives and dwells in us also because this power is the comforter that the Father promised us. This is why the Word of God tells us that we can do all things through Christ. We have been chosen for such a work and for such a time as this. One of the last commandments that Jesus gave His disciples in Luke 24:49 was to go into Jerusalem and wait until they received power from heaven. My friends, this power lives within you now. Release the power that is within. Be the Word . . . not a Jezebel!

Our lives can lead us in so many directions positively or negativity. If we don't make a choice, it can cause us to have a form of spiritual corruption . . . being dishonest or having a fraudulent conduct. The ability to develop an immoral lifestyle started within an initial thought and manifested into an action. That action led to a negative unethical version of who we have become as a people. Even listening to individuals with a corruptible spirit can hinder us negatively if we're listening to them without giving correction!

We can't live with the idea that we were born this way or we inherited a corruptible spirit from our parents. *"For you did not receive the spirit of bondage again to fear"* (Rom. 8:15 KJV). The root of bondage can lead us to fear and when we fear it can lead us into corruption. Harboring fear in your heart may lead many people to get a concealed carry permit, carry pocket knives, carry mace, and whatever else calms their fears, and sometimes that kind of power can come with a cost! Be careful what you desire; some people are just waiting for trouble and their desire for trouble could imprison you for life!

If you are enslaved to your Jezebel spirit, you are claiming yourself as its victim, and you cannot get your liberty, if you are used as its vessel of corruption. "Where the spirit of the Lord is there is liberty." (2 Corinthians 3:17 KJV) And with liberty comes accountability and responsibility. Your Jezebel spirit heeds responsibility, because it wants to blame others, and won't heed to accountability, because you're never wrong! Yes, there is a difference!

We are responsible for what we know, therefore we are held accountable to work out the information we now know about! Work out means put into action the corrections you've been given! Once we know better, we can do much better with our petition for assistance from God the Father. I heard a person surprisingly tell another, "At our current level of adulthood, it's our fault, for our shady attitudes, our lack of respect, and our dishonor; nobody's fault, but our own." He was so right! We are too old to keep placing blame for our actions on others.

That person went on to say, "You must control the person you've become; I can't do it for you!" That was owning up to your mess... real talk! This is a truth and a correction for us all to gain our own understanding of, for our characters' shaping; no one can do it for us! It is nobody's fault that you are or have become who you are; you have the ability to correct it and make changes if you don't approve of some of things about yourself!

Jezebel even exhibited the type of character she had in her spirit (this is a spiritual lesson) when she encountered a righteous man named Naboth who declined to sell her husband, Ahab, the land adjoining the palace, rightly confirming with her that to sell his inheritance would be against the Lord's command. He clearly stated that the Lord said it, therefore he wouldn't be disobedient to what the Lord said, but do you think she cared?

How do you feel about what God says? Well, of course she didn't care! If God tells you not to sell something but someone offers you much more than the value of that thing, will you sell your soul for money, think on such things! To go against what God tells us to do or not to do is just not worth it!

Jezebel was so spiritually corrupted, that while her husband Ahab moped and fumed on his bed because of his wife's lack of respect for Yahweh, she taunted and ridiculed him for his weakness. Ever been weak in spirit to the point you find yourself moping about what you wish you could get away with!

Ahab had sleepless nights, a weary heart, and now she's causing him even more agony with her mouth. She was a woman no man could truly have respected, because she had none for them. When you choose marriage without being equal to one another, you are faced with division and separation that could lead to the death of an innocent soul.

Someone could get hurt over a Jezebel attitude. Someone could die, because of the betrayals of a Jezebel. Someone could get fired, because someone lied on them. Someone could become homeless as a result of what you stole that wasn't yours. Yet, in spite of all that, this type of a woman will continue on with her selfishness, regardless of what's right.

Jezebel proceeded to have a faultless, innocent man named Naboth framed and stoned to death just because she wanted his land. When we desire to meet the needs of our flesh, we find ourselves not only destroying the lives of one man, but we find ourselves wanting everything attached to him that doesn't belong to us.

Jezebel even went so far as also having Naboth's sons stoned to death, so there would be no heirs, no one to inherit his wealth, and the land would revert to the possession of her husband the king, which meant to her. When you can't get what you want and you conspire to find another way to have what you believe you deserve, that is a direct defiance to the Lord. No one can devote their lives to taking what doesn't belong to them for their own greed and selfishness! Such a single-minded determination to have one's way, no matter who is destroyed in the process, is a characteristic of the Jezebel spirit. The Lord is not pleased, for this is the act of an impudent, shameless, morally unrestrained woman!

A spirit of corruption doesn't just happen overnight, it takes planning, manipulation, and the manifestation of negative thoughts, distorted motives, and the planting of bad seeds (uncultivated soil) that have evolved and grown in someone's spirit. You have taken all that was birthed in your spirit as pure and allowed it to become tainted and wicked, which could cause you to have a corrupt spirit, which lacks integrity, has dishonest practices, is crooked, perverted, filled with wickedness, evilness, lacking in character, spiritually infected, tainted, disloyal, has no morals, or a decaying attitude. When you feel like you're losing control of the ability to control your actions, ask God for help!

Corrupt comes from the Latin word *corruptus* which means "broken in pieces." A broken spirit is a spirit that's falling apart! Piece by piece you are coming apart! When you are falling apart, you're inside out, confused, unsure, inhibited, and your nature starts changing from good to evil. The ability to do good works is nearly impossible, for you have more feelings of negativity, more tainted views, than you have thoughts of gratitude and morality.

We have fed more into our evil being instead of our spirit-man, allowing for our wicked man, our sinful nature, to maintain power to control. We are a tripart being, meaning that we have a body, a soul and a spirit; we also have a will, mind, and soul connection with the Father that tells us when we are speaking or acting out of order! You know when enough is enough; you just lost your way on your path to defeat all!

If anyone continues to allow Jezebel's ruthlessness to rule their lives, they will eventually become less honest, less caring about others, less dedicated to helping people, less friendly, less responsive to right versus wrong, less concerned, less appreciative, less motivated to do, less of this, less of that, to the point that they will begin to believe less is best!

Even when you mean well, you still find yourself doing things that cause you to be scrutinized. That's because in your heart you did it with a deceitful, treacherous, or callous motive. As a result, no one took your motivations seriously nor had faith in you any longer! Is this you?

Although Jezebel heard of the miraculous powers of the Lord, she still had a hardened heart and refused to repent. She continued to believe in her gods and swore on her gods that she would chase the prophet Elijah ruthlessly for as long as it took and take his life.

She's not giving up her ways regardless of what anyone has to say about Jesus!

Jezebel's stubbornness and her refusal to see and submit to the power of the God led her to a dreadful death in the end. She died a deceitful woman! God cast her onto a sick bed, along with everybody who committed idolatry with her. Everybody she converted to the worship of Baal and succumbed to a Jezebel spirit died with her as well, their fate was sealed just like Jezebel's was! Anyone exhibiting this type of a spirit is always led by death and destruction, both in the physical and the spiritual sense.

I couldn't imagine being a friend to such a small-minded person, who's evil, a killer, betrayer, and a control freak. Her name even meant wickedness—one who has a corruptible and degrading life. She was like a cancer to the Hebrew religion as well as to herself. Cancer destroys everything it attaches itself too! Our spirit must not be so destructive that it destroys everything we touch! Jezebel was not only harmful to herself, but she was perceived as a bad mother, a bad wife, a bad ruler of her people and a bad person. She was dominating and controlling, and no person should believe they are invincible as she believed. She thought she was above all gods, even the God of Israel, and she died as a result of her wicked intentions.

There are times when people are given a little earthly power, then they use it to dictate negatively, at what level of power, they really have. What I mean by that is some power is just supposed to be Holy Ghost power that's not intended for us to misuse it to influence people to do what we expect of them, but it is given to us to use the power to uplift God's power. The power of God is what draws us closer to God, we just utilize it to show how merciful and gracious God is in using us for His glory.

But the moment your Jezebel nature emerges and misuses this God-given power, if you're a curser, you'll start cursing someone out, because that's how you feel. If you're an alcoholic you'll start drinking excessively, and not care who you affect. If fighting is your addiction, you might start a fight, and begin hitting someone just to get your point across. You get my point!

If you are living outside of the will of God your character reflects what's in your heart. Having a Jezebel personality is ungodly! Keep peace in your mind, live righteously that you may have your own testimony of how Christ made you a new creation.

A person who must have control over everything truly controls nothing; for God is the only one in control. A need to always be in control shows a person who fears or lacks something and uses control as a tool to keep a false identity they probably should have given up years ago. If you feel like you always have to be the boss and you're always trying to control your family, friends, spouse, every situation, everything around you and everyone's life you touch then you don't understand who you are in the Lord. Well, maybe not just yet!

Jezebel had forgotten that she was created to be a helpmate not for her to try to play the role of God. God does not expect you to bear this burden alone, so use your energy wisely by being a helper to your mate, not a reprobate. Your corruptible nature can land you in trouble with the law, in jail, homeless, or even dead when you spend all your time trying to deceive others. Nothing good comes from corruptibility. God wants you to love not to hurt. Is this you?

As her story is told from I Kings 16 through II Kings 9, Jezebel's life choices lead her to a life of destruction. We must watch how we lead and be conscience of the things we do that affect the lives of those around us. Is doing it your way greater than doing it God's way? Our reward is in heaven.

> *"Therefore, confess your sins to each other and pray for each other so that you may be healed. The prayer of a righteous person is powerful and effective"* (James 5:16 NIV).

Inhibited

II

Reflections of Jealousy– Hagar Spirits

Does your facial expression reflect your jealousies? When you talk about perceptions most people think theirs is on target and their sight is aligned with how we all see things. They believe you see things just as they do. Our ability to see, hear, and understand is exactly the way they see, hear, and understand based on their interpretation. Well, if that were so it would be a great day but we don't all see things just as they do!

Truly most people develop their perception based on how they see life through their own eyes, the sound their ears give them, how it feels to them, the aroma of life as they smell it, and what kind of taste it has left on their spirit.

Most of us see the world through the lenses of our own experiences, and our perception is influenced by our past experiences, our level of education, our values, our cultures, our preconceived notions, our present circumstances, and our perception becomes our reality, even if it's a distorted one! No two people share the same thought processes, and sometimes we have to clean our lenses, so that we can see a clearer view. When you have a limited view or there's smudges blocking your clarity, you can lose sight of what's really there; what was really intended for me to see might be missed in the blur of the moment.

Most people think they see the world as it is, but truth be told we see it as we are! We see things how they relate to us! Ask yourself these questions: "Has my perception worked within my purpose or against it? Have the things I've been subjected to left me with the entire picture God wants me to see, or did I miss something moving way too fast through my life?"

What do you see in your natural sight that coincides with your spiritual sight and what opposes it? Sometimes, the limits of our perception make living life so difficult. How do we handle life when our perception won't line up with our reality, despite all the effort we put into making it correspond to what we perceive?

What we perceive might be part of the opposition! Being caught up in that opposing place can bring turmoil within ourselves and cause us to go through life limitlessly. When you are blinded by your sense of fairness versus faithfulness, your view—your perceptions—may be the reason you can't get along with people. How do you look before you put on all the dressings? It's important to approach life with the knowledge of your purpose, and let your perceptions be governed by that purpose.

God saw us before He ever created us. He saw us completely in our mother's womb. In fact, (Romans 8:29 NIV) says, "For those God foreknew, He also predestined to be conformed to the image of his Son." He knew us before we lost our sight! We can perceive what we want seen, or we can perceive that which really. In other words: you make your own choice as to what is acceptable or worthy of your time and attention!

Hagars perception of commitment was corrupted by her jealousies and conduct flaws. She gave priority of herself and her ownership to individuals who had control over her spiritual energy. Hagar was an ancient Egyptian servant of Sarah, the wife of Abraham in the Bible. She was a tenant, Sarah's handmaid, and a slave who later became jealous of the hand that fed her. Her perception changed as a result of the choices she made while a resident in Sarah's home. Her desire to live in her present and escape her past circumstances gave her notions that later taught her a very vital life lesson. We all have made decisions that rob us of the true characteristics of God!

We have been disrobed of our pure characters, let alone godliness, now we are strangers to the Holy Spirit and deaf to His call. We act out of character of who we were created to be as a result of our frustrated perception of God's people and their enslavement. When we follow God's instructions, His requests, and seek after what we already know He requires, we find what makes for a good servant.

The Spirit of Hagar: Many people have a Hagar spirit today. They refuse to come to worship services, mass, Bible study, Sunday school or any other form of organized, collective religious activity, because they feel like there's too much vanity and financial gain going on with some pastors, priests, and other religious leaders. They believe that some of these religious leaders have made a mockery of the gospel of Christ to satisfy their own personal motives. They see these clerics as only being motivated by their spirit of greed, deceit, and selfishness. The vanities of some religious leaders have many people not coming to their congregations, because they fear the clergy will take advantage of them, but not all pastors and religious leaders have a Hagar mentality. Many fear the Lord, and they give due respect and honor to God and their call to the ministry.

Your mindset cannot include everyone just because someone failed you. Your perception cannot put everyone in the same category because you were mistreated by others. When God gives us promises and someone exploits them, it feels as if they stole what we were assured. Sarah gave her handmaid to her husband to bear him a child since she couldn't. God's promise was to Abraham's seed through Sarah not to the seed born through adultery in Hagar's son Ishmael! We can't take God's promises into our own hands and think we're capable of doing a better job than God himself!

Some people will only come into your presence because they're seeking something from you, but you are not God. They show up seeking signs, wonders, and miracles in congregations, but when these don't get delivered, they think all faith-based places are the same. God appoints and anoints but He won't give us anything we're not ready to handle. Remember, not all preachers preach the truth, some make false promises. We must seek the promises that come only from God. Hagar's son Ishmael was the seed of Abraham, but not the seed of God's promise.

God didn't promise him a thing! Ishmael was the product of seduction and persuasion of his mother Hagar, that was not in alignment with the promise of God, and what came out of Abraham's body was not and could not be of God. It was the product of sin, and so were his actions. Our actions can sometimes feel like we're doing God's will when really, it's only what we're receiving as a result of the desires of our hearts.

Watch carefully who spiritually counsels you, many so-called pastors, prophets or preachers make promises that are of their own seeds and not the seeds of God! Being a pastor myself, I must be very careful not to give my own opinions without noting that "it's in my opinion," that's why we should just give what the Lord says at all times. My blessing as a pastor isn't going to be the same blessing that God gives you, Himself! That's why it's so important to follow someone who follows the heart of Christ!

Although Sarah gave Hagar her handmaid to her husband and allowed her to bear him a child, she became jealous of the choice she herself created. After going against God's promise that she would have a son and he would become the son of promise through whom the tribes of Israel will arise, Sarah was too impatient to wait on God now her human emotions, which are usually brought on by our own misguided efforts, kicked in and her jealous nature came out with a vengeance. Don't allow your emotions to take you out of character.

When we become jealous hearted, we begin treating one another inappropriately and disrespectfully. Sarah giving her servant to her husband that he may have a child occurred because she was too impatient to wait on God and her jealousy later on led her to become flawed in her character, and in that act against God she showed that she didn't have faith in His promises.

It wasn't Hagar's fault that Sarah was impatient, but she was at fault for laying up with another woman's husband and giving him a baby, which led Sarah to despise, mistreat, and become envious of Hagar. And men, just because a woman says you should do something stupid doesn't mean that you should do it. Look at what happened to Adam in the garden in Genesis! A bite of an apple cost him so much more than he ever anticipated!

What roles do we play that cause us to fall victim because we lack patience in God? If God says wait, then wait! The Bible says, *"Wait on the LORD: be of good courage, and he shall strengthen thine heart: wait, I say, on the LORD"* (Ps. 27:14 KJV). Ask yourself, "Do I have a jealous nature?" Are you as Sarah was toward Hagar? Do you have a jealous nature? Are you drumming up arguments and accusations for no apparent reason? What have you done to others just because they have what you want? Can you truly say that you've never said a bad word about any other woman? Let that marinate for a moment before we move on!

Hagar spirits have trouble dealing with someone who has advanced beyond their expected scope. You have to stay at the level they feel you should be at, don't surpass their expectations. Their envious nature will have them cuss someone out just for having confidence in who they are and walking proudly in it (focused). It's hard for them to compliment others on their accomplishments. Even if they felt the person deserved the break, they would find a reason to discredit them (critical). This type of person is always initiating petty arguments for no legitimate reason (argumentative). They're even jealous of their friends, family, and people they don't know, but feel threatened by (jealous). They see themselves and believe that they are worth more or are better than others (simpleminded), and they look at other women just to judge their self-worth (judgmental). They truly think they're much more beautiful than most others (Vanity/Vain).

People with this type of mindset have forgotten they're supposed to be their sister's keeper not their attacker. We must watch over one another with care and if they lack, we are their earthly resources! We cannot discredit the worth of someone because they're ahead of where we are! Just because someone has a higher status or is more accomplished, or even has greater material gain, doesn't make them any worthier to God than you are!

God loves us all the same! God doesn't care about materialistic measures; He cares about souls saved. God cannot be positively reflected in our lives if we are being petty and vindictive toward one another. No one should consider themselves above or worthier than another nor should they desire what their sister has. We are to be our sister's keeper, look out for one another, pour love upon one another, and lead out with joy for one another. Is this you?

It's important to focus your attention on being careful not to judge each other (lest we be judged) or put each other down. You know that old saying, "what comes around goes around." Be careful how you treat your sister, she just might someday become the person you might rely on for a favor in times of troubles (low on food, can you lend me a hand), your boss, (the same one you mistreated or disrespected, now controls your financial and job security), or even your financial loan officer (the one who determines if your loan is declined or approved). Karma is real! Be careful not to offend anyone because you never know who you might have to stand before asking and seeking assistance from someday.

Jealousies are a reflection of how we feel about those who have more or less than we do! It can be a result of something as simple as the way one look, speak, walk, or any other means we deem necessary to hate one another. Jealousy causes us to destroy the dreams of others with our tongues, our negative actions, even with the use of our eyes. Jealousy can make us assume that we are better than one another because of our status. Are we less than because someone said we are? Of course not, we are who God says that we are and it's time to own up to it and let go of our Hagar attitudes.

If you are fortunate enough to have more material or financial gain than others, you should not boast or brag about it, and if you have less you should not become envious and jealous-hearted, like Hagar and Sarah. Envying what another person has is ungodly, unhealthy, and exhausting. It takes too much energy to always walk around complaining about what we don't have, and besides, no one wants to hear it anyway. We use up way too much energy trying to keep up with the Joneses instead of thanking God for all the opened doors He's made possible.

Start your day off by thanking God for the closed doors. Thank Him for the doors He brought you through especially for the one's He has shut on your past mistakes, the entrance He has blocked from the enemy's entry. Thank Him for the open doors He has already blessed us to see, to come to, and to go through. Don't take for granted the people God has allowed to move in and out of your lives, because they fulfilled their season. The closed doors are some of the most important blessings we could ever bear: the padlocked doors, the dilemmas we once endured have been shut!

Some of our closed doors are the ones where cancer emerges but is passed through, poverty passed on, abuse passed in an out, even doubt, suicide, and despair found an open crack but was squeezed out. Homosexuality came over for a visit, but the door was too narrow so he left, not to mention low self-esteem came and went. Diabetes, stroke, heart attack, and high blood pressure stopped by, but thanks to God we weren't home. The enemy had to flee, because the door was closed! We should be thankful for all the doors God closed that we thought were curses against us for an open door doesn't always mean good things will come through, especially if they weren't sent by God. Thank God that you have survived some of the household drama, the heartaches, and pain He prevented.

Being jealous is being foolish; having what someone else has could mean having their cancer, having their diabetes, having their abuses, having their evictions, and even having their death sentence. Be grateful for what God has allowed you to have, and enjoy it to the fullest!

We become jealous of what we see when we haven't seen what burden came in achieving it. You could have much less than you now have, but God saw fit to give you everything you have, whether it is less or more. What looks good on the outside doesn't mean it's good on the inside.

We tend to always want what someone else has, but we don't know their story, what they went through to achieve it! And sometimes, after hearing their story, you might feel like saying, "You can have it if it took all that to obtain it!" Ask yourself, "Am I willing to sweat my way through the storms, do the research, weather the tears, fight through the storms, bare the frustrations, endure the long hours required in achieving success?" Are you willing to do anything other than complain about what you didn't receive out of life? If you want it, go after it and be happy for those who have paved the way! If God did it for them, He'll do it for you!

We must earnestly pray that God changes how we feel about one another. He did not send His Son Jesus Christ into a lost world with the intention that nothing would change. We must desire change before we can receive it! I've heard time and time again from various women, "I don't have a lot of female friends because they are too jealous-hearted," or from other women who say "Nobody wants to see you have anything nice; they always have something negative to say," or what about the all-time favorite line, "Women just can't be trusted."

It's bad when we as women cannot rely on each other for support without fearing betrayal and distrust. We have become jealous of God's blessing for our sisters in Christ, their earned successes, great achievements, accommodations, even educational status. You can achieve it too by trusting and obeying, putting in the hard work, dedication, and determination. It too can be yours. God did not bless one to have the other envious. He did it to show you just how good He is, and if He can do it for one, He can do it for another. Being envious derives from within our nature, causing resentment, frustration, and jealousy. Are you so busy competing that you can't see the need for change? Is this you?

III
Mental Seduction—12-Step Program

What are you focused on that has you mentally seduced by it?

Focused on the Goal

I'm not saying that I have this all together, that I have it made. But I am well on my way, reaching out for Christ, who has so wondrously reached out for me. Friends, don't get me wrong: By no means do I count myself an expert in all of this, but I've got my eye on the goal, where God is beckoning us onward—to Jesus. I'm off and running, and I'm not turning back.

So, let's keep focused on that goal, those of us who want everything God has for us. If any of you have something else in mind, something less than total commitment, God will clear your blurred vision—you'll see it yet! Now that we're on the right track, let's stay on it.

Stick with me, friends. Keep track of those you see running this same course, headed for this same goal. There are many out there taking other paths, choosing other goals, and trying to get you to go along with them. I've warned you of them many times; sadly, I'm having to do it again.

All they want is easy street. They hate Christ's cross. But easy street is a dead-end street. Those who live there make their bellies their gods; belches are their praise; all they can think of is their appetites.

But there's far more to life for us. We're citizens of high heaven! We're waiting the arrival of the Savior, the Master, Jesus Christ, who will transform our earthy bodies into glorious bodies like his own. He'll make us beautiful and whole with the same powerful skill by which he is putting everything as it should be, under and around him. (Philippians 3:12–21 MSG)

These Bible verses teaches us regardless of what we have experienced there are associations we have, dwellings we visit, and objects we have obtained that are a hinderance to us and warns us to keep pressing on until we're able to be released from their grasp, Philippians 3 gives us a scripture of training rules to follow. *"I press toward the mark for the prize of the high calling of God in Christ Jesus,"* it also instructs us *"To watch and pray that you may not enter into temptation,"* and *"to abstain from every form of evil."* What we allow to take rule over our minds affects our lives and that deliverance from it is what we're pressing toward, the things we're surrendering to is what is tempting us and the sin we have welcomed! Somehow, we have missed the mental mark due to our blurred vision, and what we see as a result is us giving in to our temptations!

When you're missing out on your spiritual-mental seduction, the place where your mind is at ease and your spirit is at rest, you have missed your opportunity to think according to a Christlike nature, for your mind has adapted to the way *you* think without Christ. You have chosen to allow your mentality to be infiltrated by the desires of your heart and now you're permitting the intrusion to be its rule.

When you have a sweet tooth, you usually find something sweet to satisfy the craving. Once you accept the initial thoughts you find yourself lusting after within your nature, they become your candy, and as it seduces your mind it becomes your sweet thing that needs to be satisfied and once you've tasted of it regularly, it will become your norm!

Our norm is gratified with all the negative concepts of our thoughts that have fallen out of alignment with Christ's will. We have accepted the new me as normal, regardless of who we have become. Who you have become isn't always who God says that you are! Don't assume that because it's comfortable to you that it's God-approved!

What if you find yourself on a date and it doesn't feel right—he says things contrary to your beliefs, he's rude, stiffs you with the check—do you go on a second date? I hope not! But if you do, then you are training yourself to accept the damaging things people say and do to you. We are what we allow! Your mental compacity knows what is unacceptable, yet your desire to have something or someone will have you willing to compromise and accept mess just so you won't be alone. So many women settle for less for all the wrong reasons. It's time to let them know your worth! Be willing to correct people who don't appreciate what they have in you. Don't allow anyone to disrupt your aura, the energy field surrounding your being.

People will treat you the way you treat yourself if you allow it. Why would they do better toward you than you do toward yourself? You've just said "I'll compromise who I am, I deserve less than, I'm willing to make negotiation for the sake of a possibility." Be more than someone's maybe! Keep your eye on the prize, stay focused, stick with God, and remember He's the goal and He'll never see you as just a possibility!

When you let in negative energy or hang in environments that make you uncomfortable, you accept your surrounding for what it is. Your unspoken thoughts will allow that negative energy to halt your well-being, because you didn't speak out against how it is affecting your positive vibe. You have adapted to your environment instead of changing it.

When your intellect steers you into the negative, seek after a mental modification; don't consider yourself to be beneath your own goal. No one can tell you that you are unworthy of respect but you, for your attitude shows them, it steers them, toward what's acceptable and unacceptable with you! If you act unworthy of respect, your actions warrant the response you receive, so make them admire the woman that you are by being the best possible version of yourself. Let Jesus reconvene the positive forces that represent how your body functions and let your refocused emotions heal your body, your mood, and your state of mind. When your emotions change, your energy changes and you develop a balanced mind and body and your spirit is at peace and protected from the negative energy of others.

How you think about yourself, about your situation, tells others if you will accept less than your value! When you find yourself thinking against God's rule, remember that He says you are worthy; make acceptable behavior a conscious choice. God's rule is that you are above and not beneath! His first 5 rules in Exodus 20 were *"I am the Lord your God. You shall have no other gods before me. You shall not make for yourself an idol. You shall not make wrongful use of the name of your God. Remember the Sabbath and keep it holy."* Jesus didn't come to destroy the law but to fulfill it. He has rules and if follow His rules you will receive your just due and gain your worth.

God gave us a choice to live or die. No man chooses death purposefully. Sometimes, how you feel about yourself could reflect on your choices. How you live for Christ makes your choices clearer and more dignified! Being wrapped up mentally in what feels adequate instead of what is reality can result in some life mishaps! You could be dying internally as a result of not making a positive choice. *"And if it seem evil unto you to serve the Lord, choose you this day whom ye will serve; whether the gods which your fathers served that were on the other side of the flood, or the gods of the Amorites, in whose land ye dwell: but as for me and my house, we will serve the Lord"* (Josh. 24:15 KJV).

Our misguided mental seduction, the way we view things in life including ourselves, how we concur in the foolishness that sometimes get in our heads, could lead us into negativity and that could be a facet of the mental blockage we use to cover up our situations, block the truth, or stop us from reaching a level of full maturity all because we are lacking in areas we have yet to address.

How you analyze your situations, before you start to reap the repercussions, is what determines how far your reach will go. Don't be the person wishing you would have listened to wise instruction. God said He couldn't stand to look at the wicked lives of the people. They had the nerves to not even look Him in the face.

He was so angry at the way they were living their lives in great sin that He wanted to destroy them all, even after he had taught them how to live, they still refused to listen and to be taught! *"They have turned their back to Me and not their face; though I taught them, teaching again and again, they would not listen and receive instruction"* (Jer. 32:33 NASB).

It's not that we don't know, we just choose our own options: respectable or immoral. In many cases our minds' inability to grasp the difference between right and wrong is due to our choosing what feels better. We have trained ourselves to gravitate toward the things we love rather than what we truly need, whether they're good for us or not! Whether it angers or pleases, we sometimes don't care if it satisfies our selfish desires to please oneself! That's why Scripture teaches us that we have to get mature in the Lord. Maturity comes when you have the strength to walk away from anything or anyone who opposes God's word and His teaching. If it hinders your walk with God, go in the opposite direction, that's maturity. It can be something or someone that's disruptive, threatening, attempting to steal your peace of mind, who tries to take away your mental stability, compromises your values, morals, or self-respect. When you mature, they will flee!

Some situations arise as from unavoidable misguidance we face. Good doesn't always mean it's good for you! Look at white sugar: it tastes good, but it could cause diabetes, weight gain, heart disease, cancer, depression, aging skin, Alzheimer's, elevated cholesterol, and cavities, which shows that indulging in what is satisfying isn't always a good thing for you! Sometimes, it's best to substitute what we like for what is best for us, but don't substitute God for man! God is a priority, not a worldly luxury!

Do you believe your mind is incapable of separation of the spirit from the flesh to the point that it allows itself to become seducible? If you can't control your flesh-man your spirit-man won't stand a chance against all the world's luxuries! I'm not speaking about the good kind, but the ones that cause us to stumble in our walk with Christ Jesus! You know the other woman/other man type, the staggering ones, or maybe even the ones who hold us hostage to them, because they look, feel, and taste so good, the seductive ones!

The seduction of your spirit has you caught up in dilemma after dilemma for so long, that your inhibited choices have become acceptable to you, they feel right in your sight; you are being seduced by the enemy who has you believing that everything you choose will be for your good. You are spiritually dying, because you know not what you do, or you do what you know is wrong! Relinquishing control isn't easy for most of us when we all have our own agendas to manage. God wants dominion over your life, for you to declare Him as your Lord. Isn't He worth surrendering for?

What if I told you that you are still responsible for what you don't know, or don't do? Do you know that you are held accountable for what access you have to the knowledge of God? You are responsible for answering why you didn't do what he told you, showed you, made available to you, instructed, even if you didn't know. Why? If you have heard about Jesus, but never sought out the revelation of or knowledge of who He is and established a relation with Him, you still had all the resources available to you to use as a tool to learn of Him; therefore, He will ask you why didn't you gain any biblical understanding of who He was.

We're educated scholars, doctors, nurses, businessmen, homemakers, and so much more. We are people who should know how to stop the mental breakdown the *rigor mortis* from taking place within our minds. Get the facts! Yet, you fall victim to your own selves or others' mental sedation. Satan tranquilizes us with distractions. He wants control over us, over our lives, but mostly our minds, and he feeds us what we like, so we will remain in a sedated frame of mind. He tries to defeat us by hindering the natural process of our minds, by inflating our minds with ungodly thoughts, infiltrating our godly lives in order to make our true faith appear fraudulent and tainting our thoughts, having us believe Jesus is a man-made figment of our imagination. He throws darts that read: Jesus isn't real; There's no God; You don't need to pray; You don't have to believe nor confess your sins to God! But don't be deceived; Jesus is real! Satan's job is to tear down everything about God in your spirit, from the head to the tail, and destroy everything in between, and that means you too!

Satan is filling the minds of the people with ill will, negativities, and jealousies that are of the good-and-plenty rule: he makes everything look good, so you will want plenty of it. He knows if it feels good, taste good, and if it looks good, then just maybe your physical desires might indulge him by leaving behind the spirit-man's thirst for righteousness. The desires of the flesh, if fed plenty of the mess you want and like, will eventually override the desires of the righteous: our desires to be holy, to be pure, to be virtuous, to be thankful, to be grateful, to be loving and kind, to relinquish the sins that held you bound!

Your thoughts will dictate your actions and influence your life. If you don't get your reasoning in check, your thoughts can fuel how effective Satan is at getting control over your mind. Your thoughts are powerful food to the mind. When you have negative or unhealthy ones, they can cause you to worry, be sad, become fearful, have anxieties, or even lose your mind. If you focus your thoughts to energize the power of the Holy Spirit that dwells within you, it produces within you peaceful, loving thoughts filled with joy, peace, gratitude, and positivity, and you become Christ-minded. Everyone is better equipped when they're mentally focused and not operating out of their emotions.

If you don't know why you are fighting wars within your mind, then your mind is under attack. Satan is trying hard to undermine every thought of perfect peace you have within you. Once he feels as if he has you mentally incapacitated, chewing on his twisted scraps of deceit, there's no room for correction without repentance. Repent and be set free of any indiscretions you might have committed knowingly and unknowingly.

Satan thinks if he can keep you preoccupied with your wants and desires, you will forget about your godly position and possibly never seek a recovery center namely, the church or godly counsel. He knows if he can keep you confused about religion verses relationship, Holy Bible verses Qur'an, God verses Jesus, righteousness verses worldliness, if he can keep you from seeking answers and from getting the true definitions, then just maybe you won't believe that there is anything including a lamb who was slain for you and I. It's up to you to find the answers to your questions.

Scripture teaches us to ask, and it shall be given you; seek, and ye shall find; knock, and it shall be opened unto you. Scripture assures us that everyone who asks receives; he who seeks finds; and to him who knocks, the door will be opened, so what are you intending to do differently to get Satan off your trail or should I say off your tail?

The devil's beliefs are not yours; you have to get focused to claim your place in Christ. There's a doctor in the house, He's a healer, He's a heart surgeon, He's a forgiver, a deliverer, and a redeemer, and His name is Jesus Christ. If you ask, He can save you from the wiles of the devil. He will deliver you out of any distorted behaviors you have welcomed into your spirit. He will help you put your past behind you and move on in spite of what life has thrown at you. All you need to do is just ask for His forgiveness in your heart, seek after Him with all your heart, then trust and believe in Him within your heart, and you will find Him!

In order for a change to materialize we need mind detoxification; which happens when we enter into the mindset of Christ by allowing Him into our hearts and proceeding through a 12-step program to achieving a successful change by teaching ourselves what we must know and believe is necessary to our Christian process! Here are the 12 steps!

Step 1: Regeneration

Step 2: Self-Determination

Step 3: Heart Transplantation

Inhibited

Step 4: From Inebriation to Mind Transformation

Step 5: Kingdom Participation

Step 6: Mental Recuperation

Step 7: Heart and Mind Rejuvenation

Step 8: Godly Interpretation

Step 9: Dependable Capitalization

Step 10: Christlike Motivation

Step 11: Visions of Inspiration

Step 12: Selfless Justification

Step 1: Regeneration

What have you allowed in that has bound itself to you as a result?

In these disconcerting times, we face many stressing facets in our lives that can become very taxing on us psychologically, physically, socially, and financially; that drain us internally. I've been told that the past two years have been two of the deadliest years this entire world has witnessed since the Holocaust, the Spanish Flu, and the swine flu, but it still came with many blessings and faith building moments!

There were so many people who have been called to glory, who have suffered, who have been battling with their thoughts of depression and suicide, and so many who's faith suffered as a result of these enormously hard years!

So many of us have spent countless hours praying for healing, spared lives, restoration, deliverance, God's mercy, and so much more. People have found themselves stressing, worrying, filed with fears, unbelief, sadness, loss, loneliness, and the feeling of defeat, but with no rejuvenation, no hope, no faith, and no strength some will succumb to their circumstances!

Life is short, it's unpredictable, but with Christ it's worth living even with the ups and downs it brings! How can you talk about overcoming, moving forward, propelling forward? Why not! When Christ died, He was first tortured, beaten, spit on, lied about, betrayed, put on trial without cause, tempted to sin, mocked, and then He still laid down his life for you and me.

I speak on pushing past the obstacles, especially the hardest obstacles life throws at you, because they are either going to kill your dreams, destroy your future, or murder your vision! Nothing good comes from wallowing in self-pity, disappointments, or missed opportunities. Not even our losses can keep us bound to them for an extended period or we will lose ourselves in our pain!

If we are to overcome these obstacles, we need to find a way to release our frustrations, a way to deal with the death and the suffering so many of us have been forced to face that can make it hard to accept these acts as fate! How can we see the promises of God if all we feel is the drama of life kicking us down—the hurt and pain of disastrous times—and see no way out of this level of distress? The battle is not yours, it's the Lords! You are not alone! Don't try to carry your burdens on your own! Take it to the Lord in prayer! See a therapist! Fight for your will to survive this pain and believe that someday you will be a survivor!

Get to the place where God's love and power is consistently demonstrated, that place where you display the manifestation of His glory during the dark storms of your life. You won't just get there overnight! First, start by professing Jesus as your Lord and Savior. Start getting into His word that it will come forth when you need it. Call on Him in the midnight hour or anytime you feel you need Him. Find some folks who will be a designated spiritual driver for you, someone you can call on, talk to, who will take the wheel when you can't drive any longer on this road to recovery. Find someone who can pray with you, intercede on your behalf, someone who's a child of the King, not by word or deed but by the blood of Jesus! Find someone who has their own relationship with the Lord and cares enough about God, that His agape love transcends over onto you through them!

Being restored doesn't mean that you won't have tornadoes forming in your lives, it means you can learn how to endure them with Christ, if you will only trust him to carry you through your storms. Jesus didn't promise to take away the difficulties, to fix our problems, to remove our stressing marriages, our wayward children, our financial hardships, improve our job statuses, correct our imperfect processes, nor realign our living arrangements; He promised to fix our lifespans by giving us eternal life, being our comforter and our way maker.

Many of the stresses that consume our time and take us into overkill are sometimes the very things we choose—things like our mishandling of an excessive workload or always taking the overtime—we work too much and we have way too many jobs. We're on sports activity overload, we have our kids doing everything to keep them well-rounded, or we're pushing them to achieve what we didn't. Even the mishandling of our family time can cause us to be heavy ladened and we don't have time for one another, we've stopped eating together, stopped talking to one another.

Have you wondered why you're exhausted all the time? Just maybe we have way too many obligations to our friends, hanging out every weekend, coming in later every night, and later running on empty every day. Some of us can't function for God because we're too busy trying to make everyone happy at work, working longer and harder just to get that promotion, satisfying our colleagues' many personalities. It can all become a challenging life aspect that needs to be regenerated. Some life changes might be in order so that some of that energy can be given to your spiritual walk with God! God deserves you, your time, and your energy. You can't come to Him with what's left and expect Him to bless it!

Let some things or some people go if they're keeping you from developing in your walk with Christ. If they keep you from spending time with God, if they have no time for Bible study or Sunday school, if they're always too tired to get up for church service, let them go; they are hindering your relationship with God!

Everyone you love deserves some of your time, but the most valuable time you can make is the time spent establishing a relationship with the Lord. We all must make Jesus our kept promise before we obligate ourselves to others! Don't promise to put Him ahead of everything and everybody, and not make enough time to listen to Him or say a daily prayer unto Him. Your promises should always be kept. Your prayers are what develops your relationship! Your Bible reading is what brings you closer to His truths and what helps you to hear clear instructions so that you have no doubt that they came from God!

Never let people be the only ones telling you what God said, make sure He tells you too!

When your time is too consumed with stuff, you will regret the things you have missed or wish you could have a do-over! There are countless moments when we've wished things had emerged differently. If we had not been so busy, the outcome of many of our choices could have been different had we spent less of our time in striving to survive mode and more of our time getting to know God. He is warning us about putting others before Him. There's always a warning before the repercussions.

You knew at that moment when the warning signaled something was off, but you continued onward into a path of destruction anyhow. There is so much stuff we put ahead of God. If only we could somehow return to that occasion or two and either remove or modify our outcome, then, just maybe, we would be strong enough to believe that we will get through it this time, without fumbling, without the consequences.

There are moments that have had more negative, than positive effects that require redevelopment of our minds to deal with its complexity. The revamping of many life conditions could be the positive force enlisted for future endeavors to flourish. What you do today for God will be for the benefit of your future blessings! Only what you do for Christ will last! Let us wait on God for our spiritual development!

When the Bible speaks of "waiting," it has many situations one could consider in their waiting instead of *wait* meaning just, "stop," "hold-up," "stand still," "don't move;" but God means for us to "wait on Him," without canceling your God ordained assignment! Don't stop performing your God-given duties. Don't reinvent the wheel when God said reinvent yourself in me, as you are learning of me.

If the Word of God is filled with *"wait,"* why can't we wait? When we wait on the Lord, He will walk with us through all these unforeseen encounters, not only in the big things, but He'll test you to wait even

We stress ourselves out over bills, relationships, work, people, even the wrong type of love! When you are renewing areas of your life, you want it to be fulfilling, more rewarding than before. With God your reward is greater than any you could ever envision! There's no loss with Christ!

God wants us to know we deserve love, to be loved wholeheartedly, to be rescued from our pain, to be showered in blessing after blessing, but to fully receive it we must regenerate our spirits to operate effectively in love, not just any love, agape love, God's love for us! We have to learn how to have agape love for ourselves as well! Unconditional love is the only acceptable kind of love in a flourishing relationship, the kind of love God said He wants to give us; no more just loving our way through life, no more just falling in and out of love with this one or that one!

When you feel loved you want to operate in love! Christ Jesus will get us through our stressful times when we accept His love which will also give us renewed strength! Early on I used to teach my children the importance of agape love starting with just singing songs to one another. Here's one of the first we've ever sung: "Jesus loves me this I know for the Bible tells me so, little one to Him belong, they are weak, but he is strong, yes Jesus loves me, Yes Jesus loves me for the Bible tells me so." Jesus is love! *"But anyone who does not love does not know God, for God is love"* (1 John 4:16 NLT). We know how much God loves us, and we have put our trust in His love. God is love, and all who live in love live in God, and God lives in them. Love is the key to abiding with God and being renewed in our hearts!

When you help others in your weakness, it helps you to grow and to flourish while you're going through! Your emotional, physical, financial, social, even spiritual development could get you through the various experiences you have encountered in life when you are not worrying about your own personal issues. How you cope in your development is what gives you your evolution. If you can't handle your own problems, you won't be able to handle others'.

The more time you put into other people, the more you will develop and be able to handle what you have endured. We learn how to cope by repetition. Focusing on others sometimes can empower us to turn our situations around, instead of being consumed by them. Pouring yourself out on others could take your mind off your own circumstances and help you forget about what you lack or need.

Live your life as if the consuming fire of the Lord is nearby, as if this is the final straw, your last warning to offer acceptable worship to God with reverence and awe to bless His people, to love in agape form, to be changed by the power of the Holy Spirit. When you think as if today might be the day, then you will do your best to make every day count.

Surround yourself with people who are filled with the love of Christ, instead of mental anguish, knowing that this will fuel you to embrace change within your heart. Allow the love of Jesus Christ to keep leading you toward what's right, so that you don't let people drain God's purpose and plan out of you. Don't get burnt out over man-made substances, untapped opportunities, or people's burdens, but put your trust in God and He will destroy your enemies and anyone who opposes His will for your life. Our God is a jealous God; you cannot put anything nor anyone before him.

The Lord is like a fire that consumes or destroys when someone lacks belief, respect, or righteousness. He will destroy everything in His path that is against Him. Although God is holy, just, true, faithful, and righteous, He still is a jealous God and His wrath is devouring to those in opposition. Vanity is opposing God! Cheating is opposing God! Unforgiveness, lying, killing, cursing, drunkenness, slothfulness, sin, betrayal, laziness, jealousies, fornication all oppose God! Sinfulness consumes you and it will destroy you if you won't surrender it unto the Lord, repent of it, and turn away from whatever has a hold on you! Holds can curse your land and halt your blessings.

In the Old Testament fire represented a burnt offering unto the Lord as a gift of divinity, a sacrifice in His holy presence. The altar was lit by God and the priests were to keep it lit at all times, and a fire being lit by any other source is unacceptable to God. His perpetual fire was to be a reference that this was His doing, He lit it, and it was a constant reminder of who God is and the power of His might. The fire in the dwelling place of the Lord was his Shekinah glory, therefore no other source of fire was acceptable. Don't spark off fires on your own and say "God lit them with a curse." Besides that, why are we starting fires we can't control or put out ourselves? Fire hurts, burns, scorches, destroys, becomes uncontrollable, it consumes, so why would we want any part of starting one or trying to put one out! Just let Jesus be your extinguisher!

Today we live with many avenues of pain, pains embedded so deep we carry them from adolescence into adulthood, from relationship to relationship, even from mask to mask. Some pains are more complex than others, but all pain feels consuming. The hard knocks we encounter can feel as if we're being devoured by our internal conflicts: the ones so unbearable, the struggles that scared us, the spiritual wars we never faced, the losses we can't subdue.

We just want the memories gone so we bury them, hide them, cover them up and continue to carry them day by day. Part of the problem is our indwelling sin. Sin always leads us to some level of discomfort and pain. It starts out rewarding and ends up painful. Most pain isn't our fault and there's sometimes nothing we could have done to prevent it. We can be in pain due to surgery, trauma, body aches, muscle or joint discomfort, diseases, nerve damage, arthritis, injuries. Many types of pain are classified by the damage it causes to your body! How it affects you determines how it will be treated.

The pain of sin is also categorized; it is classified by the damage it does to your spirit-man! How you interact with your sinful nature determines if you will or will not continue to engage in it, or how long you will remain. How you react in your sin determines the level of pain that will follow as a result of the damage you have done to your spirit.

In order to win the war within, we must understand its magnitude, how deep sin has eternalized! Where has my sin level elevated to?

What's the magnitude of my corruptibility? What's going on within my inner conflicts? What has initiated it? What level of damage has been done? I need to also ask myself questions like Where does it stem from? How do I rid myself of its confusion? How do I alleviate this pain?

Some of us should be asking more questions like "Was it something I did?" "What or who caused the discomfort associated to my pain?" "What am I fighting against internally as a result?" "What can I do to learn how to cope?" "Even if it wasn't my fault how can I get through this pain?"

If we don't deal with our pain, it can become a lifelong battle, and the struggle will eventually become a nightmare that you will have to deal with on a daily basis. God is the solution to every life situation we're facing; that's why we have to talk to Him openly and honestly about our problems. Stop trying to come to God with lies or half-truths; He knows what we need and who we are. When our struggles are more than we can handle alone, it is an internal matter that requires His full attention! The song writer put it so clearly when he wrote, "Jesus paid it all, all to Him I owe, Sin had left a crimson stain, he washed it white as snow."

> *"For our struggle is not against flesh, and blood, but against the rulers, against the powers, against the world forces of this darkness, against the spiritual forces of wickedness in the heavenly places"* (Eph. 6:12 NASB).

"For through we walk in the flesh, we do not war according to the flesh, for the weapons of our warfare are not of the flesh, but divinely powerful for the destruction of fortresses." (2 Cor. 10:3–4 NASB95). There are numerous strongholds we have encountered that are keeping us from overcoming the pain of our battle scars. Keeping our pain embedded internally can cause a foreign-like substance to build up, it can leave us scared, and pour over into what once was a happy, satisfying, loving

space within our hearts. Our hearts are designed to handle the natural process of pumping blood throughout our bodies, so we can live a fulfilling life, but with all the foreign substances building up we are clotting and bleeding out!

These substances have accumulated into walls of destruction to cause us to feel conquered before the battle begins. We have weapons as believers that are for us to use against the pain that's causing our internal war. These weapons are for the use in the spiritual war that's going on within us and around us. Demonic forces, demons, spiritual warfare, evil beings are the things we are fighting against, not people, but what's attached itself to the people. If we don't get focused, regenerated, and ready for the battle we will continue to feel defeated and alone instead of empowered and humble in heart!

It's time to take up some weapons that actually have some power! It's time to stand firm against the schemes of the devil; time to stop handing over the forgiveness that has been so graciously given to us! If we lack for nothing and we recognize that we have the power of the Holy Spirit working within us, then let the devil know your name. When he hears your name, he should come to a stance, look around, and become concerned, because it's you, and he knows you're not coming alone. You rose with the power of the Holy Spirit who gives peace in the midst of a storm, heals the sick, gives provision to the needy, life to the hopeless, meaning and purpose, He strengthens the weak, sooths the cries of the righteous, and comforts the hurting, loves His children and restores strength to the weary. The countenance of the Lord is a calm before the storm; His face is peaceful until the devil comes for what's His!

Your faith should express that power when you stand firm against the attacks of the enemy. The war is fought among the swift at heart, the ones who recognize the enemy and the unseen spiritual battles taking place. Your countenance should change too when the enemy knows that you are coming with your battle clothes on. You are prepared, ready, equipped, and determined to fight at a warfare level!

When the devil hears your name, he should be the one standing up, looking around and concerned, not you, for he knows that you are not alone, but that you are coming clothed in the power of the Holy Spirit attached to you and reigning on the inside of you! We are children who will not be shaken; for we are the ones causing the shaking!

We need spiritual warfare armor, godly weapons, to fight with divine power, and that only comes from God. So let go and let God fight your battles, just make sure you're wearing the proper attire for the fight if you insist on handling it yourself. If you insist on dealing with your own pain alone, then your armor is improperly placed. (Ephesians 6:10-11 NKJV) tells us to *"Finally, be strong in the Lord and in his mighty power." "Put on the whole armor of God, that ye may be able to stand against the wiles of the devil."* The devil has a plan to kill, steal, and destroy you, what's your plan?

The enemy knows exactly what God has placed in you, that's what you're working with in the Spirit, and who you are to God. He even knows what God has given you: the spirit of love and a sound mind; he knows you have peace that surpasses all understanding. He knows that you will not be moved, that you are the covered in love, joy, peace, and nothing will condemn you, nothing will cause you to remain inhibited, especially not demonic forces seen and unseen.

Sad to say, but some of you regardless of what tools are place before you to use as a weapon will continue to go through your entire lives struggling when you don't have to; life doesn't have to consume anyone! The devil wants to stir up a pot of fears, insecurities, lies, and destruction. He wants to use your life as a plot for schemes, to make you forget about your plans, to strip you of your power, and cause you to cast off all restraints so you will wallow in negativity instead of your power so that you will fall back into your uncomfortable spaces and fall out of your standing firm form. He wants to influence you so that you forget about who you are in Christ Jesus.

Many of the choices and decisions being made are the result of some of us making plans without God's guidance. Your pain, your turmoil, is the result of what you have decided to do without first seeking God. Weapons are for war, you cannot enter a spiritual fight with your own skills, you have to put on your spiritual garments, so that you don't get defeated. If you would "put on" as scripture stated above , *put on what you need to survive, to get through the devils' schemes, and his attacks against you, then you will survive the attacks.* Nothing will be able to penetrate your spirit when you have on the proper attire, and when Jesus goes with you to fight in a spiritual war, you will not be defeated.

You must stand firm, know who you are to Christ Jesus, then with the belt of truth buckled around your waist or "gird up your loins," as said in the ancient days when the men would wear a long robe. Even though it was a hinderance while they were working to have on this type of attire, they still came prepared and they would use these belts to gird up their loins. They covered up their temptations; their distraction piece!

The injunction to gird up your loins has a significance for many people who get caught up in the workforce today, mixing work with pleasure. See, these belts ran around the men's waist and between their legs which represents us getting our sexual appetite under control.

A lot of our attacks occur because we haven't gotten our fleshly desires under control. Once you get your physical being, your sexual drive—or should I say your flesh—in alignment, then the rest will follow, because every other piece of the full armor of God is attached to the belt of truth. It's attached to your level of control! When you can control yourself, you're properly equipped for the battle ahead. This might have been initially meant for the men, but today women are acting just as the men did, in sexual exploitation of yourself! You can't blame others for being sexually overactive! Gird up your loins and get your sexual appetites under control!

If you don't begin with truth, you'll never defeat the enemy, and Jesus said God's Word, "Make them holy by your truth; teach them your word, which is truth" (John 17:17 NLT). Therefore, put on your belt and control your desires. Get control of your human wants, emotions, and cravings which are your nature and put on your breastplate of righteous which is the righteousness of God, so that you can protect your hearts.

If you lose focus, you will most likely forget the purpose you are called to, and you will start refocusing on your fears and distractions, and your belt of truth will fall loose and you will start redirecting all your weapons in the wrong direction—at the people we love, at our situations—instead of at the enemy who wants who you are, your legacy, your voice of righteousness, even your life!

In your obedience to God, He will give you the protection you need to secure your hearts from being wounded by sin; that's why His instructions are obeyed. Scripture says *"Delight yourself in the Lord, And He will give you the desires and petitions of your heart."* (Psalm 37:4 AMP) If we use God's method of delight, then a heart that truly is delighted in God will desire what God delights in and what He desires for you, it will love what God loves and it will do what God purposed it to do, wholeheartedly!

And, in return we can have peace with God and forgiveness of the sin that tried to make its way into our hearts. You can't ever leave home without taking up your shield of faith. The Holy Bible says that the Romans soldiers dipped their hide-covered shields into water to extinguish fiery darts throw at them. Can you imagine going into battle with fire and darts being thrown at you by your enemies? Well, every day when you wake up, Satan has darts already aimed at you to defeat you day by day! Without your faith, without Jesus shielding you and washing you that you may be restored, you would surely perish. We are being dipped in the water of the Word, and we are covered by the blood of Christ and fully replenished. Protect yourself—where's your shields? Furthermore, where's your faith?

In this spiritual battle don't leave home without taking your helmet of salvation, that's the only way of protecting your crown and keeping your mind's purity protected and secure from the lusts of the world!

Don't ever allow the enemy to make his home within your mind. Your mental stability is very important, especially if you are weak in your flesh. All of us have sinned and our sins are formulated with just a thought and if we are weak, sooner or later, we might become prey to our temptations.

The desire of your flesh can have a tremendous force on your will power, it will continue to draw you toward disobedience, it wants you to go against the pull of the Holy Spirit. That's why Satan attempts so hard at getting within the walls of your feelings—your cracks—tempting you when you desire to be wanted by others, or need to feel loved. If you continue to think about your desires, eventually you'll act on them!

The battle for control becomes a tug of war between your spirit and your flesh. What have you been thinking about lately? Do you have a helmet when you step out there? The devil wants your mind, your thoughts, your actions, and your crown to fade! He wants the good in you to become the *Girls Gone Wild*, or the Men of Distinction! He wants your virtue, your esteem, your supernatural God-given power! He wants your relationship with Christ Jesus! And if there's a crack in your armor, you are wide open! Remember, your battles are not just in the physical, but they stem from your thinking process.

Your minds are just filled with conflicts you are battling, and sometimes you leave yourself open to the wars within. The battlefield of the mind is the primary place spiritual battles are fought. We can't win the battle if we are not fighting in the spirit realm, and definitely not with our carnal man. The Lord works His truth into our perspectives to free us up, while the enemy fights for strongholds to bind us. Freeing truths are the realities we face, the stuff we surrender to God, our repentance for the freeing of our minds. When we are set free then the strongholds are broken as well!

This is a spiritual war between your new man, the person you have become in Christ, and your old man, the person you used to be; they are battling for your life! Your old man wants to keep you in your sins and your new man wants to see you make it to your everlasting life.

You must always be sure you carry the sword of the Spirit, which is the Word of God everywhere you go. It is the only piece of armor that will defend, protect, and improve us. When we are tempted, the most effective weapon that God has given to us as believers is the sword of the Spirit.

God expects us to use what we carry, what we know about Him, what's embedded within our hearts, so that the Word of God goes wherever we go. Do you have your sword with you? If you spend time reading your Word, studying Scripture, and learning how to allow it to lead you then you will have an effective weapon with you always. When you allow it to be delivered off your tongue against the enemy effectively then you are carrying the sword of the Spirit. Continue to use it to speak over yourself, encourage yourself, and to use your spiritual words as a weapon to fight off the attacks of your enemies.

When the devil tried temptation after temptation, lie after lie against Jesus, He used the sword of the Spirit to defend himself. He had the Word hidden in His heart and when temptation came, He was able to use what He knew about the Father as a tool against His enemy. When the devil tempted Him three times, Jesus responded with the truth of God's Word every time. If you haven't studied it, you can't use what you don't know. This is how we defend ourselves and how we go into offense against our enemies, by using the Word of God—every time, every-day, everywhere! You are taking time to pull off your inhibited form when you take back your voice. You are unveiling your newness, and you have unmasked your inhibited nature with just the power of the Word of God! The devil can't have your inheritance!

You should not allow your life battles to overwhelm you when you can just plug into your power source, which is God. *"[Y]et for us there is but one God, the Father, who is the source of all things, and we exist for Him; and one Lord, Jesus Christ, by whom are all things [that have been created], and we [believers exist and have life and have been redeemed] through Him"* (1 Cor. 8:6 AMP).

God should be the only one consuming our lives with anything. While on this journey here are all the tools you will need in every battle described in this scripture:

Therefore put on the full armor of God, so that when the day of evil comes, you may be able to stand your ground, and after you have done everything, to stand. Stand firm then, with the belt of truth buckled around your waist, with the breastplate of righteousness in place, and with your feet fitted with the readiness that comes from the gospel of peace. (Ephesians 6:13-15 NIV)

This is all you'll ever need to win your battles!

The apostle Paul went on to give more details in how to win in spiritual warfare, he said.

In addition to all this, take up the shield of faith, with which you can extinguish all the flaming arrows of the evil one. Take the helmet of salvation and the sword of the Spirit, which is the word of God. And pray in the Spirit on all occasions with all kinds of prayers and requests. With this in mind, be alert and always keep on praying for all the Lord's people. Pray also for me, that whenever I speak, words may be given me so that I will fearlessly make known the mystery of the gospel, for which I am an ambassador in chains. Pray that I may declare it fearlessly, as I should.

With everything else discussed above never forget prayer too is a necessity! If you don't have a prayer life, you're not in position and that's when Satan will come for you! *"The effectual fervent prayer of a righteous man avails much"* (James 5:16 KJV).

When you're praying, you'll feel your inner man moving into a newness that's beneficial to everyone who encounters you. The people who take the time to know you will be blessed by the way you wear your crown. You cannot be a hypocrite. One moment you're up and the next you're down. As a new creation with a new mindset and with restored vision, you're able to see things new. Continue to admire your sight through God's eyes and not the world's vision.

This will allow you to be more prompted to walk on a new road, a straighter one to make your journey without delay, and talk with a new tone that includes the love for God, and His people. What benefits are more substantial than the ones God has for you in getting to the maximum level of your growth? You are what you do and how you do it, so guard your gates! Be mindful when it comes to negativity or anything that preoccupies your spiritual space.

My God, His reward is worth the change. Change is in your best interest, for God is the greatest reward we could ever receive. When you grow spiritually it is of great benefit to everyone who meets you, because they can see the benefits of being faithful through you, through your witness!

If you believe that you are the best creation God made when He formed you then put Him on display! Never forget to show your gratitude for what He has done. The beauty of His glory is displayed because we were designed in His image. What a Father who showed us His love and the gleam of His image for us to exhibit daily! How could you imagine looking any other way?

Take care of who you are, when you neglect yourself, you're neglecting what the Word of God says about you! Your reputation, regeneration, your rebirth, being born again, you're reawakening from a dead spirit, won't occur if you don't believe your mind can be transformed from the way it used to be. To be born again is to wake up and thrive so others can see what you believe! When you believe in who you are, you change the game! Your faith has made you live so do not open yourself up to things of the devil! One quote I love is "when life gets too hard to stand, kneel." Get on your knees and ask the Father to guide and help you overcome the things that keep trying to steal your seed.

In the book of Genesis, Eve, who's name meant "to live" or "to breathe," gave Adam a forbidden fruit to eat, which he ate bringing sin and death into the world, which led to the repercussions we face today. As a result of their disobedience, God removed them from the garden of Eden and sent them elsewhere to regenerate, redevelop their minds, seek forgiveness, and take time to think about the crime they had just committed against Him in the sanctuary He created just for them.

We can find ourselves put out of the shelter of God for our disobedience. They had everything necessary for a fulfilling life, but lost it all due to a corrupted mindset. We can say the serpent tricked them, but remember they still made the choice to walk in the disobedience! They chose to walk with the negativity of God's enemy! A Facebook friend I have said, "Negativity can only affect you if you're on the same frequency, so vibrate higher."

That's why you must train your spirit to listen to the spirit of God to be transformed into His Spirit! To recognize that God is still on the throne comes through letting go of the mistakes of our gardens. Your mind is a garden, your thoughts are the seeds that fertilize it and bring forth the beauty of your harvesting, either you'll see the flowers bloom or you'll see the destruction of the weeds choking out your growth! What you grow is based upon what you allow to get in your mind!

Psalm 91 (NLT) reads,

> *Those who live in the shelter of the Most-High will find rest in the shadow of the Almighty. This I declare about the LORD: He alone is my refuge, my place of safety; he is my God, and I trust him. For he will rescue you from every trap. and protect you from deadly disease. He will cover you with his feathers. He will shelter you with his wings. His faithful promises are your armor and protection. Do not be afraid of the terrors of the night, nor the arrow that flies in the day. Do not dread the disease that stalks in darkness, nor the disaster that strikes at midday. Though a thousand fall at your side, though ten thousand*

are dying around you, these evils will not touch you. Just open your eyes, and see how the wicked are punished.

If you make the LORD your refuge, if you make the Most High your shelter, no evil will conquer you; no plague will come near your home. For he will order his angels to protect you wherever you go. They will hold you up with their hands so you won't even hurt your foot on a stone. You will trample upon lions and cobras; you will crush fierce lions and serpents under your feet!

The LORD says, "I will rescue those who love me. I will protect those who trust in my name. When they call on me, I will answer; I will be with them in trouble. I will rescue and honor them. I will reward them with a long life and give them my salvation."

Bad choices occur when you react before you interact! It's very important to take time to meditate. Think before you respond! Focus your attentions on "The Me Factor" when getting your mind stable. Ask yourself, "Is it for me that I'm doing this?" If you're doing anything for anyone other than your own personal growth it will eventually collapse! Stability is missing in the lives of so many great people. People with great minds that let in the weeds! When you're unstable you make bad choices that might not have been made otherwise based on your current situation. There is renewed hope in the life that is found in you when you remember that God is in you, He doesn't need to come and gather you home, for he has never left you! He is waiting on you to welcome Him back into your life, back into the unwelcomed choices you made without consulting Him! When you give your all to the Lord, you are making the best and securest investment into your future life with Him.

Brother Stacey Spears, a good friend of mine, would say, "Don't sleep on ya own common sense!" And he would love to counter your excuses with, "Forget all the reasons why it won't work and focus on the one reason it will." Such a wise friend is he, especially when he said, "Some people miss the message because they are too busy looking for the mistake." Remember the struggle you're in today, the hard times you're enduring, the mess of stress, is there to develop the strength you will need to make it through your tomorrows as well.

It is important to pay attention to what you watch, listen to, read, even the people you hang out with. What you subject your mind to is what you are chewing on either spiritually or worldly! One or the other is feeding your emotions, your spirit, or your physical body the meal of your indulgence. My mama used to always tell me "A hard head makes a soft behind," I didn't learn what she meant until it was too late! She said "what goes around comes around" and "what goes up must come down," but I still had to learn the hard way!

One thing I can say is that she never gave up on me, when she said, "you will reap what you sow," and I did, that's when I finally got the message and decided to get my life right and now, I'm reaping the harvest God promised me! I finally got it together once I understood God's word, *"you will seek me and find me when you seek me with all your heart."* (Jer. 29:13 NIV) I only wish I had listened sooner!

When you enter into "The Me Factor" you're saying it's okay for me to be a better version of myself. Loving yourself is a healthy facet in gaining love for what you do, how you benefit from the love of your achievements, and even how love enters into you. I don't believe anyone should be considered to be selfish by saying to others 'I love being me," "I did it" or "Thank you, I did my best," but in some cases we misuse our gifts by taking credit for them. Our gifts came from God, not us!

If you struggle to truly believe in yourself, it might be hard to see God as your everything! When you don't recognize that all things are done through the grace and mercy of God who allowed you to do all things in becoming the individual you are today and acquiring all He has provided for you to have, it is a dishonor to Him. It's okay to say you're an achiever, just don't take credit for the achievement; give thanks to God for the strength in your laboring, getting through your hurt, weaknesses, confusion, loneliness, even the lack. He gave you the strength, the healing, the hope, the answers, the clarity, the peace, the provision, the purpose, and the love you needed to make it through it all; that's why He deserves the praise, honor, and glory!

The fact of the matter is to encourage yourself and to be an encourager in the Lord! Encourage one another to accept their "me factors." Be careful who you listen to, not everyone wants what's best for you. Some people don't want you to achieve; they will not speak good things into your life to better it! Misery loves company, don't be the one who's miserable!

You can't give honor to God when you are low in spirit! It's okay to say "I did my best," but always conclude with "Thank you, Lord for giving me everything I needed to make it happen!" God gets the glory and honor always! Give God all the credit for being the God over your entire life's benefits! And never be ashamed of getting spiritually balanced! *"For I say, through the grace given unto me, to every man that is among you, not to think of himself more highly than he ought to think; but to think soberly, as God hath dealt to every man the measure of faith"* (Rom. 12:3 KJV).

When we ask ourselves some vital questions and consider the answer God always takes forefront. The song "I Never Could Have Made It Without You" comes to mind every time I think about what God has done for me! He deserves the glory and honor for every part of our lives! No one should go into the "me factor" believing it's all about themselves! We cannot think of ourselves more highly than we ought to. In doing "The Me Factor" you are learning to be a better Christlike person. "The Me Factor" is just a self-evaluation while you are sitting alone with God seeking answers, as He reveals them to you, write them down, so you won't forget. Start by asking God questions like "What is it that you require of me, Lord?"

So many people have asked the question, "How do I know what the will of God is, for me?" Or "How do I know if I am hearing from God?" My answer to them is always, "You have to first believe in Him as your Lord and Savior and trust Him with your entire life, not a portion or just some things, but everything, then begin seeking an understanding of who Jesus is, to you." If you seek him, you'll find him! Once you have an established relationship, just like anybody else you love, when they are speaking to you their voice is clear and recognizable! The closer the two of you become, the more you love talking to one another, for you are building a lasting relationship!

We'll never fully know everything about an omnipotent God, but day by day you'll begin to get a clearer picture of who he is to you. Learning what God's will is for your life involves you getting alone in prayer with Him daily and seeking His guidance. When you don't know, make a realistic list of what you have or have not done for Him, so that you can determine where you should go from here. If you are truly following and seeking after Him, you'll find the answers as long as your list isn't filled with lies. The only person you'll be lying to is yourself, God already knows! No walk is easy, but it's worth the benefits!

Write down what you are committed to doing for Jesus, for life. Be realistic! Don't vow anything you're not ready to commit to. The Bible says it best, "Moses *said to the heads of the tribes of Israel: "This is what the LORD commands: When a man makes a vow to the LORD or takes an oath to obligate himself by a pledge, he must not break his word but must do everything he said"* (Num. 30:1–2 NIV). Don't make an oath that you cannot commit to!

If your list is filled with what you want Him to do for you, then you're not in a marriage with Jesus, you are just courting Him for your own personal gain. You have not made a commitment to honor and cherish Him, in sickness and in health, till death do us part. We are brides to the bridegroom, this is a marriage, we are united together for life! Our level of commitment must be equally yoked! Therefore, never tell God what you think He wants to hear.

Be determined to do a genuine self-evaluation, a written process, and an assessment of yourself in order to gain the truth of who you are and who you want to become? Once you know God's will, act on it by regenerating your mind back toward Him. Death without Christ is eternal damnation! It's time to wake up and get your mind restored back to Christ Jesus! I read that "in order to carry a positive action, we must develop a positive vision." Let your vision be uncompromised by letting your God be the source of your vision.

Regeneration is a radical yet gradual change that doesn't happen overnight; it's something you will have to work at. After regeneration, you come alive, you should begin to see, hear, and seek after the divine things of God. Then you will begin living a life of faith and holiness. You'll start wanting a life filled with more and more godly things and less and less of your worldly practices.

The more God you have, the more the Word of God and life of Jesus Christ will start to form in your heart, and you will become partakers of His divine nature, having been made new creatures. It's God, not man, who is the source of our transformation; we cannot take any credit! New creatures are people who have new natures! They have been renewed. They have come alive in their spirits. Dead things, including the mess and the distress that you used to carry and do, have all passed away. When you are renewed, you will gain your clarity and see your way more clearly!

Being led into a life of regeneration is necessary, for our sinful human flesh cannot stand in God's presence and say we are holy, nor sanctified. The only claim we can make is that we are saved by grace! If you are regenerated you will make living righteously an acceptable part of your life every day, not just occasionally. What God did for us at the moment of our salvation, along with His sealing it has guaranteed us birthrights.

> *"[W]ho is a deposit guaranteeing our inheritance until the redemption of those who are God's possession-to the praise of his glory"* (Eph. 1:14 NIV). It guaranteed His adoption of us. *"[T]o redeem those under the law, that we might receive adoption to sonship"* (Gal. 4:5 NIV). It guaranteed us His reconciliation of us.
>
> *All this is from God, who reconciled us to himself through Christ and gave us the ministry of reconciliation: that God was reconciling the world to himself in Christ, not counting people's sins against them. And he has committed to us the message of reconciliation. We are therefore Christ's ambassadors, as though God were making his appeal through us. We implore you on Christ's behalf: Be reconciled to God."* (2 Corinthians 5:18–20 NIV)

God cannot be taken for granted.

Regeneration is God making us spiritually alive, our eyes were blind, we couldn't see, and as a result of our faith in Jesus Christ and our acceptance of His death, burial, and resurrection, we are regenerated at that moment of us believing. You cannot look at regeneration as an option, it is not optional, for *"flesh gives birth to flesh, but the Spirit gives birth to spirit"* (John. 3:6 NIV) if you are reborn again, it is only of the spirit alone. When you have been renewed in Christ, your spirit is living again!

My husband always says "spirit recognizes spirit," which means you will be recognized as a child of a king and your spirit won't be comfortable around the children of the world, for they are not of the same family structure!

Our physical birth prepared us for earth and our spiritual rebirth, our regeneration, prepares us for heaven. Before salvation, we were degenerate, corruptible beings, but after salvation, giving up our will to God's will, we are regenerated. We are being led into peace with God into a new life with Him.

Through salvation we are gaining an eternal son-ship, a relationship between father and son, with God and our regeneration process begins with the process of sanctification wherein we have become the people God intended for us to be. We are justified by Christ alone; no work of our hands can give us regeneration. We don't need restoration or renovation or reorganization; we need rebirth in gaining our regeneration And for that we are no longer captive to a lost world, for we are only visitors passing through!

As captives we have all been set free.

> *The Spirit of GOD, the Master, is on me because GOD anointed me.*
>
> *He sent me to preach good news to the poor, heal the heartbroken,*
>
> *Announce freedom to all captives, pardon all prisoners.*
>
> *GOD sent me to announce the year of his grace— a celebration of God's destruction of our enemies— and to comfort all who mourn,*
>
> *To care for the needs of all who mourn in Zion, give them bouquets of roses instead of ashes, Messages of joy instead of news of doom, a praising heart instead of a languid spirit. Rename them "Oaks of Righteousness" planted by GOD to display his glory.*
>
> *They'll rebuild the old ruins, raise a new city out of the wreckage. They'll start over on the ruined cities, take the rubble left behind and make it new. You'll hire outsiders*

to herd your flocks and foreigners to work your fields, but you'll have the title "Priests of GOD," honored as ministers of our God. You'll feast on the bounty of nations; you'll bask in their glory. Because you got a double dose of trouble and more than your share of contempt, your inheritance in the land will be doubled and your joy go on forever. (Isaiah 61:1–7 MSG)

May the Lord bless you and keep you always! May the Lord make His face to shine upon you, and be gracious to you! May the Lord lift up His countenance upon you, and give you peace of mind! Amen.

Step 2: Self-Determination

Are you reassured of yourself or easily intimidated by others?

In our process of becoming self-determined women and men, we are no longer being defined by others, we have set bounds on what you can say about who we are. We will not be compromised by morals or values that are not becoming of our natures just so we will be accepted. We are ready to make sensible, intentional, and fulfilling decisions that fit the character of who God says that we are without permission! Now that we realize our greatness, we're willing to evict anyone who doesn't respect our level of self-convictions.

My son Darius said "One important thing we must remember as we look to self-improve our lives in this year is 'soil development,' just like a seed trying to grow in bad soil, we cannot become everything we are designed to become in bad environments. Plant yourself in healthy environments around people who will pull the greatness out of you and uphold you to a standard." Wow, that's real growth! We need people to hold us accountable in our soil-development, so we don't regress. When your soil is fertile your soul is reaping the harvest.

The process of defining ourselves accurately comes from our self-determination to find our true natures. It shows that you have come to a conclusion that your way isn't always working and now you are willing to be led toward your true definitions. There was a young man I met some time ago who told me about how he lost everything including his family because he was determined to always be right! He revealed that he was in leadership, a pillar within his community, but wasn't willing to compromise his negativity for the good of the people who loved him, now he has, in his own words, some rebuilding to do!

God gives us what's already within our reach to find our paths to His loyalty. We have to learn to utilize what we have. Part of who you are is found in how you utilize what you have to grow as women. The use of the tools God provided for us to study His Word not only helps us define who we are to Him, they help us to understand the factors to getting aligned with Him.

"The entrance and unfolding of your words give light; their unfolding gives understanding (discernment and comprehension) to the simple" (Ps. 119:130 AMP). The unfolding of God's Word should bring us revelation, it should enlighten us, and open our eyes to the kingdom of

God once we have an understanding that it is His Word radiating as our light. When you read and abide in the Word then you grow in it as a partaker of what you now have learned from it.

You can't just say you are enlightened by the Word of God and live as if you have no real expectations that a change has to transpire. Without you allowing His Word to change your outlook, there will be no light and your bulbs will eventually go from dim to blowing completely out if you never connect to the source. Your enlightening of the Word comes through your understanding of who God is, then standing boldly on the knowledge of Jesus Christ and what is right, what is true, and what you know to be honorable, because you know Him! To be changed is to spend time in the Word.

As a young woman carrying the weight of the world upon her shoulders, I found it hard managing a full-time job, six kids, a husband, and going to school. Lining up with God's will was difficult! I couldn't manage my time to develop a relationship with Him. As a result, I lived with mental sedation; always tired, feeling overwhelmed, and under-appreciated! I lacked the ability to cope with my life and blamed it on the life I was living. I allowed the enemy to tell me that I could do better and be better if I hadn't made the choices that I had made. Later in life as I matured, I realized that God allowed things to happen to prepare me for the task He had in store for my life, once I was fully in position to receive the assignment. Watch what you give your attention to, it might be what's interfering with your assignment!

Being mentally seduced is an interference of the mind seeking after the things of the flesh instead of the spirit. When we allow our minds to seduce us into mental deficit, we can lack the ability to escape without believing we must be our own sacrifices. The sacrifice has already been made; all we need to do is to make the right decisions in our living for God. Let your lives be the meaning of your love for life, not your lack of living it right.

The Bible says, *"For those who live according to the flesh set their minds on the things of the flesh, but those who live according to the Spirit set their minds on the things of the Spirit"* (Rom. 8:5 ESV). As women we hold extreme power over the hearts of our mates, therefore if our minds are filled with fleshly feasting, we're always thinking seductively, relinquishing our God-given power of peace and serenity, our worth, without any biblical requirements, then how can we expect them to trust their hearts to us when all we've offered is our flesh. Know your worth if you goal is to become more than just their pastime. No one should use you to pass time until the next time! Show some self-control!

We cannot give our crowns of glory over to everybody who compliments us or admires our crowns! God created us in such a way that your jewel is for His glory! Your crown is for His deity! It's your power cord, your virtue, your honor, your righteousness. Don't lay it around, move it anywhere, or just give your crowned jewels to anyone! In other words, don't be worldly with it; it is costly to lose! Everyone shouldn't see your decorated jewels, because your crowns are the authority of your precious jewels!

"For to be carnally minded is death, but to be spiritually minded is life and peace" (Rom. 7:6 NKJV). Don't let your lack of independence have you partaking of any and all things that come from having a carnal mate with a carnal mind. Allow yourself to be guided by a spirit-led mate with whom you are in sync with his spirit, and not just his fleshly actions. A man respects a woman who has respect for herself! If he loves you, he'll help you straighten up your crowns, and wait for your jewels to shine again!

When we are in sync with our roles as godly women, as the helpmate or helper within our relationships, then we can be effective caretakers of the souls of our mates, gently loving and sensitively nurturing their spirits. We can then relinquish our aggressions and freely give up our need for control. When your mate has earned your respect and trust, don't fear letting him have your heart. If you are properly aligned in holy matrimony, it comes with ease, especially when you are equally yoked with your mate and your Christ. Now you lack the desire to feast on meals all over the urban and rural area! You Boaz is out there if you can be patient and wait on him.

I know in the ways of the world today that it is hard to wait! But for some to retrieve and reclaim your God-given free will, you need to find the freedom of your jewels release within your celibacy. Your abstinence allows you to hold the key that unlocks the hearts of your mates when they are led by God. This promise of abstaining includes outercourse!

When this same power has already been misused or abused, it becomes a woman's tool to disaster, rendering her powerless, allowing intercession of the heart to become manipulated and seduced instead. Even a woman who has made a compromise within her jewels can still reclaim her powerful position in practicing voluntarily. There are some who would say this is undoable because the body desires what you feed it!

The Bible tells a story about Potiphar's wife, a conniving woman who caused interruption within the "oneness" process between herself and God. When you give up a portion of your values to unworthy people, it interrupts God's process. And, you're coming together as one in heart is now brokenness, but the bond between Father and child is always mendable.

Genesis 39:7–23 tells how Potiphar's wife was a woman who was a seducer, manipulator, liar, and deceiver. She almost destroyed a life with her defiance of God's laws. If you have a godly man, you two should always be working toward oneness; don't give Satan power over your cohesion by allowing division within your relationship. Be determined to make ends meet so that the moment Satan throws darts at you, you show unity! Have a spiritual extinguisher ready to put out the flames of any unforeseen outbreaks. Extinguish the attack on sight, don't wait until it divides!

Equally yoked people are less likely to be divided when times are rough, if they agree with the standards of God! Unequally yoked people can come together, but they will have a harder time standing in the gap for one another, because they don't have the same values or believe in the same things! The phrase "Unequally Yoked" is described in 2 Corinthians 6 as, *"Be ye not unequally yoked together with unbelievers: for what fellowship hath righteousness with unrighteousness? and what communion hath light with darkness?"* (2 Cor. 6:14 KJV).

The (NASB 1995) version says, *"Do not be bound together with unbelievers; for what partnership, have righteousness and lawlessness, or what fellowship has light with darkness?"* Yet sometimes we still choose our partners by their looks, abilities, and our feelings, instead of starting with the character of their godly love!

Let's me break this down because so many of us find ourselves in relationships with people who are not reborn again, therefore the relationship is unbalanced! We believe in different things and that divides us! Let's first understand what is a yoke? I'm not referring to the yolk of an egg you can cook, but the yoking up together! A yoke is a wooden crosspiece that is fastened over the necks of two animals and then it's attached to the plow or cart that they are to pull. It's the piece that helps us balance one another.

There's so many people, places, and things that are yoked up to us that have to be released from our spirits and removed from us, so that God can begin to shine through our lives. Many years ago, I wrote a message titled "What Does It Mean to Be Unequally Yoked?" The summary of the sermon went something like this: The phrase "unequally yoked," is taken from 2 Corinthians 6:14 in the King James Version of the Holy Bible and it carries a level of standards: *"Be ye not unequally yoked together with unbelievers: for what fellowship hath righteousness with unrighteousness? And what communion hath light with darkness?"*

The New American Standard Version says, *"Do not be bound together with unbelievers; for what partnership, have righteousness and lawlessness, or what fellowship has light with darkness?"*

The Message was received with a wide-eyed view for many of the women I was speaking to because many of them were living within a lifestyle of unequally yoking. I was later asked "What should I do?" I am not here to give answers to problems of the matters of the heart nor the matters that God will answer if you ask Him. If you want a relationship with Christ you have to surround yourself with people who want what you want.

In doing some earlier research, I learned that a yoke is a wooden bar that joins two oxen to each other and there was a connection and a burden that they pulled, because the oxen were "unequally yoked." They were united, whereas one stronger ox and one weaker, or one taller and one shorter were linked together to show how to bear one another's burden as a team. Yet, they were unequal, because one was weak and smaller while the other stood upright and strong in spirit. They're placed together for training so that they will eventually become equal to one another. The spiritual principle is that the one that's unbalanced, lacking in spiritual growth, needs help becoming who God created them to be.

The weaker or shorter ox would walk more slowly than the taller, stronger one, causing the load to go around in circles. When oxen are unequally yoked, they cannot perform the task set before them equally. Instead of working together, they are at odds with one another. Just like a marriage that is divided or unequal.

The purpose for the yoking up is for the growth of the weaker, shorter oxen or Christian, so that they can mature and learn how to align themselves to the Word of God.

Surround yourself with Christlike people who will help you grow while you're feeling weak in spirit. You will always be weak if you stay disconnected from yoking up with Christlike people who can help you in your walk.

When the unrighteous walks with the light or with a righteous Christian, that person if they are mature in Christ must be available to help train, to help prepare, the weaker oxen or weaker Christians, who still wants to stray or go the wrong way. But how can you be ready if you still insist on straying yourself?

In 2 Corinthians 6:14 the apostle Paul addresses the church at Corinth about the effects of a Christians life when they are unequally yoked to people, places and things of this world. He discouraged them from being in an unequal partnership with unbelievers. He says in the letter that believers and unbelievers are opposites, just as light and darkness are opposites. They simply have nothing in common, just as Christ has nothing in common with *Belial,* a Hebrew word meaning "worthlessness," which Belial is also known to us as "The Devil" who's unworthy to dwell with us.

The word *worthlessness* refers to Satan and his worthlessness here on earth. He is worthless to us as well. Satan negatively influences us with corruption, wickedness, and skepticism, this is why we, as Christians, should separate ourselves from all wicked worldly pleasures that cause us to fumble. Christ separated Himself from all the approaches, devices, and tactics of Satan that would have caused Him to be separated from His Father; therefore, we are to do the same!

We were considered worthless yet Christ resided among the worthlessness and He never let Himself be influenced while living within the world. He never partook in any of the wickedness of it. He maintained His purpose for which He came: to save you and I. We are to follow the example of as His followers and not allow anything to interfere with the plans God has for us!

When you're attempting to live a Christian life with a non-Christian as your close friend and ally, it will only cause you to spin recklessly; you'll find yourself going around in circles trying to figure out the right amongst all the wrongs you're living. There are many women today who are wondering why it's not working out; why your spirit can't find what God has in store for it. Have you considered who, what, or the things you are yoked up too? Everything attached to us is spiritual! The distractions that we allow can hinder our spirit-being and affect who we are in Christ!

The people you have soul ties with who are not on your level are a distraction. The people you have welcomed into your spirit space who only came to make you believe they are there to leave a deposit are a distraction. The people who have only made withdrawals from you are a distraction! The places that you have visited without cause are distractions!

Where we go, what we do, how we entertain have to serve our kingdom purpose or they will only distract you from your kingdom agenda! When you are distracted, these things will dwindle down your dignity, your self-worth, your resilience, your time, your faith, and leave you inhibited!

You cannot expect to continue to be unyoked Christians and be mad when you fall short or cause your own selves to stumble if you haven't done what's necessary to get stronger! Stay focused even if you take a nosedive, stay determined even though you're losing everything, stay in prayer while you're feeling discouraged, stay on track even if people slander your name, stay in church especially when you're mad and even when it feels hard to do!

Sometimes this is why you find yourself going in circles, landing back where you started; you're not yoked up to the same size oxen, you both aren't as strong in faith as you hoped, and you both are not living righteously in this walk! You are still weak in spirit! When you are equally yoked, the two of you when yoked up are unshakable! Your union will be blessed! Keep walking, until God yokes you up with the right person who's in pursuit of you!

This is why Scripture tells us what we must and must not do *"Be ye not unequally yoked together with unbelievers: for what fellowship hath righteousness with unrighteousness? and what communion hath light with darkness?"* (2 cor. 6:14 KJV) If you're not strong in faith nor spiritually stable, you will find yourself repeating the same life lessons we've discussed earlier; this is the place in your life where you're going in circles and can't understand why!

In a world filled with unbelievers who have opposite worldviews and morals, even their business decisions will reflect their worldview and not comply with yours and you could feel pressured to leave your Christian principles behind for the sake of a business gain.

In Genesis 2:24 God has a plan is for a man and a woman to become "one flesh" in marriage with Him as the third string within the marriage. God never intended for us to marry and become unequally yoked by design, for this union comes with a cost! You don't have the same standards; therefore, it becomes difficult living without compromise and what you do, see, and hear has become an egotistical distraction in your life!

If you want things to line up, don't just yoke up with anybody, anywhere, in any way; be available to be a light in a dark place, get ready for God's service and to receive His people that you may be yoked up with to help them grow and not to be pulled back to where you once were.

Set a standard for your life right now, one that you won't allow Satan to compromise by killing, stealing, or destroying what God has positioned you for. Take back what the devil stole by honoring God and His kingdom intended participation! You must be ready, none of you are exempt from God's kingdom agenda. It's time out for living among those that cause division. We must live like we believe, as if our faith is strong, that it is evident in our choices.

This bar joins two oxen to each other and onto the load they are pulling it to accomplish a purpose. It's the same measures we use when we are working together to accomplish a common goal! But an unequally yoked team is an unbalanced team. When either one of us is too weak to pull the haul, we yoke up equally to accomplish the task. When you are unequally yoked, you struggle to perform the task set before you. This is what happens when we pair up with people who are not like-minded with us. Instead of us working together, like the oxen, we are at odds with one another, unbalanced. We are divided! Our views on Christ don't align, because one of us doesn't know who He is! While one is praying; the other is complaining! While one is worshipping; the other is gambling! You get the metaphor!

Have you yoked up with someone that you regret? Now the butterflies have subsided and you feel like your life is spinning in circles. You're going slower than you expected, because the partner you're attached to is choking the life out of you. God wants you both to be linked up with Him before you link yourselves to one another, so that you will understand your purpose as one with Christ!

The goal is to grow up so you can train others on how to run in this race for disciples. When we put on our yoke, we might have to put our hands to the plow over and over again before the weaker, or shorter, oxen catch on and learns what the requirements are in order to continue on without giving up. It's very important in any relationship that we choose someone who has overcome and is able to be a trainer and a strong Christian leader! Otherwise, unless they know Christ Jesus, they are unequal to the eternal life Christ is preparing for us upon His return.

Some people deny Christ for various reasons; therefore, they are not of Christ and useless to us as His believers. Unbelievers are the reason why we are called, that we may show them that He is real and usher them into the presence of His glory that they too may desire to receive Him as their Lord and Savior. Satan is worthless in comparison to our worthiness in Christ Jesus! It's like having a union with Satan himself when we yoke up with people who don't believe in Jesus Christ! Worthy is the lamb who was slain for all, but only the children of God will reap the benefits. He died for us all, unbelievers, sinners, and lost souls, but everyone must confess Jesus Christ as their Lord and believe in their own hearts in order to acquire what He has offered His children!

Satan is equal to his own kind and they are practicing their own religions, paganism, wickedness, and unbelief governed by the principles of Satan, not God. As Christians, no one should join any religious cults, but should be separated from the things of the wicked. You shouldn't partake in anything that separates you from the truths of God.

Christ Jesus separated Himself from every form and fashion of wickedness and deceit, and from all the tempting practices, purposes, and ideas that Satan made look pleasing to our natural sights. We cannot be the children of God and the world as well! Christ had no partaking, no union, no tasting, in absolutely none of them and He expects us to do the same, to flee, and when we don't, we find ourselves spinning in circles instead of being in control of our self-worth!

We cannot expect to continue as unyoked Christians and get mad when we fall short. Our shortcomings could cause us to stumble and others as well as if we don't do what's necessary to get stronger! Stay focused, even while you take a nosedive, stay determined while you're losing everything, stay in prayer while you feel discouraged, stay on track while people slander your name, stay in church even when you're mad. If we are yoked up to God and you are off course, the time will come when you will need to hear that you're in need of a stronger, larger oxen to walk with you until you get in step with the vision!

If you find yourself going in circles, landing back where you started year after year, it could be time for a change, for the right two working together when yoked up are unshakable! Therefore, I repeat the words of the apostle Paul, what we must and must not do *"Be ye not unequally yoked together with unbelievers: for what fellowship hath righteousness with unrighteousness? And what communion hath light with darkness?"* If you're not strong in faith and spiritually stable, you will find yourself reiterating the same life lessons, and you'll never stop going in circles!

The unequally yoked person will find themselves in a personal relationship that tempts them to put off the godly perspectives just to get along for the sake of their relationship, and then they will find themselves compromising their morals, and their integrity, to make things work between them and their worldly friends!

When you waver in your worldly ways against your spiritual principles, it's easier for Satan to use his bait to reel you in, and if your principles can become compromised by him, you might find yourself wavering on your morals too! It's like having a target on your back saying "pick me." The Bible warns us: *"Therefore, my beloved brothers and sisters, be steadfast, immovable, always excelling in the work of the Lord [always doing your best and doing more than is needed], being continually aware that your labor [even to the point of exhaustion] in the Lord is not futile nor wasted [it is never without purpose]"* (1 Cor. 15:58 AMP). Don't become the world's daily pick! It's worse to be married and in union with someone and have to live every day with a complicated relationship because you are opposites! No one wants to be with someone they don't see eye to eye with!

If you want things to line up don't just yoke up with anybody! Don't get caught anywhere, in any way with a bad yoke partner. Be available to be a light in a dark place, get yourself ready for God's service and be available to receive His people. Get ready that you may yoke up with people to help them grow; not to be pulled back to where you once were. Set a standard for your life right now! Make a decision of what you won't allow and stick to it. Command that you won't allow Satan to sabotage, confuse, or tear down anything that God has promised to you. It's past time to take back what the devil stole!

The apostle Paul states *"We are often troubled, but not crushed; sometimes in doubt, but never in despair; there are many enemies, but we are never without a friend; and though badly hurt at times, we are not destroyed"* (2 Cor. 4:8–9 GNT). People of God, it may appear easier to live your lives based on how your trials and tribulations steer you, how you go through them or not, but one thing for sure is that everyone shall have trying times.

It's how these times are managed. There will be days when you feel exhausted from trying to figure them out! Even, sometimes you will feel so overtaken by your trials, that you will insist that you must get right with the Lord. Oftentimes we believe that we shouldn't have a rough day in our lives when we believe we are in right standing with the Lord, but the pressures of our tribulations should never cause us to forfeit our privileges, our blessings, nor our God.

The enemy wants you to feel crushed, troubled, doubtful, and to lose hope so that you will fall out of alignment with God! Give up when your pain has crushed your spirit, but whatever you go through stay in your Word and continue to trust God. You will not be destroyed! Even if you have already yoked up with an unbeliever, never stop trusting God to make a change in your situation. He's able to do exceedingly, abundantly above all, especially, what we have caused on our own. Give it to Him and let Him fix it for you!

Step 3: Heart Transplantation

Why does my heart feel broken into pieces?

What is seduction of the heart when it is unleashed into a society filled with lust, violence, and deceit? It's now a weapon of mass destruction that's filled with lust over love. It has become a heart gone sour—one improperly filtered, and now it has been filled up with years of bitterness, selfishness, vanities, depression, misuse, abuse, unhealthiness, loneliness, illiteracies, waywardness, foulness, and so much more; leaving behind the residue of a scorned heart.

If it doesn't receive the proper nutrients it was designed to receive—love, kindness, hope, comfort, peace, goodness, or warmth—then you are left with a heart filled with no ripe fruit, no hope, no joy, and limited room for proper affirmation. Your love dwindles and now a loveless aching heart is leading you with no passion for love, only the lust for an act of seduction. It's without the ample power to love so it can be easily seduced and abused! It will have you believing that everyone who says, "I love you" means it!

A powerless, misused, and abused heart filled by the power of flesh is now set loose to operate outside God's realm of protection, and these are the hearts that wind up teaching others the wrong way to be loved. Then you become our Sunday school teachers, singing in our choirs, ushering at the doors as gatekeepers of our churches (our greeters/ushers), and you struggle to show love. These same abused seductions within your hearts are awakening inside and outside of God's house and that's why people find themselves not really knowing what real love is as a result of a failed heart's desire to be loved. We have to know who we are and love who God created us to be, so we don't allow ourselves to be misplaced in a position of disgrace instead of honor.

Love has to become of importance to getting our hearts transplanting accurately and in gaining back the adoration we are due. Love for ourselves and others have been stolen in the midst of life's circumstances, relationships, and unwarranted situations. Find the love you lost and add to it. Add some kind words, a smile, or maybe just give out hugs occasionally. A hug will go a long way to someone who's in need of one. Satan no longer has the power over you to continue in this cycle of non-caring. We cannot command one's love, demand one's love, or take away love, but we can fall out of love if we don't nurture our love languages for one another and stage a level of seduction that is tainted because there's no sincerity in how we love on one another.

God wants our courtship with Him. He wants us to be captivated by His love. He wants use to dance together in love with Him, not just becoming infatuated with a false sense of love, but being in tune to the beat of His heart and in godly love with one another as He is in us. We have lived among many deceitful people masquerading as holy rollers or people who think they know more than God Himself! We've lived in the flesh or with worldly natures and with the mindset of seducers who lurk all around and invade our weakened hearts. Check yourself, it just might be you doing the contaminating. A decent, respectable, God-seeking person will want to find the reason for the tears within their heart then seek Him for the strength to change their course. If you ask, you shall receive, so don't be afraid to ask.

A redirected heart can mend enormous broken fences, scrapes, bruises, any and all distractions, and close tears ducts. But nothing can be accomplished if you never ask God to do the mending and believe that He can and will. Too many tears in any garment will ruin the lining of its fabric. It will eventually fall apart if it continues to have tears in it. Let God mold you and put you back together again.

Once you're willing to attempt to make changes in your life, the key is the willingness. Some of us refuse to even try; we're happy just the way we are. Have you ever met people who believe that everybody else has problems, and there's absolutely nothing wrong with them? It's like the minister who preached a convicting sermon meant for everyone to reevaluate themselves, but there's always someone who looks at others saying to themselves "I hope she paid attention; she sure needed to hear that," but what about you, did you pay attention too? The message was for us all.

You're inhibited when you can't find it in your heart to love, forgive, or reinvent yourself.

Love is bigger than you are. You can invite love, but you cannot dictate how, when, where love expresses itself. You can choose to surrender to love, or not, but in the end, love strikes like a lightening bolt, it can be so unpredictable and irrefutable. You can even find yourself loving people you don't like at all as a result of love. Love does not come with conditions, stipulations, an addenda, or a timeline. Like the sun, love radiates independently of our fears capturing the warmth of our hearts.

God chose to love us unconditionally, without limits; why is it so hard for us to do the same? No one is perfect, but we all deserve to be loved wholeheartedly and without prejudice! Your principals can become compromised when you waver on your morals of love. *"Therefore, my beloved brothers and sisters, be steadfast, immovable, always excelling in the work of the Lord [always doing your best and doing more than is needed], being continually aware that your labor [even to the point of exhaustion] in the Lord is not futile nor wasted [it is never without purpose]"* (1 Cor. 15:58 AMP).

We have to learn how to get in sync with one another and in tune with God. Where can we enter the internal wilderness experience development line, the line that leads to God and His glory without wandering aimlessly and disobediently so that He can develop us? What corners are worth turning to experience time alone with God? Begin by praying for one another and ourselves, seeking reconnection back to Christ.

> *"Love is inherently free. It cannot be bought, sold, or traded. You cannot make someone love you, nor can you prevent it, for any amount of money. Love cannot be imprisoned nor can it be legislated. Love is not a substance, not a commodity, nor even a marketable power source. Love has no territory, no borders, no quantifiable mass or energy output."* Pinterest Quote

> *"Love knows no limit to its endurance, no end to its trust, no fading of its hope; it can outlast anything. It is, in fact, the one thing that still stands when all else has fallen."*

(1 Cor. 13: 7-8a J.B. PHILLIPS New Testament).
The only love that has no bounds is the love of God.
God is Love.

Some of us are not as godly as we think we are. We barely pray for one another without there being some sort of retribution, like helping one another is a punishment and we've been found guilty of the crime. How can we not give of ourselves to someone else or be in Christ and say we love God but not love each other? *"Search me, O God, and know my heart: try me, and know my thoughts: / And see if there be any wicked way in me, and lead me in the way everlasting"* (Ps. 139:23–24 KJV). We need to ask God to examine our hearts and our motives, and if there be any wickedness in us, lead us according to your ways, Lord.

In our society today the times have changed. It's considered honorable to buy loyalty, companionship, attention, even compassion, but someone's love cannot be bought. Love will come, or it will not. It has its own will and it will come in its own timing. It's not predicated on how we plan it or if it will be returned back to us. Love has no bounds, no commitments, no reasoning, and it cannot be forced upon another. That's why the greatest love comes from God who is love and gives it generously to us all.

God gives us free will to choose to love Him back and all He requires is that you reciprocate it back to His people as well. Our love cannot be turned on as an incentive. It cannot be turned off as a punishment. Only pretending to be love can be used as a tool to lure somebody, as a hook for a bait and switch, or imitating someone else's method of love, insinuating you're in love, when you're not. When you are in love, it comes freely and it's genuinely from your heart. Ask yourself, "What is your heart demonstrating?"

When you show love toward one another it doesn't mean that your love allows for destructive and abusive behaviors to go unchecked. If your spirit is being attacked, your love for one another speaks out against the injustice and protests with God's people when harm is being done. Your love antennas will register a rise in love or sink due to a lack thereof. The sincere love from God points out the consequences of hurting one of His own, especially when it comes as a result of spiritual warfare, such as the devil using someone to cause you not to be lovable. The attacks against you affect the love you show toward anything or anybody trying to harm you, that's why God directs His love toward us so that we will know how to continue to love the unlovable.

Satan sends attacks every day that are designed to make us fall out of love with God and His people. Just because we sometimes fall short, our love allows room for anger, grief, or pain to be expressed and released positively. We should never use negative circumstances as a tool to retract our love reports for one another. Love does not threaten to withhold itself if it doesn't get what it wants. Love does not say, directly or indirectly, "If you do wrong, I'll withhold my love." Love does not say, "God loves me more and you less." Love does not say, "If you want to be loved you must be of a certain demand or make a certain promise." It was freely given to you and that's how you should bestow it upon others as well.

God is love and He cares what becomes of you because He knows that we are all interconnected with Him. God's love is inherently compassionate and empathetic. God exhibit the true nature of love and God's love cannot be manufactured, manipulated, or self-possessed. Our love for God will allow us to honor His sovereignty and gain respect for every soul He places in our hands. Love is its own law and not the law we choose to follow. The Bible said that David was a man after God's own heart meaning even when he fell short, he knew that God was the only one who could restore him whole so he asked of God for everything that the devil stole from him including what was once the genuine love in his heart. And God restored him whole!

Step 4: From Inebriation to Mind Transformation

What has you intoxicated by it that you are distorted as a result?

God want us to proclaim His liberties; He has given us the license to obtain our liberty. We can either hold a license to sin or a license to serve God, either way we must choose who we will obey. Satan uses your old man mentality to get you to do his will, and some people have willingly allowed him to lead them. Now you can choose a better teammate if you want to be delivered from your deformities. When you put yourself out there detached from God, you are using improper bait. You can't catch fish with candy. Satan wants to show you how sweet it is when you need to know how will it work for my good. Is what you are reeling in from a good batch or a bad batch?

It's important to know what you're pulling in on your line, because you could have reeled in a batch of substance abuse, gambling addiction, drug addictiveness, behavior disorders, or alcoholic tendencies. Whatever gets you going is what you bait with. It is time for you to decide to stand strong and steadfast in the faith, so you can break this unit of separation and remove what is contaminating your batch. We need to know how to use the proper bait so we will know what's working for us or against us and what's not working at all, then we'll know what type of batches we are spiritually producing.

Breaking down the barriers and getting out of your drunkenness, your blurriness of your life choices that have led you into a confused lifestyle will not be easy, but it's worth the pursuit. You are in the act of committing spiritual adultery by allowing a separation of your spirit from God to lead you into corruption.

When our natural man leads, it causes us to work from a corruptible nature or mindset. The Bible says, *"Whosoever therefore shall be ashamed of me and of my words in this adulterous and sinful generation; of him also shall the Son of man be ashamed, when he cometh in the glory of his Father with the holy angels"* (Mark 8:38 KJV) It's a shameful feeling knowing God is not pleased with us, because our ways are not His ways, but we still say we are Christians. Pleasing God has restrictions; you can't do it how you want, but how He expects!

We are to profess Christ in all we do and say, especially among each other, not allowing the flesh to persuade us otherwise. Some restrictions are caused by us putting limits on God! Once you take the limitations off God you can get out of your rut and begin to claim your transformation in Him. Tell Jesus you are willing, ready, and able to try again this time with Him, and repent and turn away from yourself.

Let us examine a person who may be inebriated or in a drunken state of being before coming into their transformation. This type of person is like us before we came to Jesus. They are oblivious to the fact that they are absorbed in mess and that it has caused them to be incapacitated in spirit. We are blurred to what is really going on in our lives.

Inhibited

We are killing ourselves because we do not know any better. Our ability to think righteously is distorted by our wants and needs for things we think give gratification instead of those things that bring restoration.

A person who is drunk doesn't see what we can see about them. We see that they have exhibited behaviors of addiction even when they cannot see it themselves. We see they are unstable when they believe they are okay. We have witnessed them in a state of denial all while they are unable to remember what they did and that we actually saw it take place. If we can see it, God has already seen it and He knew it before you partook of it.

Addicts in their addictions have a hidden agenda, they are sneaking around trying not to get caught. They can't hold themselves up, always telling lies about their addiction, and they believe they can quit whenever they feel like it, but it never happens nor do they ever feel like it until something forces it upon them. Some addicts become so intoxicated that they cannot hold things stably, yet their addictions are evident in various areas of their lives, especially, when they're trying to remember what day it is, or what happened yesterday. It sometimes affects their work and everyday routines. Walking alcoholics can continue with their daily meet and greet process without ever blinking an eye and know they are drunk. They engage in their forbidden drinks thinking they are hiding it, but God and others already know. If you are pouring your desires into another container to conceal what it is then yes, you have an addiction that's now a problem you can't control on your own.

We see it in their eyes, their walk, their lack of remembrance, we even hear it in their slurred conversation. Why do you believe that you cannot overcome? Is it a family curse, and you fear of not fitting in if you recover, loosing friends, not being able to party like you used to? There are thousands or people who have overcome an addition and so can you with the proper assistance!

When you are facing an addiction you spend money frivolously on your desires, with no regard to the important things such as family, bills, food, or shelter. You have no stability! Addicts will take a little from all of them to feed their habit. They spend way too much time feeding the addiction rather than living their lives. They act out and start fights when they cannot have their way or need a fix.

Do you realize that addicts have no bladder control. Their bathroom sometime become a cup in their car, on their couches, or even on their or your bedroom floors. As an addict you sometimes treat people badly not realizing your burdens become your family's as well. Our loved ones are suffering, because of some of our choices! Some addicts are always trying to explain their situations to everybody, and it's usually never ever their fault according to them. Take ownership of your choices regardless of what happened to cause them! We can't have addictive personalities and not know we are drunk.

When enthusiasts drink, they usually never have just one, but they have an all-day or all-night binge, or they drink until they pass out. Addicts mostly enjoy drinking alone or they get together with anyone who wants to be their drinking buddy for the moment. You have no enemies when you are drinking; you get along with everyone especially when you are all indulging together; you have the same common denominator—getting drunk.

We are still working through the various personalities that people have and sometimes ignore because it's too hard coping with who they really are without feeling embarrassed, but we must get to the root so we can get the results. This is a type of personality that detoxifies your mind from getting spiritually sober. When you're intoxicated you eat anything and everything, or nothing at all, so losing weight is never a problem. Even your bathing is sometimes in a pool of your own bodily fluids. You can sleep almost anywhere and even on top of anything, including your own front lawn or in the neighborhood park. You have a perfume of your own that attracts flies and bees like flowers. When you arrive everyone feels the need to put up their purses and watch their belongings, because you tend to love to borrow what's not yours.

And what's with the bad dancing when you fall to the floor and on people, you can even wake up in beds with people you don't even know. Now I can understand why you need a cigarette to get through the pain of your hangovers. And you think you are okay without God! No judgments here, inhibited is for everybody!

If this hit home, do not feel that you are being singled out or talked about. You are not alone. God wants to show you how much He cares and is willing to teach you how to get through all the things that you believe will have you forever. God wants you to surrender and come back home.

Whether it's a form of behavior that you are exhibiting or your actual testimony, you have to make up your mind that inebriation is a behavior, one that you want help recovering from, because it doesn't look good on anyone! Anyone fitting this description needs professional help as well as spiritual counseling, so they can receive the support you need.

While we are counting down our 12 steps it's important to know about the Twelve Steps Programs of Alcoholics Anonymous so that we can get an insight as to being addicted to a dying world's system throughout the next seven steps:

First, you have to admit that you are powerless over alcohol—that your lives had become unmanageable.

Second, you have to come to believe that a Power greater than yourself could restore you to sanity.

Third, you have to make a decision to turn your will and your lives over to the care of God as we understood Him.

Fourth, you must make a searching and fearless moral inventory of yourself.

Fifth, you must admit to God, to yourself, and to another human being the exact nature of your wrongs. Confession.

Sixth, you must surrender, get yourself entirely ready to have God remove all these defects of character.

Seventh, humbly ask God to remove our shortcomings.

Eighth, make a list of all the people you have harmed and become willing to make amends to them all.

Ninth, make direct amends to such people wherever possible, except when to do so would injure them or others.

Tenth, continue to take personal inventory of yourself and when you are wrong promptly admitted it.

Eleventh, seek deliverance through prayer and meditation to improve your conscious contact with God, as we understood Him, praying only for knowledge of His will for us and the power to carry that out.

Twelfth, having had a spiritual awakening as the result of these steps, we tried to carry this message to alcoholics, and to practice these principles in all our affairs.

Even after going through the 12 steps, someone still has not made up their mind to be transformed and be spiritually delivered out of their addiction. Maybe hearing the behaviors of an addict might make you think about a life transformation and spiritual renewal.

We all have some form of addiction in some area of our lives that needs to be addressed. God does not want us just being alive without the benefits of living righteously. For the fear of the Lord is to be impressed with Him, inspired by Him, and in sync with Him; it can only be accomplished when we are transformed by Him! Don't let Satan keep you stuck in an addictive nature.

Step 5: Kingdom Participation

What does kingdom participation mean to you?

When you look at yourself in a mirror do you see your inner being? Can you see what is going on within you? What if you could feel it even if you cannot see it? The nature of who you are is within! How you receive the energy from within your spirit is determined by how much involvement you put into your well-being! *"A cheerful heart is good medicine, but a crushed spirit dries up the bones"* (Prov. 17:22 ESV).

The relationship you have with yourself is the one you will draw the most strength from. How you love you, your healthy self-love, is your best love!

Kingdom love is also accomplished by the love you have for yourself as well as the love you have for the ones attached to your life: your family, colleagues, place of worship, school—even your comrades—play a role in your goodwill. What is attached to you in love will build your kingdom! Your kingdom is you, and no matter what challenges you are up against, you will win; you have unstoppable self-love residing within you.

The kingdom of God is at hand and God is reaching forth to you to show His love toward you. Make sure you allow room for God not only to reside, but to reach out His hands unto you for His kingdom is inside of you. When you have been granted a kingdom reservation, you have received the mercies of God! Make sure you are conscious of God in all your thinking, doing, and speaking.

Your kingdom resides everywhere you allow God to go with you. Has God been welcomed in the company of everyone you know, and everywhere you go? When He comes with you, you are telling God that you are okay with His presence surrounding your world. The power and supremacy of God begins in you. It begins with you saying "yes" to God. Your submission is required for God to take up residency! Even if you hide it or won't submit it to Him, He still sees it!

Once you say yes, then God can rise up automatically in your heart and He can begin the process of deliverance and sanctification. All you need to do is to say yes, acknowledging to Him that He is the Messiah; He is the Savior of the world; He is the *El Shaddai*; He is God Almighty! Who would not want a relationship that restores, heals, cures, protects, loves, and also meets us everywhere and satisfies every need that we have? When God extends His hand toward you, take ahold of it, be guided by it, and accept what's in it for your good!

If you have no relationship with God, you are not a participator of His kingdom promises. Remember the feeling of losing the one you love because of failed promises, that is nothing compared to squandering your relationship with God! You will miss the rewards of His promises! Respect the fact that He is the promise! God's promises are a product of the rapport between the two of you. You are involved in a love affair between you and Him, and when your love affair kindles, be passionate about the one you love! Love Him wholeheartedly, stay faithful and remain committed! Show how much you care by being available to be loved!

God promises that those who believe in Jesus, and are baptized for the forgiveness of their sins, will be saved, He promises that all things work together for good to those who love and serve Him faithfully. He promises that He will never leave you nor forsake you. He promises that you will be an heir to His throne. He promised us victory over death, He promises that we are kings and queens, He promises that he loves us, He promises that with Christ all things are possible, He promises to supply our every need, He promises that His grace is sufficient for us, He promises that his children will not be overtaken with temptation, and He assures us that a way of escape will be provided, He promises his people eternal life, He promises to bless us if we will follow His instructions. Every promise carries a condition attached—if you to do your part, obey the Lord your God and stay committed to His calling—you will reap the blessings attached to His promises! Who else do you know that can fulfill such promises; no one, but God!

In order to participate in God's kingdom, we have requirements that must be met. One thing for sure is we must stop forming habits that knock us off the course. If God is to be uplifted and we are getting fit for His kingdom, then we need to knock out the bully controlling how we stand up for Him! No one can just break their habits while wandering in their desert complaining about the habit that has overwhelmingly grown past their level of management. You must fulfill the conditions to manage the habits.

We have our valley moments, but our mountaintop experiences are met on top of the mountain where God will be, the valley is just where we find ourselves, so we can appreciate rising above them. Your mountaintop is the place where you meet with God for His answers, for your directions to your battles, to conquer your giants and be challenged beyond your expectations, and to correct your distorted behaviors. The giants we face don't stand a chance against the plans He's giving us to surpass the days of our deserts. Jesus was in the desert being tempted by the devil for forty days, yet He came out ready for the task at hand: to teach about the kingdom of God! While you're in your deserts, what teachable lessons are you learning?

If you want to break the habits that are hindering your relationship with God, you need to redevelop your thinking habits. Breaking negative habit-forming ideas must start in your mind by replacing old thoughts with newer, fresher ones. By pressing your thoughts away from the way, you normally would respond to a newly defined way, refining how you see situations you face that no longer meet the new established way you have mentally processed in your newness. I read that with motivation you can change your mind in a matter of time, but you cannot change anything that you don't process as a problem. You have to put off your habit-forming tendencies to be effective in your cycle of change.

Look at the 21/90 rule, which shows that if you commit to a personal or professional goal for 21 straight days, after the third week the pursuit of that goal should have become habitual. And if you continue to do it for another 90 days, then it should become a permanent lifestyle change. If you are earnestly trying to change a bad habit, it takes repetition, dedication, and determination.

If we are to participate in God's kingdom, kicking our bad habits will be necessary. Getting in proper position and having a purposeful attitude and a posture of gratitude will require that you dismantle your will and your ways to God's. Your viewpoint has to lean positively toward God so that He may break the habits in you that you've built against Him. This is why going to church has such great benefits in learning about God and His promises as well as who He is, and who we are in Him. He's challenging us to participate within the body of Christ, to work with other believers, to grow spiritually mature; that will help in how we proceed within God's kingdom practices. All He simply needs is for us to welcome, accept, and abide by His will and He'll do the rest.

Step 6: Mental Recuperation

How are you recuperating?

When you rose this morning and prepared yourself for whatever your day held, be it work, school, or whatever, were you mentally prepared to meet your day? Were you fully alert and focused on the task or does the task have you fixated on being unprepared? Are you well rested and properly prepared for today's assignment, that you're able to withstand the time you need to invest to accomplish your obligations? If not, there could be repercussions if you're mentally weary!

I wasn't always ready when I first started in ministry. It was new, unpredictable, and it felt cold at first! I found working in ministry exhausting! It was even sometimes overwhelming! It came with many pros as well as cons! It gave me the feeling of restlessness, that you can feel impelled to the point of thinking you must live with it, because you were chosen by God to do it! You have to learn how these lessons affect your life and recognize the signs that there is an attack against your spirit arising that you are unprepared for so that you don't find yourself still forming and not taking root so that you can grow up in your assignment. If you haven't received the experience you need to make it over the hump you will definitely feel the bump of the fall!.

It will become your fledgling lesson, one that an underdeveloped person might encounter and be unprepared for when a situation arises and weighs down on you at spur-of-the-moment. Without the proper amount of preparation we tend to be apprehensive about the task. If you're nervous, you're liable to make errors in judgment with the life problems of others as well as with your own life. I soon realized that relaxation was critical to ministry and any other God-given assignment. At times the time needed for mental relaxation or recouping from ministry seemed to be nonexistent! Especially when you are on call to anyone at any given time day or night. Physical and mental recovery is a must no matter where you work or what you do professionally!

Mental recuperation is recovering from the emotional stress of a bad case. We must spend time discovering better methods of dealing with the stresses of ministering to God's people. We come to God to put our burdens down upon that we may find our rest. *"Come to me, all you who are weary and burdened, and I will give you rest. Take my yoke upon you and learn from me, for I am gentle and humble in heart, and you will find rest for your souls. For my yoke is easy, and my burden is light"* (Matt. 11:28–30 NIV).

My sister-in-love Elder Cynthia Turner said in a sermon at The Call Worship Center Church one Sunday morning "We too often remember the hurts life brings. But we seldom remember the lessons the hurts taught us. In doing so we are doomed to repeat them." Life lessons are repeated when we do not take time to rest and listen to the voice of God and let Him direct our paths. Are you on the right path? Are you in position to hear from God, mentally? When we lack rest, we welcome unwanted problems into our lives such as, pain, disease, depression, obesity, and worse! Your body needs to have a fighting chance but it can't fight when it's weary and burdened down and you are restless! Remember, being a Christian doesn't change what you deal with, it changes how you deal with it!

Why inhibited? Well, let me tell you why! Most women start their lives off innocently then independently, but somewhere along our paths a lot of us find ourselves so overwhelmed and underappreciated! Some marry the wrong men; others date the wrong men. Some of us are working in fields we hate; others are overworking. Some of us have wayward children and some of us cannot have the children we want.

And the list goes on and on. We are never told thank you enough for our stretch marks, cesarean scars, and hanging breasts; yet we still make it to every event and every game. We cook, clean, wash clothes, dry watering eyes, and do amazing flips to make it all work out for everyone who depends on us, but we love beyond measure through it all.

Some of us press on, some become depressed, some committee suicide, some turn to addictions of various sorts, some run away from the hurt and pain to disrespectful acts, even some just stay and turn themselves inside out, but most just cover it up among the other masks we're already wearing. Being inhibited is not about everyone but at some point, most of us we have felt inhibited!

The life we're living today may feel exhausting, overwhelming, distorted, yet we continue on in spite of that. We are built for longevity, to last, and we're tougher than our feelings. We can get squeezed so tight that it amazes us that we haven't deflated; it's because you are recuperated and you held up to the task.

You overcame the situations you faced! When you feel life closing in around you; you cannot be as effective in your ministry without the proper mental recuperation. Your families suffer if you are not at your best. Take time to smell the roses as my grandmother always used to say.

When was the last time you gave yourself a break to just be you? Do not let your life get twisted up to the point that you don't exist.

You must smell the roses and enjoy the warmth of me, myself, and I. Relaxation and personal quality time makes for a healthier and happier you!

God expects for you to rest in order to be your best! Pray for peace, love, strength, and joy while gaining your wings of restoration! When an eagle flies, he attaches his wings to the wind and soars with the wind in the direction he wants to go. We must learn how to soar with wings like eagles and soar in whatever direction we want to go toward in our self-fulfillment. Soar in whatever state of life we are in; just do not give up your own expectations because you're overloaded. Let your wings guide your life toward the direction God wants to take you without hesitation. Mental recuperation is recovery for us from them! Getting us to the place of resting in the Lord!

> *"Do not be anxious about anything, but in everything by prayer and supplication with thanksgiving let your requests be made known to God. And the peace of God, which surpasses all understanding, will guard your hearts and your minds in Christ Jesus"* (Phil. 4:6–7 ESV).

The things that weigh on your mind can either exalt you or delay you! How you handle your thoughts reflects how you handle your life. You can't be intoxicated, overly exerted, negative, lazy, weary, and not live a poisonous life. The poison is coming through your image, out of your mouth, in your walk, and it could be pouring out onto your co-workers. In many places it might even show up in your children's attitudes toward you. Our poison spreads in our relationships when we are anxious. Christ knows your relation with Him isn't growing, because your spirit is full of poison!

What poison is running through your veins, pouring out upon your peace of mind, damaging how you are mentally and spiritually recuperating? Some of you are too anxious about everything and have forgotten that you are the temple of the Holy Ghost and you cannot feast on anything you desire. *"Or do you not know that your body is the temple of the Holy Spirit who is in you, whom you have from God, and you are not your own?"* (1 Cor. 6:19 NKJV). God wants to light a flame within your heart but you have to cast away the poisons: all laziness, all anxiousness, all uncertainties, all wickedness, and be ye doers of the Word!

Once you have recuperated mentally you will be sincere in your thinking, humble in your judgments, kind in your heart, and available to hear when counseled and instructed wisely. Ask the Lord Jesus Christ to *"Restore unto me the joy of thy salvation and uphold me with thy free spirit"* (Ps. 51:12 KJV). God wants to restore the joy some of you once had and feel as if you may have lost it due to the fierceness of life.

When we find ourselves in this condition, ask God to restore your joy, which is your fellowship with Him. You desire to have a fulfilling relationship with Him; you're tired of the consequences of your sins for your sin only hardens, hinders, and handicaps your heart and your life! You sin grieves the Holy Spirit and He wants to restore joy unto your heart again!

Step 7: Heart and Mind Rejuvenation

Has it begun, again? You know, the mess!

My earthly beginning was built on the concept that I'll grow up someday but not fast enough. As a child I thought as a child, now that I've matured and know right from wrong my question is, why am I still experiencing so many abundant beginnings?

Mama never said there would be so many days like this, so many abundant beginnings! Meaning, why does my life feel like it keeps repeating itself and I can't get off the roller coaster I'm on. It's a repetitive cycle!

Today's world being filled with its great temptations and ample portion of offenses is extremely hard on the natural mind and can become very discouraging. There's neglect of the poor, abuse of the innocent, rules of injustice, disease of the body, offenses being acceptable, and those are but a minuscule part of the recurring problems that weigh us down spiritually and then some!

The reason we are feeling forced to deal with the desires of the heart, the war of the flesh, and our misguided life decisions is that we believe there's no consequences when we do it our way versus others. Wouldn't it be easier if your choices came without any consequence or at no cost? Wouldn't that be great if nothing we did came with a price? Absolutely not, then you would make even more wrong decisions and eventually destroy your bodies, your minds, and hinder your ability to discern righteous from unrighteous. Everything you do and say and everywhere you go would be acceptable, because there would be no cost for your actions. We are witnessing this right now in our society. So many people have stopped caring about repercussions, which is why we must deal with ours! Once your ulterior motives advance, so does your negative actions. Then there will be consequences to face.

When you find yourself in a crumbling mode, spinning out of control, unable to cope, medicated, and feeling defeated, it has gotten very serious. Your life has been accepting more bad choices than good. God wants us to turn toward Him for the answers before we have to deal with the consequences!

What is the force behind making some of our decisions, for no one can choose them for you? Can you live with it? Have you asked yourself, "How can I keep my bad choices and decisions from reaching the core of my heart?" First off, the decisions we make in life should not hinder the joy of gaining victory over your situation. If they make for a worse situation, they are a bad decision. The way you prevent them is to control your surroundings! Some decisions can feel like they are out of our hands, because we've allowed them to get out of our hands and out of our control.

This is when life sometimes seems difficult to bear even, discouraging in our circumstances based on a bad decision(s). If only we knew how to turn back the hands of times, we'd go back in time and choose more wisely! That would have been a plan, but we chose another route instead and now we have to reverse the road we're on.

Jesus is our hope and our joy. He is the one who can show us how to overcome these obstacles. He is the resource we need to stop the destruction of our bad decisions and halt the destructive behaviors that took us astray. How we lie down and get back up lies in how much we trust Him and give over to Him. When we accept Him as our savior, we'll find out that there is joy and peace in the midst of our despair, and we can stop our life's negative routines from reoccurring.

Jesus created the beginning and He is the start and the finisher of all things, including you and I and our bad decisions. When we go back to the beginning, where it all began in our lives, we can learn how to put an end to the destruction and start another new beginning. It's never too late to restart doing the right things.

It is okay to begin again and again until you find your rightful place in the Lord as long as you are earnestly seeking after Him. Your start isn't always the same nor will it begin again at the same place! The very first words of the Bible are *"In the beginning God created the heavens and the earth. Now the earth was formless and empty, darkness was over the surface of the deep and the Spirit of God was hovering over the waters. And God said let there be light and there was light. God saw that the light was good"* (Gen. 1:1–3 NIV).

In the beginning we can assume that there was emptiness, singleness, formless, and of course darkness covering the earth. The Bible declares how God changed it, how He brought forth what was necessary to make that change happen. It tells us that God began to create. He not only brought forth a difference by creating day but night. He made a change in what was empty by adding life, He made a single man a married man, He gave form to the shape of the world, and He brought light and life to a dark place. That's all God wants to do through us. He wants to change us and create from the darkness, emptiness, loneliness we carry within our hearts. God fulfilled His masterpiece with you and I and the earth was no longer void nor formless because God's image was now present.

God created us to be His witnesses, not for the purpose of filling a void in His life, so why are you filling your void with everything else except Christ? Each of us has a beginning—the beginning is where the cross met humanity—and we cannot experience our beginning until we meet the one who was in the beginning and that is the grace that went to the cross on our behalf! His grace was supplied and that grace is what we rely upon to be corrected and then transformed.

The hymn writer Isaac Watts wrote "At the cross, at the cross, where I first saw the light, and the burdens of my heart, rolled away, it was there by faith, I received my sight and now I am happy all the day." This writer recognized that life starts at the cross and that is where your life will begin to take form and lift your heavy burdens.

As you grow in faith, you are able to see the light, regain your sight, and recognize Jesus as the source of your light. All this was accomplished just by starting at the cross where Jesus died for our sins. This is our starting place to begin our course of assurances, just by shining the light on Him.

If God made a change and saw that reinventing one's circumstances, one's life, was good, then why do we deny the fact that restructuring is for the better? God wants us to have a desire for change, a desire to revamp our lives, let go of our bad habits and negativity toward one another by changing our way of thinking.

When we lack the desire to recreate ourselves, we are leaving ourselves in a powerless position. Our claims of value now become even more costly; our initial grandeur has a greater cost with lesser value when change is avoided. It costs us more to regain the promise than to change that which we have already been given. What sacrifices are we willing to make to be grand for the Lord?

God has given us teachers, instructors, trainers, even coaches along the way who have had influences in our lives. These chosen people have in some way given us proper instructions, teaching us right from wrong. We are also given instructions in His Word of what is right and wrong.

The Ten Commandments that God gave to Moses in Exodus 20:1–17 clearly state right from wrong. To follow these commandments, we must have a willingness for change; it just does not happen overnight. We have to work on it daily and diligently.

Step 8: Godly Interpretation

Can you interpret effectively?

Sometimes these words aren't used enough, because people take offense so easily, but I'm going to say it: some of you need to "watch your mouth" because it's keeping you hostage! Here's another popular sermon I wrote that discusses how others interpretate what we say! The scriptural reference is taken from Proverbs 15:

> *A gentle answer deflects anger, but harsh words make tempers flare. The tongue of the wise makes knowledge appealing, but the mouth of a fool belches out foolishness. The LORD is watching everywhere, keeping his eye on both the evil and the good. Gentle words are a tree of life; a deceitful tongue crushes the spirit. (Proverbs 15:1–4 KJV)*

. . .

> *The heart of the godly thinks carefully before speaking; the mouth of the wicked overflows with evil words. The LORD is far from the wicked, but he hears the prayers of the righteous. A cheerful look brings joy to the heart; good news makes for good health. If you listen to constructive criticism, you will be at home among the wise. If you reject discipline, you only harm yourself; but if you listen to correction, you grow in understanding. Fear of the LORD teaches wisdom; humility precedes honor. (Proverbs 15: 28–33 KJV)*

Is your tongue tied to righteousness, or do you need to watch your mouth? The tongue has the power to choose good over evil! The tongue as a weapon can have destructive tendencies when improperly planted. It lands in one of seven hazardous areas of our lives that we need to watch. These are our hot spots, our hazard zones, within our spiritual planting operations. When we're hazardous we are like a warehouse filled with no quality control, no environmental protection, no poison control, no fire hazard, no hard hat areas for our safety, no loading docks, and no safety and security zones or personnel. We become hazardous when we don't watch what slides off our tongues and lands on the assembly line.

1. **Our Quality Control**: These are people who measure whether existing products meet a standard of quality. They determine the standards by which quality will be judged and establishes the process of how the products will be improved upon to meet quality standards. They keep records of the information they find that they may create paths for improvements. They identify what caused or is causing the problem and work to improve its quality to meet standards or expectations.

God want's us placed under a quality-controlled atmosphere, one that meets the standards, has good measures, and establishes a divine relationship when it comes to how we act and speak, how we communicate, and what comes off our tongues, but there's an established process and a proper order to meet His expectations. We have to determine what's causing the problem and create a plan to work at getting to the acceptable standards of God.

The word *tongue* refers to the spoken word. How we represent what's on the inside is by speaking with a controlled tongue. God's Word is what should be coming out of our mouths and nothing else is relevant if it doesn't uplift Him. We are the walking Bibles! Are we meeting the standards of it? Proverbs 13 says *"The one who guards his mouth preserves his life; The one who opens wide his lips comes to ruin"* (Prov. 13:3 NASB 1995).

We all know that the tongue is only a small part of the body that can create a battlefield when misused or it can create an atmosphere that measures up to what God requires. Like enjoying a moment of meditation, you experience the joy of peace, calm, and solidarity, but only if we are using our tongues as our spoken word. Proverbs 15:4 NLT states, *"A deceitful tongue crushes the spirit,"* the tongue obviously cannot crush the human spirit, but the words the tongue produces can. Proverbs 12:14 NASB 1995 says, *"A man will be satisfied with good by the fruit of his words, And the deeds of a man's hands will return to him."* We must work at it in order to measure up to the standards at which we should be speaking.

2. **Our Environmental Protection**: This is the practice of protecting our natural environment, on controlled and governmental levels, for the benefit of the environment and humans. Some degrading/corruption is taking place, so restraints must be made and awareness must be created that the impact of our activity on our environment is as minimal as possible.

What is God is trying to get you to understand is that you must set the climate changes in your atmosphere. A gentle (*soft*) answer deflects anger (turns away wrath), but harsh words make tempers flare and stir up anger.

The climate is the condition of the weather. It has gone from either hot, warm, cold, wet, or even dry on any given day. Our climates can go from mad, sad, happy, angry, to glee at any given moment. For some of us it's usually more negative than positive. Set your thermostats on low then slowly, gradually raise them according to your taming level at the rate of your maturity.

If your environment speaks with ruin, you can't expect it to be protected from the environment that you've created. You've place yourself in an unproductive environment that can't reap a harvest, because you're speaking against your inheritance. Stirring up trouble purposely has consequences! *"And the cares of this world, and the deceitfulness of riches, and the lusts of other things entering in, choke the word, and it becometh unfruitful"* (Mark 4:19 KJV).

What you speak creates an environment, either of peace or discord. The tongue of the wise makes knowledge appealing, but the mouth of a fool belches (pours) out foolishness. Manage, nurture, and protect your environment and the environment around you by recognizing when to speak and when to be silent. Silence mean "I'm going to shut my mouth on this one, because it does me nor my walk with the Lord no good to make a comment."

Your silence is you using the power of quietness to soften the blows of the tongue. The environment needs protecting from the degrading words of man, because it has reached toxic levels that call for restraints. *"For by thy words thou shalt be justified, and by thy words thou shalt be condemned"* (Matt. 12:37 KJV).

3. **Our Poison Control**: This is someone who educates consumers and health care providers about potential poisons and what to do if poisoning occurs. They must know quickly about a million different drugs, pesticides, chemicals, snake bites, bee stings, terrorist attacks, and even plants and be able to give reassurance to others. Their job is helping others or even advising others; they must be prepared to assist. They work to prevent an epidemic. It requires a calm spirit, patience, the ability to listen, communicate effectively, work under pressure, and the ability to absorb information rapidly.

The Lord is watching everywhere, keeping His eye on both the evil and the good. He protects us from potential threats of the evilness of this world and Satan who roams among us. He knows all, sees all, and is in all places assisting us with tapping into the power that lies dormant inside some of us, encouraging us to calmly get up, listen to instructions, diligently work, communicate with Him, and study the information He has given us as a tool for growing our faith.

Not all of us can cast out demonic spirits, heal diseases, or speak prophetically over someone's life, not because it's not in us, but that we spend more time speaking with poison. Poison control is controlling what rolls off our tongues so easily. God hears all!

When you continually try to prove your point in a situation, be right, talk back, speak ill, lie, curse, yell, or speak disrespectful notions out of your mouth, you're not in agreement with becoming a spiritual poison control specialist, you are playing a part in stirring up the pot of poison. You're stirring up negativity by using your words just for your own benefit to be right. This releases your power back into the hands of the devil who loves taking what's good about you and using it against you. Every battle isn't always won with your mouth.

The power of life and death are indeed in the tongue, the life or death of discord. There's a disagreement going on with your good words and your bad ones. Who's winning? We must choose to live and not drink of the world's poison. You can shut it down (and win back your peace) by letting your silence shine brighter than your tongue's lashes! Shut it down with a silent smile and start speaking Jesus; He's your mouth's antidote!

4. **Our Fire Hazard Team Leaders**: This team works together to eliminate and to have an effective and controlled fire hazard zone. You must have a fire and safety watch team. Someone must take responsibility to watch out for fires, for hazardous situations stirring up, maintain proper conditions and requirements, stop operations from mishandling combustible materials, sound the alarm when necessary, and maintain the inflammables in the proper place. Have extinguishers, hoses, and hydrants ready and handy for use.

When it's watch night time, it's time to watch our tongues (how we talk to people), watch what we do (hiding my secrets), watch the intent of what we're saying (am I nice or naughty), watch our steps (where we go), watch our delivery (what we say to each other), it's time for a neighborhood watch so that you can tame or block your tongue's slashing. It's time to extinguish your mouth's mishandling of words. Some of you have tongues that are fire hazards; setting off wild fires every time you open up your mouth. *"Gentle (wholesome) words (tongue) are a tree of life; a deceitful tongue crushes the spirit."* (Prov. 15:4 NLT)

A deceitful tongue can create: white tongue patches. cold sores, scars, blisters, fungus mouth, bacterial mouth, chapping, and diseases just by the way you speak. It's scaring and stirring up the neighborhood around you! We're ready with our anointing oil and ointments, holy water and spiritual warfare to ward off and wash your mouth out! Effective immediately, the call worship center has a new watch night in effect! Flames have sparked, fires have been set, torches burned, but now there are controlled and effective fire extinguishers in place to douse the flames of your words.

We are taking responsibility for the sake of our Savior's name when you're setting off sparks in His ministries. We're putting out the burners when you're trying to roast in the sanctuary. There are effective methods when your fuses ignite and you blow your top off at a moment's notice. The conditions are right for defusing any combustible spirits and wayward tongues.

There's no room for discord among the saints of God, because the fire fighters are in operation. Our deacons and trustees are on point to shower down and remove all combustible(s) including, the tongue slashers. We have firefighters present to control hazardous waste, but our ultimate lifeguard walks on water and can choose to just let you burn if He so pleases. Thank God, for he gives us the ability to choose our own fate. Just make sure you stay in the fire and safety zones.

5. **Our Hard Hat Area:** When you wear this hat, it gives you the highest protection against electrical hazards, high voltage shock, burns, and against the impact or penetration hazards that flying or falling objects can cause. You're protected from the oops of the job.

God knew when He created you that there would be some hardheaded believers and some stiff-necked folks who will try to see how far their deception can go and get hit with rocks, because they weren't wearing their hard hats for spiritual protection. Instead of standing on the solid rock, which is Jesus, they continued to speak corruption, slandering people, cursing and disrespecting God's house and His leadership. We're in a race to the finish running for Jesus with people verbally knocking us off our spiritual course; you can't get to the finish line if you're not truly running in the race for souls. This is the reason our firefighters are forced to tame your tongues with their fire extinguishers.

Once you step outside of the will of God, you're stepping outside of His protective will as well. Speaking recklessly in a danger zone can get you electrocuted, burned in a lake of fire, or even hit by falling debris. Please, protect your mouths!

You will get a spiritual shock from the impact of your toxic tongues. The tongue is used throughout Scripture in both literal and metaphorical ways, especially in Psalms, Proverbs, and James. The Bible says it holds true whether we're speaking of spiritual, physical, or emotional "life and death," your tongue holds the power over how you choose to live for God. The heart of the godly thinks carefully before speaking; the mouth of the wicked overflows with evil words. Speak with the heart of God toward His people!

The power of the tongue is a picture of how we plant seeds in our lives from our mouths and how important it is to think about the consequences of our actions before spitting hazardous seeds at people. We have the choice of either planting bad seeds which produce poisonous fruit or we can plant good seeds which produce good fruit. Either way we're planting one or the other and only time will tell whether a harvest will come or there will be devastation.

Psalm 140:11 KJV says, *"Let not an evil speaker be established in the earth: evil shall hunt the violent man to overthrow him."* Don't add fuel to a burning bush, it will only escalate and become a bigger problem and do more damage. When a fire starts, pour the holy water on it immediately and diffuse its flames.

When you step into a hard hat area, it's a cautionary zone telling us to safeguard ourselves from what could happen without our protective gear on. It's for our own good, our protection. Ephesians 6:11 KJV says to *"put on the whole armor of God, that ye may be able to stand against the wiles of the devil."* If we keep telling you that you need to watch your mouth, control your words, speak good and not bad, you have been cautioned. God isn't pleased and you're operating in disobedience, so protect yourself! Guard your hearts in peace and love that you may be able to speak peacefully and in love.

6. **Our Loading Dock**: Loading and unloading takes place here in the storage rooms of the building. This is where we can store up our good deeds and unload them when we need them.

What has attached itself to your loading docks that is hindering your storage vessels of good versus bad? Loading up a lot of information about someone and then unloading it with everyone else means your storage space is empty of good deeds for use toward your fellow man and that you need to be available for God to empty you out of yourself and then fill you back up with His righteousness.

Be careful when gossiping about God's people. Once you start a rumor about someone you can't take it back. Gossip starts subtly and it's destructive. It can begin with just a simple phrase like "did you hear about," "guess what I heard," "do you know that," "you know you can't tell her anything," and before you know it, you are part of the gossip, caught up in it; but if you're smart you know you can't believe everything you hear.

When you participate in gossip, you are loading and unloading on someone else's docking station and not your own. By the time the gossip makes its way back around to the originator it's has taken a totally different story line, because everyone gossiping has added their own dirt to the pile. And remember, if they gossip to you, they'll gossip about you, so watch what comes out of your mouth! If we load up with God then we can unload to God! Let God be your only loading dock!

The tongue is filled with corruption when your loading dock is empty or your storage place is full of mess. When you haven't taken the time to put in God's goodness and His love and speak gently about His people, it's easy to just say whatever comes to mind. A foul mouth hinders your spiritual growth. When we place our faith in Jesus, the Holy Spirit begins the process of making us more like Him, conforming us to only His image and that will begin to change how we speak toward one another. The Lord is far from the wicked, but He hears the prayers of the righteous.

7. **Our Safety and Security Zones**: This is a zone dedicated to support a safe environment in which we can learn, live, teach, and work free from potential dangers, suspicious activities, need for assistance requests, and emergency situations that we do not become a victim of our environment.

We know that the tongue is a metaphor for the spoken word of God and the word *tongue* is often referencing our spiritual walk and being a disciple for Christ. Disciples are made by their decision to follow the instructions and teaching of Christ and use that teaching and instruction as a rule of conduct to govern their lives.

First Thessalonians 5:23–24 NIV says *"May God himself, the God of peace, sanctify you through and through. May your whole spirit, soul and body be kept blameless at the coming of our Lord Jesus Christ. The one who calls you is faithful, and he will do it."* God's Word is our safety zone and we should be secure in it knowing that although there's dangers seen and unseen God will come when we call on Him. We don't have to be afraid to live in our environments scared that we'll get sick, go hungry, die, or be mistreated. These potential dangers exist, but when we put our trust in God, He will keep us, cover us, and give us comfort.

How do you feel when you put on your best, get a haircut, spray on your favorite cologne, put on your smile, and head toward your destination? It feels like power when you know you are at your best and others can see that you are "The Man" striving, you're on a mission, and you're secure in yourself!

Well, how do we handle people who, despite all our efforts, still won't speak a kind word to us or about us or see anything positive in us? Can you still speak well of the ill-willed? As Christians, we need to remain in control when faced with conflicts.

What is needed for a believer to grow and be a disciple of Christ is to be able to control their tongues, even when someone isn't in control of theirs. Be the Word, live it, breathe it, then share the knowledge of it with someone positively. It's our safety and it secures us. If we put on our best for the world, we shouldn't give God less.

It isn't important that we always have the last word. Even if we're right, we don't always need to defend ourselves until the end. If someone tells us something that may or may not be true, don't waste energy stating your case or becoming rude and defensive. Saying nothing and just letting well enough alone shows that you are growing spiritually. A cheerful look brings joy to the heart; good news makes for good health.

This journey requires that you have self-control and if you can't control your tongue, you can't say you have self-control! If you blow up at others because they make corrections to your possible self-destructive thought process, then you're lacking self-control. Being able to speak good into others and even making alterations to the way they receive some things is growing them up not tearing them down. Age doesn't mean maturity; not even being in church all your life means maturity. If you listen to constructive criticism, you will be at home among the wise.

How you process the information given you, be it negative to you or positive, if you're able to keep moving in Jesus's name and are willing to reevaluate what you've heard before you become offended, that is maturity. But watch how you speak to God's people who He has placed in your life to help you move from glory to glory, to the glory of the Lord. Proverbs 13:2 KJV says, *"A man shall eat good by the fruit of his mouth: but the soul of the transgressors shall eat violence."*

When you speak with meekness and a soft tone with self-control it gives you more power than a slanderous tongue which only reaps destruction when your tongue speaks ill by any means. We are speaking the Word into existence. The Word tells us in Proverbs 21:23 NASB 1995 *"He who guards his mouth and his tongue, Guards his soul from troubles."* The tongue can become a weapon if not properly used. When used improperly it carries backbiting words, disrespect, hurt, corruption, slander, decay, and disease. The tongue, when it's used in weapon form kills instead of heals. If you reject discipline, you only harm yourself; but if you listen to correction, you grow in understanding.

There's power in the name of Jesus. If you consider your choice words before you speak, it carries love, peace, happiness, contentment, security, righteousness, and the fruit of the Lord. Isaiah 3:10 NASB 1995 tells us to *"Say to the righteous that it will go well with them, for they will eat the fruit of their actions."* Either you will eat of good or you will eat of bad, but whatever you speak will show its fruit. You are reapers of what you sow. Look at the power of the tongue and the need you must have for the Holy Spirit to have full reign in your life and over your tongue! Controlling our tongue and holiness go hand in hand! Fear of the Lord teaches wisdom; humility precedes honor.

James 3 says this:

Likewise, the tongue is a small part of the body, but it makes great boasts. Consider what a great forest is set on fire by a small spark. The tongue also is a fire, a world of evil among the parts of the body. It corrupts the whole body, sets the whole course of one's life on fire, and is itself set on fire by hell. All kinds of animals, birds, reptiles and sea creatures are being tamed and have been tamed by mankind, but no human being can tame the tongue. It is a restless evil, full of deadly poison. With the tongue we praise our LORD and Father, and with it we curse human beings, who have been made in God's likeness. Out of the same mouth come praise and cursing. My brothers and sisters, this should not be. Can both fresh water and salt water flow from the same spring? My brothers and sisters, can a fig tree bear olives, or a grapevine bear figs? Neither can a salt spring produce fresh water. (James 3:5–12 NIV

In the name of Jesus, watch your mouth, because your words do matter. How you use them does matter. For you to tame your tongue, you must change your heart. Your heart influences your tongue. It affects what's good and bad in your heart, and God wants us to think before we speak that our words are soft and subtle and they never stir up anger or trouble. Amen.

Inhibited

Step 9: Dependable Capitalization

What are you depending on?

Where it all began...the molding of a godly woman!

You can depend on God to see you through when you realize that you can depend on Him even when others let you down! You are not defined by the thoughts, actions, or opinions of what someone thinks about the life God gave you to live for Him.

I've found gospel music can be a tool of comfort during my storms. There was a time it was used for only secular means, but now it's all about my God! This song resonates throughout my spirit because it's what I'm asking God for now!

"Inhabit My Praise, Oh the Presence of the Lord" (Written by Rodney Posey)

(Recorded by Rodney Posey & Praise and also Beverly Crawford)

To be honest, the habitation of my spirit-man wasn't easy! I didn't feel that I could depend on anyone. Allowing God to reign over my life started off very rocky for me! Like so many other people contemplating their decision to surrender to the will of God, my spirit-man was in roller-coaster mode, up then down, happy then sad, secure then insecure, faithful then unfaithful.

If someone is constantly being let down, why do we expect them to depend on a God they barely knew? You've been taken advantage of by so many that now you are feeling like people are still trying to capitalize off your sufferings. Now you expect them to lean and depend on God to change their misfortunes? But the answer is still, yes! It won't be easy making your decision if it's based upon having an entrapped spirit. If your truth still has you trapped in your wilderness, ask God to show you His truth about who He says that you are, then anything worth having, you are willing to work hard to get out of the adversary's clutches.

On my journey to becoming spiritually renewed, it wasn't a poof, and it was done moment for me! There were no bright lights and loud noises that rang in the wind; not even a simple sound of a pop went off in my spirit! I didn't get an immediate revelation as someone spoke prophetically over me and I instantaneously received a new way of thinking. None of that told my story!

I didn't even focus long enough to listen to the truth early on in my conversion! Hearing the Word of God was going in one ear and out the other. If I could have only gotten it from the start that would have been great, but unfortunately that wasn't my testimony! I had trust issues that I couldn't shake free of and dependability was done with one eye open and a security camera watching your every move!

You see, in gaining my own divine revelation of who Christ was, it took more than a few words and beautiful songs to get me motivated to change my ways! Being let down time after time and mistreated by the ones who said they loved me and capitalized off my weaknesses meant for me that it would take a miracle to overcome this level of mistrust in men!

It wasn't even my getting convicted about my unscrupulous actions that triggered a positive response in me and I just couldn't wait to repent. No, I continued to do things just as I thought they should be done and even thought that doing it my way was the best possible way! We just discussed this type of character in the past

I felt if you wronged me once I'll never give you a chance to do it again and my guards were at full stance against all people. God was showing me a better way, but my scars ran too deep! I couldn't even trust Him yet, so I stayed astray!

In my disobedience I never realized that I was walking with a rebellious spirit! What would it take for a stubborn spirit like mine to be subjected, to learn to trust, to be set free? I was told once that I had to stop accusing people of planning to do me wrong the moment I met them. I didn't give them a chance and that was hindering me from gaining a relationship with God and man.

Not having a relationship with God at this point began to concern me. That thought was truly what made me have a change of heart.

What had been instilled in me over the years of watering eventually brought about a conviction. God wanted to heal me from my inability to see the good in all people especially within myself.

Finally, I was able, willing, and ready to listen to the voice of God. My inner man made me listen as I thought, *What if Jesus came for me, at any moment, would I be ready?* I thought about all the times my grandparents said we never know the day, hour, or moment of the Lord's coming, so be ready!

That thought scared me more than any other words, shortcomings, or life disappointments I endured. I'd heard so much that could have crushed me like a bug had God not been keeping me even though I wasn't where I should have been, but deep down I knew I wanted to be right with God, so I surrendered! Sometimes, it's better to stop allowing yourself to just fall and pick up the pieces that haven't served any good purpose and discard them. Toss out the misuse of your time and gather up what the spirit preserved for its use in you.

Ask God to help you learn how to trust His people and put your guards down if you are going to learn how to be used by Him. Over time it will begin to happen. You'll stop finding ways of escape or looking for a motive for everyone's actions. The realization that you were operating in a stubborn spirit will stop you from entering a fire zone in your stubbornness. Admitting this truth to God will rid you of what's concerning about people. The revelation that you're not living up to God's potential will help make your new life relevant.

Make your decision to give your will over to the Lord and come to the realization that you cannot do it on your own for there is something greater and more satisfying in store for your benefit that you are missing out on and you need to experience that side! If you don't like how your mess makes you feel, then make a decision to change it. At some point you should get tired of doing things your own way and failing at them and at that point you'll welcome the day you change!

To get to the fullness of what God has for us we must surrender, so that God can redirect our paths and pull us out of the hole we continuously dug for ourselves over the many years of disobedience! Get prepared to see the revelation of God. Obedience carries a shockwave of satisfactory salute to our spirits and gives us hope!

God wants to mold us into ways, shapes, and forms of greatness and change the ways we've developed on our own, shape the scars and imperfections we've endured, and form what He started as perfect back toward His designed perfection! When the clay is being shaped, it's being tried, pressed, twisted, put through the heat and pressure before the shaping is ever applied. It's gone through the molding phase before it's ever given color or put on display.

Some of us are still in our molding phases. Without this phase there could be no display of faith! We must be pressed down, shaken together, and run over before we can reach greatness! Greatness comes as a result of our subdued pain and comfortability. But, speaking the Word of the Lord over our situation will relieve the pressures associated to it.

Step 10: Christlike Motivation

Are you getting motivated yet?

Do you remember your first love: how you felt, the plans you made together? When we are in love, the first thing we do is commit ourselves to one another. We support one another's dreams and ambitions. We even go above and beyond the call of duty to provide and please at any cost! Our love toward one another is what motivates us to stay in the relationship and press at all cost to keep it alive.

What if our motivation toward all people was Christ-centered? What if we were exceptionally drawn to the love of others and we were inspired to please Christ to the point we just loved? Our Christlike mindsets would keep us wrapped in love, the place where our Christlike motivations seek not only to please, but to be pleasing—the place of love, where we're lovable to the unloved!

Jesus Christ was given to mankind to show us how to love unconditionally and to motivate us to do the same unselfishly. Many have failed, and others have given it some serious attempts, but why attempt to motivate anyone if it's self-focused only, if you have already decided who you will or will not love?

If I won't focus outside my own selfish ambitions, then I will never meet the mark of my full maturity in Christ! When we come together as people who have big dreams and great life wonders, loving beyond our wildest dreams must be a priority and it must be a priority for the majority! Set your altitudes toward the masses and make it a priority to reach them in love for your own self-advancement.

Priorities must change, most of your time can't be built of self-importance! Get equipped to gain a return on yourself, but don't forget to carry along others. Advancing past society's expectations can't be achieved when your focus is just on your own advancement. When you're climbing together as a team putting your mind to the plow for others will help you expand to a much greater height!

Pleasing with a Christlike motivation is pleasing done the way God intended, because its inspirationally focused and motivated! You please God when you take time to extend a hand. No one can reach heights above the clouds if they just intend to stay in a state of self-service, un-forgiveness, or if you continue on with a lack of inspiration. If you are overcoming being inhibited you must overcome selfishness! Inhibitions slow you down, keep you in fear, and sometimes hinders your Christian walk when you're unmotivated.

Being self-conscious about your commitment to change isn't about being self-serving, it takes selfless motives and groundwork! When you plow you can't just work in your own yard or only on the surface, you have to dig beneath the surface, and figure out ways to overcome the things that are unresponsive to your life goals. Sometimes, you have to help your neighbors with their yard too or theirs will deteriorate and devalue yours. If you have an inhibited mindset toward growth, then you won't grow. You will only see surface work with no internal effects of your laboring manifesting, then your divine change isn't present either.

Everything is centered on God's kingdom. How we grow for His use is a part of our kingdom purpose. We must dig deep enough within ourselves to pull forth the messy parts and release it in order to utilize what's intended for kingdom use.

Your spiritual renewal comes as the result of experiencing Christ in all His glory daily. You are gaining life lessons from the knowledge you're receiving as a child of God. We need godly experiences and the newness that comes from us escaping the darkness and engaging within the light, which is only to be found in our relationship with Christ Jesus. Every day is another day to welcome a new day of prayer, positioning, gaining power, and participation with God. It's all for a divine purpose. If you don't pray, you'll never come into the understanding of who you are nor what Christ has for you. If you don't know who you are, or your assignment, you won't utilize it in this faith walk, which requires you to use the power given to you in order to partake in this Christian race.

Cliché—think about it—if you never make up your mind to just do something different, you will probably continue to do nothing but think about doing it, without applying any other action. You'll continue to interpret things as you see fit, because you haven't sought out other options. Becoming proactive for Christ isn't easy, but it is necessary! How you interpret the things relating to your life will determine how effective you are with its application.

Maybe this isn't your character, but for a lot of people doing nothing works out better in their lives, because it's easier. It's easier to wake up, go to work, hang out among friends, eat, go home, and prepare for the same routine tomorrow, or whatever your daily routine entails! It's much more convenient for me, if you don't interfere with my routine! Don't become the person who says no to Christ because it's not on your schedule.

We sometimes become complacent or satisfied with our lives just as they are and claim it to be what works for us! Being a disciple for Christ is a lot of hard work! That's why so many prefer the world's way more often for there's no expectation. You live according to you own life choices and you don't have to answer to God for your decisions. You don't have to respond to people who are inconveniencing your life. There's no out-of-the-way notions; no one bothering you, asking you for rides, pick-ups, drop-offs, grocery runs, or bugging you to go out of your way! Your day is already laid out, so please don't disrupt it! Just in case you forgot, you will still have to answer to God whether you believe you're His child or not! We all will have to give an account of what we did with our lives and who we helped along the way to better theirs for Christ.

Christianity requires us going out of our way to pick up people then take them back home, visiting someone who's sick or shut in after work, even going to the grocery store for a senior citizen, cleaning up someone's home who's unable, or just sitting and listening to a dying patient; it takes dedication and being patience. It won't be easy, especially since we too have busy lives and we don't feel like it. We're tired, and we have our own agendas, but only what you do for Christ will last. Let your life be remembered for having a loving spirit, one that leaves a residue of Christ behind. If you choose Christ, you must live how He plans your life. Some people do it only because it's their job, others do it out of kindness or obligation, but the ones who do it for the sake of Christ will reap the rewards of being faithful until the end.

When you find yourself questioning God, don't only ask questions like, "How am I expected to be available to help others on top of my own agenda?" Sacrifice comes with a level of commitment attached that we sometimes fructuate with fulfilling for other people Today I'm committed to helping myself, and then maybe by tomorrow I might be able to fit someone else in. This can be selfishness instead of Christ-centered. God will give you strength for today, if you ask for it. The fluctuations in your schedule will cease and the strength will find you as you carry on in spite of its inconvenience.

We fluctuate based on how we feel day by day! Being true disciples for Christ requires self-sacrifice and determination to please God strengthened by infusing into your spirit the faith that, with Christ, all things are possible. You must believe you can do all the things necessary but still know when to say no! No, might be necessary if your health is affected. God will give you a discerning spirit when you're being taken advantage of. He will let you know when it's time for you to press on or when it's time for you to renounce for the sake of your spiritual well-being. Just ask Him before you say no to something because of how you feel. Nehemiah 8:10 (NIV) said "The joy of the Lord is my strength."

If I'm inhibited, I'm hindered and presently unable! I just need God to help me find my strength in Him and help me start stepping up and outside of my norm! Psalm 28:7 (KJV) said *"The Lord is my strength and my shield; my heart trusted in him, and I am helped: therefore my heart greatly rejoiceth; and with my song will I praise him."* Find a way to gain the strength necessary to go on in the name of Jesus Christ and do it with exceedingly great joy, regardless of your current circumstances. Somebody has to be available. Will it be you or someone else? Our joy is to the glory of God. When we gain strength and the kind of joy that shows our level of dedication, He gets the glory. This kind of joy can only come from God. It equips us with the strength we require to put our trust in Him for our joy. Your happiness is conditional, but your joy is of the Lord!

What steps are you taking in gaining back your joy and managing and maintaining its importance within your life? The joy of the Lord has to become your strength. Your responsibility, your self-sacrifice, your determination, so that you can sometimes include others, as well as your family, and this can help you make the sacrificing feel mutual. Do a self-care test on how you're allowing God to pour himself back into you, so that you will not get burned out while doing good deeds for Him.

What that could mean for some of us is to stay in prayer, make sure you keep up on your own health by getting yearly exams and tests, exercising, singing, dancing, running, reading, and whatever else helps you to relax, to find strength, and it will help you continue to feel good about yourself. In becoming a servant of others in need and not just tend to your own selves is very challenging; you have to activate your charity and make others a priority. Loving all God's people isn't easy; it's hard to do, especially when all people are not lovable! But it is a prerequisite!

When you apply for a job, accept the responsibilities that comes with it, then you have to uphold the position with all integrity. Taking this job requires surrendering yourself to a higher power regardless of whether or not they're appreciative. It involves praying for people, visiting the sick, feeding the hungry, teaching the Bible, going to church, Sunday school, Bible study, even tithing, and so much more; this is only a part of our charity! God will provide whatever we need to stand in agreement with His will and finish our assignments!

God wants us to be pro-active Christians, or at least try before you say, "It's not going to work!" Get up and get out! Keep moving! Be about change! Don't allow Satan to tell you lies that you don't need to do one without the other. Get to know the truth for yourself! Once you know, then you're held accountable for what you know!

Ask God to reveal who you truly are so He can show you areas of your life that need His attention. When you ask God to show you the truth about yourself, be certain you are ready for the revelation of who you really are! Reality isn't always a pretty picture, but the mirror doesn't have the ability to lie.

Changing will require your responsiveness: Nothing will have a hold on you once you set the acceptable standards for your lives. You determine what can stay within your personal space and what has to flee. Salvation is a spiritual rescue attempt that once God did it, it set you free; the outcome is you stay free! Don't allow the fear and doubt to divorce you from your dreams. Breaking up from the wrong things sometimes happen because we're so used to letting go instead of working it out. We're divorcing our dreams, because they haven't come true yet! Instead of dissociating ourselves from the fear, the distraction, the doubt, the temptation, we detach from ourselves from our godly purpose.

Once you've been rescued, it's your responsibility to remain free from things that enslave you within your old nature or puts limits on where you're heading. Satan would love to keep you enslaved and bound in chains to your past; that's the lie that we will not allow to continue! That's the distraction we're separating ourselves from.

Don't become slothful or idle while waiting for your dreams to manifest, because there's no rewards attached to sleeping away your lives and becoming lazy within it. You can't achieve any gains if you're unproductive in life.

Lack of motivation only brings suffering to a person who does nothing with themselves or becomes idle while attempting to get better. Too much of anything isn't good for anyone nor too little. Too much sleep, overeating, or not doing enough can cause someone to become useless, lazy, and unproductive. When you're lazy, you don't want to work, you don't have an incentive to be effective for your family nor others, because you are unhealthy physically and spiritually.

That's the reason it's hard to make an effort at living righteously when you start. People who are physically or even spiritually unhealthy will make excuses to go back to their confusion, strive less to continue to move ahead of what's hindering them, and sometimes never look back again because they are too weary to fight the battle coming up against them. They have no strength so they give in and feel defeated.

God did not free you up for you to willingly return to your darkness. You are now a light in this dark world. Be a beacon of light that overcomes and transforms the darkness! Shine your light so bright that everywhere your foot threads glows! A dark room only remains as dark until you shine the light in it! Turn on your radiance! Pick up your slothful body and start with a smile, laugh, show your joy, especially in the tough situations! That's how we grow our faith, by being exceedingly joyful through it all. Get healthy, this is a fight to the finish and you have to shine for God's glory.

Ever wonder if you're that person who's idle, sitting in a safety seat, unproductive, gotten too comfortable, and asked yourself, "Am I sitting in a seat of hinderance?" One thing that hinders our walk with Christ Jesus is when we believe we are fine just the way we are, and from where we're seated nothing is wrong with the person we are today! Some areas we've chosen are good, but honesty is the best policy. Be honest about the areas that you need to focus your attention on. It's time for us to step up to the plate and be accountable for the words we allow to come out of our mouths and actions we may not be taking seriously. The stuff we step into and ignore the smell, still gives off a stink. Even the negative thoughts we think toward others can hinder us!

There are times when we become our own worst enemies. Open yourself up for improvement. Everyone has room for development if they will allow themselves to expand! There are 22 powerful A.W. (Aiden Wilson) Tozer quotes on the internet titled the Glory of God and the Nature of Man. This one touched me personally, "The reason so many people are still troubled, still seeking, still making little forward progress is because they haven't yet come to the end of themselves.

We're still trying to give orders, and interfering with God's work within us." Focus on your own progress and not that of the people around you and see what happens!

We can all use a little practical improvement in some area of our lives! When you decide you have "arrived," meaning you don't need to change, or you assume you have it all together, that's when you need to be afraid of whom you have allowed yourself to become on the inside and the lingering smells that you've adapted to.

This is the effects of fumbling and falling into the "temptations of the flesh." As an example: what we see that tempts us, if it's not defused, will eventually work its way into our minds; if we keep watching long enough, it begins to manifest itself in our daily thoughts; if it lingers there too long, it can start to manifest itself into our hearts; and if nothing is done to dislodge the intruder, it can manifest itself in our daily actions. Nip the temptations at first sight and stop ignoring what you know is evident!

You first saw it and were reluctant, then you started thinking about it, so you began to taste of it; it felt and tasted really good and now you're physically acting it out, stumbling over the things that you know will only cause you to stray away from God, things that you know should be shut down upon your first thought, right from the start! You can't watch anything on television, listen to everything on the radio, or hang out in certain places that you know might cause you or others to fumble!

The Bible says this:

> *Woe to the world because of the things that cause people to stumble! Such things must come, but woe to the person through whom they come! If your hand or your foot causes you to stumble, cut it off and throw it away. It is better for you to enter life maimed or crippled than to have two hands or two feet and be thrown into eternal fire. And if your eye causes you to stumble, gouge it out and throw it away. It is better for you to enter life with one eye than to*

have two eyes and be thrown into the fire of hell. (Matthew 18:7–9 NIV)

This scripture is a warning of how serious it is to stumble or cause someone else to stumble; it's not worth jeopardizing your life over.

It is very serious that we not cause ourselves or others to stumble in this Christian walk, God wants us to aid one another in love. Love shouldn't hurt! It shouldn't be used to gain or to repay evil for evil. People who say they are the children of God should always want to do their best to press forward in righteousness!

First Corinthians 13 says this:

Love is patient, love is kind. It does not envy, it does not boast, it is not proud. It does not dishonor others, it is not self-seeking, it is not easily angered, it keeps no record of wrongs. Love does not delight in evil but rejoices with the truth. It always protects, always trusts, always hopes, always perseveres. (1 Corinthians 13:4–7 NIV)

There are areas in everyone's life that God wants to perfect. It's evident in how we live that not every area of our lives is all together and that's the space He wants to work in. If it wasn't, why would we need a savoir to die for any of us! Satan would have no need to bother anyone if there was no God.

There is a God and He has given us mercy and grace and His courteous good will. He gave us what we don't deserve, and his compassion and kindness are shown to us in spite of who He knows we really are. God is holding back the wrath that we truly deserve and allowing us a choice to change our wicked ways if we choose to do so. Although the choice is yours, it will not be easy, but you just have to be willing! No one can make the decision for you! In one of T.D. Jakes sermons on Youtube he said, "God gives favor according to His purpose and maneuvers you into a position of influence so you can effectively change situations for others." The wrath of God is His divine chastisement. It's not a retribution anyone should want to suffer through.

A friend of the family wrote these words on a facebook post for us to meditate on:

> Pray your way forward for divine alignments, for favor, for resources and for open doors pray with all power! God cannot bless something that is not in order. Self-work has to begin by overcoming you before you can overcome them. We have to get out of our own way, so God can do a great work through us for we are God's masterpieces. We didn't create ourselves, develop our own organs, or arrange our own DNA, we didn't deliver ourselves. God breathed into dirt, and we came into existence. He gave us life. — Rev. Clifford Daniels.

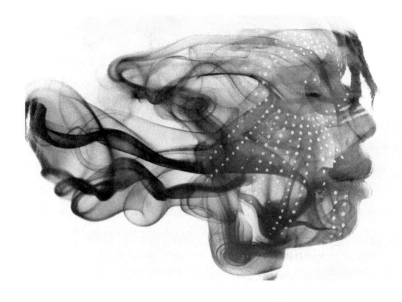

Step 11: Visions of Inspiration

Do you have a vision?

As women seeking godly direction, why do so many of you feel that you have to stay as you are? Why wouldn't anyone want to get better and better and better and never feel satisfied with the statement, "I've done enough?" The better isn't in your ability to gain fame and fortune. It means being content with what you have or have not accomplished that can take you higher in Christ. We should always be seeking to mature in the Word of God as lifetime scholars of His Word.

In Philippians 4 Paul said:

> *Those things, which ye have both learned, and received, and heard, and seen in me, do: and the God of peace shall be with you. But I rejoiced in the Lord greatly, that now at the last your care of me hath flourished again; wherein ye were also careful, but ye lacked opportunity. Not that I speak in respect of want: for I have learned, in whatsoever state I am, therewith to be content. I know both how to be abased, and I know how to abound: every where and in all things, I am instructed both to be full and to be hungry, both to abound and to suffer need. I can do all things through Christ which strengthened me.* (Philippians 4:9–13 KJV)

If you're stubborn, you may afraid of being redirected, but your stubborn nature may hinder what possibly could be a major turning point in your life. It might cause us to seek after self-satisfying materialistic things and lack focus in areas that build guarantees, esteem, and assurances. Some of us really could benefit from being told to turn back around, go back to the drawing board, and let us help you build some things back up that got misdirected the first time around.

Inhibited

If you are a person who never believes that someone could really mean well by telling you the truth about your bad attitude or behaviors, if this is why you are willing to remain in your current circumstances doing the same things you've done in the past, reaping the same old insufficient justification of your works while still pondering over why you continue to do the same unsatisfying things over and over again and again, then maybe you do need to consider this possibility. Consider the possibility that leads one to say, "Let me reevaluate my situation and just consider the possibility that there might be room for improvement in an area or areas of my life."

I remember a woman who complimented a jacket I was wearing and she stated that she would love to have one just like it. I took it off to let her see how it fit her, but it was too small, so I put it back on. To my dismay, the woman was very sweaty and now so was my jacket. I felt so uncomfortable at that moment with her sweat against my skin but I endured and never said a word. Why? I was the one who took off my clothing and gave it to her. I took it off and I put it back on; it was nobody's fault but my own! It was an eye-opening experience. We make some decisions and regret them immediately afterwards! It reminded me of how often my decisions wreak havoc as a result of me not first considering the consequences!

If you're continually finding yourself wondering how you fell back into this same old rut and why you are still at the same place in your life you were years ago, then consider your approach from another angle. You're presently riding the roller coaster of a lifeless change, meaning you've changed nothing but your job, living arrangements, relationships, hairstyles, clothes, makeup; now, change your methods, without touching anything spiritually significant. Change what truly matters inside you: your way of thinking and your approach to your way of thinking about life can't remain the same year after year.

Approaching things cautiously, yet vigorously, actually taking the right amount of time to weigh the cost and outcome of what you want to receive the truth of, and putting in the time necessary to think about the effect your choices may have if the facts are accurately defining you. Will your choices have a positive or negative impact on your life? If it were to come true, if it was to manifest, if it is to really make a significant effect on your situation, what would you be like then? If you have determined that it is a combat against your spiritual well-being, spring into action to work at making a positive change in your life happen. Nothing happens until you first decide you want it to. You are a product of the environment you grew up in, but your environment is not the only source of your growth. What you *do* is how it happens.

When you spend time just thinking about changing without getting out of that stagnant mode, you'll find yourself remaining unresponsive way too long and becoming spiritually dead. That could be the reason why some people feel like they're caught in a never-ending unchanging cycle of self-destruction. At this point, they get depressed, feel lonely, stay drunk, and use drugs, trying to escape their problems. To continue living as if it's not a problem is the problem. If there's no effort, there's no change; you're just doing harm to yourself. Life doesn't only predict good, there will be the ugly, the bad, and the indifferent days as well. Live life according to where it takes you and fulfill yours wherever you are within it.

Make an unpredictable statement in the course of your life changes. Be bold, courageous; be creative in it. Get out of that rut! Start to take steps that shows your resilience! Tap into your survivor mode, that place where the enemy hates to see you get too! Stop allowing circumstance to have its way with you and cause you to believe you need other means to cope with the life choices you've made! You are an overcomer regardless! Don't allow Satan to brainwash you with his nonsense; nonsense makes no sense. Doesn't Scripture teach us that we should have no fears, set no limited boundaries, and have no regrets? It's time to start believing so you can get through and eventually walk out of it and into something greater. Let your vision align with God's Word.

Satan is a liar and the truth is neither in him nor of him, so don't sit back believing you're nothing, useless, or can't be forgiven for everything you've done. With Christ you are everything, created to be worshippers! Victorious! A Blessing! Righteous! 2 Timothy 3:16 says that "All Scripture is inspired by God and is useful to teach us what is true and to make us realize what is wrong in our lives. It corrects us when we are wrong and teaches us to do what is right.." His word will inspire you to believe it is God-breathed, and it is the same breath that breathed life into you from dust.

People tend to still keep going backward, going down instead of up, until enough is enough. Can you sincerely say, "With Christ all things are possible and now I can trust in the one who breathed His breath in me to help me make a change?" The importance of change is having the desire for it; talking about it isn't enough. Some form of action must be present in order to achieve a change of course; it is a daily requirement.

We need to walk this thing out every day, getting to know Christ deeper and consistently, believing in Him for a full understanding of our purpose, and gaining a knowledge of who He is, then we will be able to change internally. Once we get the knowledge of Him it will evidently show an outward change of direction in our lives. It will become truth in action. Action plus Christ equals spiritual success!

Kathy Troccoli wrote, in the Women of Faith Study Bible (NIV) a reflection that read:

> "I am constantly reminded of the faithfulness of God and that His mercies are new every morning. What I was yesterday, what I felt yesterday, what I did yesterday is covered by His grace. He remembers it no more. He throws it as far as the east is from the west—as I turn, as I repent, as I offer him my sins, my failures and even the consequences of my choices. There is so much beauty to the morning, and there is so much beauty in a heart filled with certainty that the Lord has once again come

to fill, restore and heal. His steadfast love never ceases. His mercies never end."

Up until now, a lot of us have felt somewhat the same way about our spiritual walks of life, that we are living a Christlike life doing what we are supposed to do as Christlike citizens. But are we? Can we get up in the morning freely experiencing life at its fullest and truly be at peace within? With no remorse?

The Bible tells us so much about getting our peace which leads to a peaceful mindset Matthew 5:9 (ESV) *"Blessed are the peacemakers, for they shall be called sons of God."* Matthew 11:28–30 (ESV), *"Come to me, all who labor and are heavy laden, and I will give you rest. Take my yoke upon you, and learn from me, for I am gentle and lowly in heart, and you will find rest for your souls. For my yoke is easy, and my burden is light."*

John 14:27 (ESV) *"Peace I leave with you; my peace I give to you. Not as the world gives do I give to you. Let not your hearts be troubled, neither let them be afraid."* John 16:33 (ESV), *"I have said these things to you, that in me you may have peace. In the world you will have tribulation. But take heart; I have overcome the world."*

Ever found yourself reminiscing about your life's choices and thought . . . hmm . . . What if it became known? All the secret places, thoughts, actions—what you actually thought about, even if you haven't acted on them? The bad life choices you've made even after giving your lives to Christ? The times you're not proud of, the immoral, unforgiving places and things you once feared being known, what if anyone knew? Well, God knows and He loves you anyhow. He already forgave you for that. Don't be that woman who has a *Que sera, sera* (whatever will be will be) type of attitude, as if the hidden secrets are just between ourselves, praise God none of it has been revealed!

There's no need to be ashamed any longer of having such a selfish attitude; you have been renewed, rejuvenated, and restored. And if you are still a work in progress, you too can still have true repentance in Christ Jesus. God is not to ever be taken for granted. He is a Holy and Just God, a God of order, a righteous God, the ruler of the heavens and earth. That should let us know we are not okay as we are! When you turn it over to God, you will come into a level of peace like you've never encountered before.

Do you realize how significant Christ's death on the cross was, the importance of what Christ has done for us by coming back for a lost sinful world, taking our sins upon Himself and coming back to life with all power in His hands after being dead for three days, and giving us the Holy Ghost and the spiritual gifts we require to use in our defenses against the wiles of Satan's attacks? Satan wants your peace of mind; he wants to fill your mind with meaningless thoughts and attack your God-given defenses.

Christ's death on the cross gave us direct access to a loving God from whom we can now ask for forgiveness directly and repent of our own sins without feeling inadequate or inferior because we know God loves us with all our imperfections. No one can ever take us out of His hands once we accept Him as our Lord and Savior.

Some of us believe that because God is a just and forgiving God you can not only think about sinning, but you're free to act your thoughts out, visiting every forbidden zone you can, and believing that you can just say, "Forgive me, Lord" and continue doing wrong, because you know you can ask for forgiveness. Yes, we are saved by grace and mercy and our repentance of our sins gives us forgiveness from God, but we lack a clear understanding of what repentance means. Repentance is a vow to walk away from your sin and not be guilty of forever. What is hidden to others is still visible to God and it will still have to be answered for. If you repent, do your best not to repeat the offenses again. True repentance is turning away from that which we have done wrong and turning back to God with the promise that we will never to do it again! Don't play Russian roulette with your life by giving God promises you can't keep, and don't say "I promise," knowing you will do it again before the day is out.

Tell God you're sorry and ask Him to help you with your bad choices and mean that with all your heart. Until we are able to fully understand this concept and stop just saying the words, we impede or obstruct Jesus's judicious rule. We don't make the rules, He does!

We have a tendency to believe or think that if our sins are discreetly done and if we are careful, if no one finds them out, then our sin is excused or overlooked because no one knows about it. Well, God knows your heart's desires. Stop mocking His grace and become truly sincere in your desire to change your ways.

Having gracious failures instead of exaggerated faith are the best defenses we can learn how to play. The plays of the game are: maintaining your endurance—(reading and studying God's Word), setting up the defensive line—(defending what goes into our hearts through God's Word), and allowing the offensive line time to rest—(the things that we are offended by must be put to rest). The winner is the one who endures until the end. Will you win or lose? Are you in the game?

Who has the courage to put themselves out there on the front line for Christ, openly exposed for the suffering Savior, the One who sees and forgives all? When we allow ourselves to be unveiled for Christ, we are at the fullness of change, and that takes the ultimate walk of faith. If we have a lack of faith, this can cause us to lose in the game of endurance.

Some of us fear desiring to be changed, because it hurts to be found out, exposed for who we are inside. But this could be the greatest perspective on your life to bring you into the fullness of God. You should welcome being exposed because it's for your own personal growth.

The climax of self-exposure opens too many avenues of criticism. It reveals your financial tortures, your abuses, your mental challenges and suicidal tendencies, the domestic violence stigmas attached to you, the sexual desecration or your level of immoralities; whatever you're hiding or that has attached to you affects your ability to trust or believe in others for support. Jesus already knows the trouble you've seen and endured. Don't dread talking about it or letting people know what you've been through based on the assumption that they're going to become judgmental of you. Some will, but don't allow these anxieties to deny you the ability to welcome your redemption. Identification is the key starting process of elimination when purging yourself of your sinful natures. It will be a rewarding experience once you've recognized how great the reward will be for you enduring your weaknesses.

First, the problem must be identified. Next, action must be taken to close in the gaps. Then, we need to apply some Jesus's pressure to our open wounds. Jesus came that we might have life and that we might have life more abundantly. Jesus wants us to be healed from the sin of self, shame, and damnation—from ourselves.

We lack true understanding of the meaning of *who* we are and *who's* we are, which has caused us to go into hiding from ourselves. It's only you that you are hindering from growing when you allow yourself to be trapped by circumstances. It's not my intention to say what you are doing is correct or incorrect, but it is for me to say that what you do from now to eternity will render you right or wrong, just or unjust, spiritual or spirit-less, heaven-bound or traveling on hell's trails.

We are in need of finding truth from this day forward. One of our most treasured assets is not on the exterior (our outward beauty) but internally (our inner man). As 2 Corinthians 4:16 (NIV) states *"Therefore we do not lose heart. Though outwardly we are wasting away, yet inwardly we are being renewed day by day."* Our denying the need for change is affecting our hearts, *"for where your treasure is there will your heart be also"* (Matt. 6:21 KJV).

As a people, we are concerned about the here and now and not as concerned with the return of Jesus. Will we be ready or will He arrive to find us caressing Him with our unchangeable heart's desires. Don't think you can look at Him face to face and tell Him the mess you tell others? "I'll change when I get ready; as a matter of fact, I don't need to change." "I'm fine just as I am," "I'm set in my ways and it's too late to be trying to change me; this is who I am," "You can accept it or not." I hope you don't believe your own lies; He's still coming back to judge our ways whether we are ready or not. It up to us to be ready in our hearts when He returns.

Matthew 15:11 (NKJV) says *"Not what goes into the mouth defiles a man; but what comes out of the mouth, this defiles a man,"* and Matthew 15:18 (NKJV) tells us also *"But those things which proceed out of the mouth come from the heart, and they defile a man."* We urgently need to make a drastic change while we still can, at whatever age we are. Our mouths are destroying our hearts.

As long as we still have breath in our bodies, it's never too late to change what's in our hearts. It's only too late when we've taken our last breath and the time has come for us to go home to glory. God allows us time to make decisions and His Word shows us how we should make them. We are never too old to start changing. In fact, the older you become the wiser you should become too. Being hardheaded only leads to trouble. As my grandmother always told me, "A hard head makes a soft behind." I never knew exactly what she meant until I did something she told me not to do; my behind was set on fire and at that moment I'd wished it was as hard as my head.

I found that it's just best to wait for the Lord so we won't be stuck in our stubborn ways when we are old. *"The Lord is good unto them that wait for him, to the soul that seeketh him."* Lamentations 3:25 (KJV) It takes a special kind of patience to wait on God, especially for one who is older and set in their own ways. Listening to God for guidance. With patience, will help us not to always be impatient, hardheaded, or unwilling to submit to a better way!

Being hardheaded even after God has told us the truth is part of the reason we find ourselves on a lonely highway confused about where to go—the road we know as "Hell's Boulevard"—asking ourselves, "Why didn't I just turn around and go back the other way? We know it's the wrong way, but we keep on going anyhow. We keep right on going until we run into another dead-end road after another. We turn ourselves around only to find even darker lanes waiting ahead of us: there's "Depression Lane" waiting, "Loneliness Boulevard" lurking, and "Self-Pity Road" is waiting to steal whatever we have left. It has gotten so dark and lonely on Hell's Boulevard that you're forced to pull over, because it's so dark where you are your GPS can't even find where you are anymore!

One more wrong turn and guess who's at the next dead-end road, arriving just in time to get in on the act, but "Bitterness Street," and the devil never travels alone, he took you down "Doubt Court," and had you traveling onto another lonely highway just so you could keep him company. This is at that place where you begin to show hatred for one another because you are so unhappy within yourselves for all the wrong turns and bad decisions you've made where you've put the blame on the people who took you down the wrong roads. These roads may have thrown you off track, but with Christ all you have to do is turn around and get back on the right road and follow His directing from here on out.

At some point, everyone has carried some kind of bitterness toward someone or toward something done to them by someone. It may have taken place years ago or yesterday and we are still harboring ill feelings toward that person or about that thing, and if we asked why we don't like something or someone, we might not even remember the details anymore. And if you do, it's because you're still harboring the ill feelings associated with the pain within your hearts. There are some incidents in your lives that are severe enough that you may never forget them, but by the power of the Holy Spirit you can get through it and over it with the support of one another and the help of God.

When your heart harbors un-forgiveness, people find themselves sometimes yelling at others about nothing often out of frustration. Some of us rise up out of those frustrations with a "leave me alone" attitude, that means exactly what it says. When you don't get things done your way, or if you're mad and feel like nothing's going right no matter what you do or how hard you try, don't fight or cuss out others because your circumstances have overwhelmed you traumatically. It's not always anyone else's fault that Satan has chosen you to torment this season. Hold on; your change is coming. God has you close to His heart and there's nothing more valuable to God than you.

Seeking after the proper understanding of yourself will also start the process of how you get a better understanding of who you are in Christ. Start believing it is all for you; it's not just words, but it's in His actions of love that you must receive. We are created in the image of God; we are the lethal weapons He uses to bring love to life on earth.

God said in Genesis 1:26–27 (NIV), *"Let us make mankind in our image, in our likeness, so that they may rule over the fish in the sea, and the birds in the sky, over the livestock, and all the wild animals, and over all the creatures that move along the ground."* So, God created man in His own image, in the image of God He created him; male and female He created them. Together we will get through this and stand in unity as sisters in Christ, because we've survived more than was expected of us. We are more alike than we ever imagined! We are the commonality—what we are made of is the same in so many ways—and that shared grace is what Satan wants to destroy in us all!

Step 12: Selfless Justification

Are you defenseless?

When you are defenseless, feeling unvalidated, or maybe less than your wholeness, you might tailor-make your life decisions by accepting the negative evaluations of people who really don't know you anyhow. Your refining is God-driven and purposeful by His design of who you are. God designed you with the qualities necessary for you to reach the heights of your perfection. The moment He created you; the molding began to define the man or woman that you would become. The definition of your greatness is not predicated on anyone justifying your greatness other than Christ Jesus! You are working through your transformation and that self-renewal phase of your life is between you and God! He realigns our behaviors and develops our virtues as we gain spiritual growth and develop a relationship fitting to His calling and choosing of us.

God knew He identified you in Him from the beginning. He knew it would be impossible for you to be anything else, even if you chose to change something that was of His genuine design. Some women will place selfless actions above their genuine purpose, which could deflect their design, purpose, and make you forget that you are invaluable! You are beyond estimation to God! No price can be put on your value. He paid the price and now you are priceless to Satan! Sometimes women tend to search for value anyhow, wanting to be the perfect specimen, but you already are so don't water down your worth.

Do you know what reflects the *genuine* you, what is said about you to be truly authentic? Or are you *fraudulent* by default? Do you sometimes use or desire to use man-made vehicles to improve your self-worthy design? Your refined, subdued demeanor is a part of your uniqueness, but your drama could speak out above your worth and tell you that all of the extra designing of your self-worth is necessary; it's the only way to identify with what man expects of you. No man deserves to put a value on your design, but the man of God.

Some of the redesigning can just be a personal preference or a necessary healthy life-changing decision, either way, what has it done to carry you forward in your spiritual walk? Your self-worth is a realistic self-view! I see me and the me I see is; whose view? What is the view you see? No one enjoys thinking anything negative about their character even when we know we are not walking according to our value and no one deserves to put a point-of-view into your mix either. It's hard enough accepting our own faults, but when it comes from others it feels demeaning because it's not always intended or offered for the perfecting of our designs. The questions we ask ourselves will help define the answers to some of the weight of life we're carrying and why we desire to change what we see within one another. Is the new design for the uplifting of God or for the purpose of man's approval?

Never let other people become your reasons for any self-alterations or decisions unless it is a God-driven decision. Your peace of mind starts with asking yourself, Who am I? Psalms 139:13–14 (NIV) says, *"For you created my inmost being; you knit me together in my mother's womb. I praise you because I am fearfully and wonderfully made; your works are wonderful; I know that full well."* On so many levels we long to fit in. Wanting to fit in with the crowd, fit in a particular group, be on a certain team, be accepted, fit the preferred size; most of us won't get in where we don't fit in, no matter what! Some people, places, and things are just not supposed to have a space we can find our fit in.

When you desire to be the newest version of whatever it requires to fit in, you lose a little of what is already fit for perfect use in you! You're rooted and grounded in whatever you have fit yourself to! The most-high God wants you rooted in Him, and that's where you will find your perfect fitting.

Sometimes, fitting in requires that you take a step back and breathe deeply to assess what you have planted yourself among. Is it a stereotypical mess? When you relax it gives you a chance to clarify, if you are properly grounded in God. It helps to anchor yourself to a firm truth and assess if you are not compromising who you are for what others lack confidence in within you! Corrie Ten Boom ended one of her quotes on social media with, "Worry does not empty tomorrow of its sorrow. It empties today of its strength!" There was a list of 20 things on team Fearless quoted by Napoleon Hill that was said to have changed millions of lives, one being "Strength and growth come only through continuous effort and struggle."

What kind of life do you crave? To crave something implies you have already tasted, enjoyed, or done it more than once and that now it has become good to you. What thoughts have you put into action to satisfy that hunger and thirst for what you're craving. Has it given you a better quality of life or has it stolen something from your life? Accepting the power of God over your will is essential in order to gain an improved quality of life, one where you crave divine greatness. Your thoughts have to portray what you want, how you expect to achieve it, where you desire to go, and how your actions are going to bring it forth. What thoughts have you put in place to gain the quality of life you desire? What have you thought about lately! Does it fit the character you are portraying or is it perfectly aligned to what your heart are really all about?

The expectations of this world are affecting some of us negatively! We have gotten side-tracked. What you are doing has you believing that it's okay to partake of some things beyond your limits. You feel as long as you say that you know who you are in Christ, as well as whom you are to Him, you can go into territories that swing both ways and not become affected by what's in those rooms! When you know it's going to cause you to waiver from your beliefs or from what's right, make sure you're saying "No, this is not fit for my kingdom time-lining!"

All things can't be attempted unless you have set boundaries, a known self-limitation, you understand what you're not capable of and what's your limit before your flawed character is drawn to sin. After the mishap you'll spend so many unnecessary hours recouping and trying to regain that which was lost! God wants us to know our self-worth! He wants us to know we're fine just as we are. If we're not true to ourselves, we can't be true to anyone else, especially God, so don't let these things that revolve around this world become your top priority! Never try to fit in a size that's too small for your faith.

I have personally experienced many moments of pain as a result other people's misguided sight; therefore, they teased me and treated me unfairly. I was not defined by people who didn't see my worth. I sought change from God and He gave me wisdom beyond my years to change how I saw myself first in His eyes. Gaining the strength of self-assurance will keep so many people from standing in a mirror disgusted with the view and making choices based on another person's view!

Our choices are sometimes driven by our natural desire to please and to hold on to things or people, although it might not be a good rational choice. Some of us are genuine, others are just real good replicas! And I don't mean your actions; I mean spiritually! The masks we are wearing only conceal us to the viewers, but you can see them clearly and God knows they are there. Make sure you don't allow the outward appearance to make you turn into an ugly duckling inwardly. Make positive changes that lead to positive results.

When you are putting together the pieces of your lives you have to first know where they fit! Know your purpose and believe in the God who made you and said it is very good! Sometimes, we aspire to only change our outward appearance, with the intent of remaining genuine inwardly, yet we don't always keep true to ourselves. We can so overdo our changes that we don't even recognize the man in the mirror anymore. We've done so must to change what's on the outside that we sometimes manage to change the portrait of the inside too.

We can relate to beauty being exhibited on the outside as a makeup artist does, yet we must work hard at keeping our inward beauty as well. We can find ourselves sometimes admiring the creation of what we used to claim as "the wow factor" with the new weave, body shape, acrylic nails, even in the style of clothing we choose to wear; that was about the extent of the recreation we're exhibiting. But this superficial recreation doesn't have an effect on anyone inwardly, it only recreated an outward manifestation.

Many women can relate to being tired of hanging breasts, wrinkles, stretch marks from child birth, and weight gain from menopause, or even having their body altered by unforeseen reasons that they had no control over. They begin to notice how the ones they love look for another recreated version of them. Some have added beautifications that makes them feel pretty again and desired by their mates, but don't let the extras change you as a person just to please another person.

Learn how to trust your creator so that you will love yourself with or without transformations, where you are okay with or without makeup and it doesn't matter, with or without designer clothes and bags and it doesn't matter, where car brand names don't matter, satisfying others' opinions don't matter, where what matters is that Jesus is your benefactor! He matters!

We must decide at one point in our lives, not to become so focused on the outward façade, and the materialistic mess to the point that we don't care what anyone thinks about us. What's on the outside matters too, but what's inside matters more? No one should only approve of your exterior posterior without concern for your content. When we're only worrying about one without the other, we can become self-absorbed and callous! In the attempt to please people, we can become so absorbed that it's hard for God to recognize us too. He wants us to be a partaker with us not just watching us be selfish takers!

In many cases our outward appearances have changed so considerably it now reflects dramatically inwardly. God sees our hearts (what's inside), that why we have to be careful that nothing causes us to become vain and selfish people so that it affects the purity of our hearts.

I like to think back to the way I use to be, out of gratefulness, and it helps me stay rooted and true to myself and especially to God for changing me. I was no longer that woman filled with ungodly, I wasn't her any longer. My breaking point was when I met the man God chose for me and I made a decision to be a better godly woman for myself and my family. This decision was for me! God brought me a godly man, one who helped me to realize that I was worthy of happiness, respect, greatness, and I didn't have to settle for less. He added a gentle touch to my magnitude which meant more to my life than achieving greatness alone. He became my completeness, but I had to love me for me first!

In the beginning was a great struggle, but we survived the storm that was meant to destroy us and take us off course. We decided to live and weather out the storm together on one accord with God leading the way! And that was the start of a great marriage and the start of a godly union. William Ellery Channing is known for his quote on social media, "Difficulties are meant to rouse, not discourage. The human spirit is to grow strong by conflict."

Being alone doesn't mean you're any less than, it simply means God is walking with you as your bridegroom instead! In my life I've found that God purposed my husband and me that's why we walk wholeheartedly as a unit. I was able to let down my guard and trust him as well as walk side by side with him on this Christian journey. My faith in the Lord helped to remove all the baggage I carried within and my lack of trust and my hardened heart all started to change as I started to learn more about Christ Jesus for myself. I wore great disguises and had gone "Broadway" in my acting skills.

Sometimes as women we wear great cover-ups when it comes to some of the things we do, some portions of our lives we want hidden, and some of the places we've chosen visit. We become so good at our cover-ups, shielding our mess, and masking the secrets we don't want anyone to know about! It might feel wonderful if you fool us, but it's pitiful in the sight of God.

You can fool us, but God knows all! In some way this is like a game of Russian roulette where the winner lives and the looser dies. The Bible tells us *"For he that soweth to his flesh shall of the flesh reap corruption; but he that soweth to the Spirit shall of the Spirit reap life everlasting"* (Galatians 6:8 KJV). God can help us release this inadequacy we carry as the forbidden fruit. He does desire us to eat of it!

When my husband and I grew spiritually, we realized that parting with our old nature gave us healing, power, and control over Satan. We were no longer ashamed of whom we used to be or the things we used to do. That was our old man, it doesn't matter what anyone thinks of the old you or me except God, for He alone is worthy to be praised for who He has changed you and me to be, and now that we've been converted, we are new creations. *"Therefore if anyone is in Christ, he is a new creation; old things have passed away, and look, new things have come."* (2 Corinthians 5:17 HCSV)

We are new creatures in Christ Jesus! Don't allow the people who knew you back then to create a hole in your new foundation. Revealing ourselves is now a way of escape, a release. Allow yourself to be set free and release the love for yourself on your fellow man.

Change starts with making sacrifices for the Lord. John 12:25–26 (KJV) says, *"He that loveth his life shall lose it; and he that hateth his life in this world shall keep it unto life eternal. If any man serve me, let him follow me; and where I am, there shall also my servant be: if any man serve me, him will my Father honour."* I hope this is all the honor you need. So, love *you* more than anything or anybody, except God, that it reflects from the inside out and your reflection shines through revealing the beautiful new you. "You are fearfully and wonderfully made!" Show that to your old haters of the new you.

IV

Extravagantly Rare

How rare are you?

What does it mean to be rare (one of a kind, peculiar, extraordinary, uncommon, exceptional, singular, the best choice, precious, scarce, and excellent)? In the book of Ruth in the Holy Bible, Ruth displayed all of these characteristics. She followed godly direction which exhibited not one but all of these traits. In our attempt to uncover who we are inside we must search "further in and deeper down."

When you open up the inside of something you can dissect its content, you can begin to discern what was wrong with it, and determine what has to be done to correct it and what it will take to fix the brokenness within its core. Once your content is opened, you can start to see the problem inside, then you can dig deep down inside and start the fixing process to make a better you. Micah 6:8 (KJV) says, *"He hath shewed thee, O man, what is good; and what doth the LORD require of thee, but to do justly, and to love mercy, and to walk humbly with thy God?"* Here's how to know what God truly wants from us, He said to "do justly," "love mercy," and to walk "humbly" with thy God. Do what is right with Him and when your spirits are humble you can be instructed. He can lead you, but you must allow Him to help you work out the internal problems you are carrying. Let Him blaze a trail through your rough and hostile terrains so all those who come after you will move with ease on their journeys.

A good question to start with is, "If I were split apart, what would be seen? Would I be identifiable, or so disfigured you wouldn't know what's what or whose who? Are there unrecognizable spaces within me? Would I need dental records to be identified, because of the distortion?" Our actions and life choices not only affect us but they affect everyone who comes in contact with us.

Matthew 4:19 (NIV) says *"Come, follow me," Jesus said, "and I will send you out to fish for people."* Let your life be revealed as a witness for Christ by your life and your words, even if you think it, you do not have to say a word. It's written all over your face and in your body language when you did it, therefore it counts against your intentions, which affects someone else's life because your motives were not right for doing it. We must have a desire to do right in order to achieve righteousness, it doesn't just come, you have to ask God to give it to you and mean what you say. Be committed to change and desire it greatly in your hearts.

Psalm 21:2 (NIV) *"You have granted him his heart's desire and have not withheld the request of his lips."* Therefore, ask and ye shall receive.

What makes a virtuous woman? Is it her success, beauty, designer clothes, affiliations, position, title, size or color? Absolutely not. Being virtuous is being rare, pure, righteous, chaste, being pure in thought or conduct and saying to yourself, "I am choosing to be a different individual. I am on this Jesus journey and I choose to be the me God created me to be. One with power, character, and moral fortitude."

Being virtuous gives meaning, purpose, and direction to our lives. Choose how you want to live your lives whether you are a child, teenager, young adult, mother, grandmother, or great-grandmother; you know when you have made a bad choice. We must let the depth of our goodness permeate every fiber of our virtuous being.

Everyone has a choice as to how and what they are willing to do and how far they are willing to go. We are the ones who determine our walk of life and who we will be influenced by. It could be a mentor, parent, teacher, grandparent, aunt, or even a sister who gives us direction, but it is ultimately up to us to choose to follow sound instruction and godly direction or to forfeit their advice. Whatever you choose, you have to live with your life choices. Are you rare? Is that you? A virtuous woman is a rare woman!

Ruth was a woman of virtue, she was more appealing because she was faithful, she was not vindictive, nor was she a brawling, whorish, or an adulterous woman, ill-willed, loud, or rude. She was a young widow who maintained extreme loyalty to her mother-in-law, The Bible tells us in Ruth 1: *"Don't urge me to leave you or to turn back from you. Where you go, I will go and where you stay, I will stay. Your people will be my people and your God my God"* (Ruth 1:16 NIV). Ruth was willing to follow Naomi who converted her from being a Moabite woman to a follower of God. Do you know her God, is He your God? She was unwavering, shining her light among darkness. She was like a lighthouse, alluring, warm, and bright.

Ruth was a virtuous woman to Naomi, whom she gracefully made the choice to stand by and take care of; all they had was each other therefore they were a support system for one another. Ruth was willing to be led by Naomi and followed God, not always having to run the show and be in control of everything. She was warm-spirited, obedient, supportive, gentle, a kind spoken person. She also was encouraging in nature, content (happy with herself and her choices), and she definitely was inviting. She was a woman who drew you in, she didn't push you away.

Even when things were not good, Ruth was a woman you wanted around; she was loyal. She loved her mother-in-law. (She had to be a lovable, a very gifted person in spirit, to tolerate her mother-in-law even after the death of her husband.) She was admirable, modest, and courteous. She was like having a best friend who always had your back—loyal. Is this you?

If you want the full outline of Ruth's life read Ruth 1 and Proverbs 31:10–31 in the Bible. Ruth symbolized what virtue was. She made it look easy to do. Her actions help us to understand what is required and teach us how to conduct ourselves victoriously!

It's not easy being a Christian with all the temptations of this world, but you should love the Lord enough that you are willing to try. Try with all your heart, with all your soul, and with your entire might to get it right. One of my favorite scriptures says, *"And it shall come to pass, if ye shall hearken diligently unto my commandments which I command you this day, to love the Lord your God, and to serve him with all your heart and with all your soul"* (Deut. 11:13 KJV). The key word is *diligently*. Do it to show that you care enough about the work of the Lord and how you love and serve Him faithfully with all of you heart and soul.

The Word of God teaches us and gives us the necessary tools to successfully meet the goal of "love," because God is love. In getting right with God, we have got to learn how to have an abundance of love for one another, there has to be a start with each other. In our getting right inside as well as out, we need to take godly responsibility and show Christian support (love) for our sisters (we are all sisters in Christ).

We need each other's help in this spiritual walk (take responsibility for one another). When we're engaging in earthly things (things relating to our flesh) instead of giving our hearts to God (pursuing righteousness), eventually we will feel like something's missing spiritually (satanic attack). Things will creep up on us when we're too distracted by life, too busy for one another. When we're isolated, the spirit becomes deprived and the flesh begins working in our weaknesses. When your flesh is under attack, it may seem like things are falling apart around you, that's when you let the devil know that in your weakness you are made strong in the Lord.

Unfortunately, we don't always know how or why this cycle started nor how to stop this downward spiral before it starts making our lives feel empty; it's an internal infestation that is having a negative outward appearance. You must learn how to let it go and find the source of what is missing before it has total contaminated you and is attempting to have control over your entire being. Remind yourself that Satan will not get the victory over you. Release that negative energy by writing down what has hindered your spirit, pray over it, and then burn it.

Burning something that's a hinderance changes how it feels, how it looks, and even how it works against you. It no longer carries power over your energy. When you burn something, it changes how you see it, for it is different now. Now that the appearance of it has changed, so has its effect on you. So, all you need to do now is learn how to wait on the Lord, stand, and be still until it totally disappears from your view. All the flaws, disappointments, inadequacies, worries, fears, scars, even the negative people, who have made you feel unworthy have gone up with the smoke!

Joyce Meyers, a noted scholar to the ministry of God's Word said on social media, "I believe that one of the significant reasons so many of us are burned out and stressed out is because we don't know how to be still" and "Because their minds don't know how to be still, they don't know how to be still."

It's easy to lose our way and become consumed within when the fire is burning but your smoke is still rising. You are burned out and stressed out because while you're waiting on the mess to incinerate, you start creating other remedies. Instead of letting everything completely disappear, you're substituting your faith with fictitious methods and then call it a victory because it worked out this time. Be still, take your time, and wait until you are able to move forward past your blazing inferno! The time spent filling up your life with forbidden forces and ungodly resources has to be put in the blaze.

We have begun to believe that we are in need of more and more stuff, doing nearly any old thing to fill our emptiness. We're thinking we have to have someone, find something, seek out any and every thing but God to fulfill us. We are forgetting all about our commitment to Christ and the extent of what He has done for us. You know the old saying "if I was a fly on the wall." I would hate to know what would be said if we saw or heard what the real you was doing and saying.

Have you ever wondered what story would be told about you in the end? It might be based upon a misconception someone has about you because of what they may have just heard about you. And it may be accurate, because they saw you in action themselves! But the one true person that it really matters to is God and what He has witnessed.

When people go into hiding their recklessness, they fall into many ruts. How far will you go to overcome this emptiness? With the misuse of your bodies, lying, deceitfulness, betrayal, once it starts, does it ever end? When you're willing to go beyond normal limits to cover up your mess, you can find yourself covering up one act of bad judgment and misguided decisions after another. The more you cover, the more the blemishes seem to reappear.

Our hearts are the center of our being, our core; if our hearts aren't right, then how can we get rid of the blemishes? It will take more than a mask. Start by praying; prayer works. Then by reading and studying your Bible; it gives such great instructions. Once this is consistent and working in your life, become a mentor to someone who needs help with their blemished lifestyle as well.

Nothing will prosper nor be spiritually fulfilling, no matter what you do or how effectively you think you're doing it, if your heart isn't right. Having a long overdue heart operation might be just what the doctor ordered for some of us. We are becoming heartless, lost beings as a result of our leaky aortic valves.

Many women just want someone to trust and talk to about the heaviness weighing on their hearts, someone they can call upon in their time of need. Can you handle hearing someone say, "I am not okay" Will you brush them off? Will you give the typical response, "Oh, I'm so sorry to hear that" or "I'll keep you in my prayers" and just move on? Do you really care about the way others feel when it doesn't touch you personally?

Sadly, we have become a "careless society," unconcerned about others. We would rather not deal with people and make ourselves believe that "she's okay" as long as it does not get in my way, affect my day, or take me out of my way. Are any of us really, okay? We can all use a godly attitude adjustment at times.

Before we can focus on our heart's identity which is a part of our charisma, our character references, our self-worth, let's first discuss the glorious and beautiful features that are the common dominators among us all. To ensure that we receive the best possible godly instructions that will change our lives, we must understand the "Wow" effect we all carry! When you see one another as Christ does, regardless of anything else, you'll come into your wow moment and say, "Wow, we are the same in so many wonderful ways." We will appreciate what gives us our common denominator and start treasuring one another's differences.

We all share similarities yet we are still different; my ways are not your ways. When we develop ways that separate, cause division, give us a negative reputation, or are unpleasing to God, it can cause our hearts to bleed out! We must understand the repercussions of a lost heart running rapidly astray. If we're not careful and contain how we use it, it will grow enlarged, instead of being upright. We will resemble the Leaning Tower of Pisa. It's standing tall but tilting over, just waiting to collapse any day. That's the nature of a weary heart, it's tired, overexerted, infested, and beating off the charts, and if you don't receive a spiritual transplant, you will definitely have heart failure!

God is and shall always be an awesome God who will strengthen you in your time of distress; Yolanda Adams, wrote a gospel album in 1998 titled Songs of the heart and one of her songs Still I Rise is one of the most uplifting songs about being shattered, but not broken, wounded but time will heal , Yet still I rise, high above the clouds, in time I feel lonely, yet still I rise, above all my problems." We need to realize that we all have so much in common and together we can rise high above it all. But sometimes, because of a weary heart we can be evil in our God-given differences toward one another or we can choose to be a reflection of our creator, and operate from the image of Christ that we all share. In Genesis 1:27 (NIV), *"So God created man in his own image, in the image of God he created him; male and female he created them."* Whether we like it or not we are all made from the same makeup.

There's someone who has been down at least one of the roads you have been on or that you might be on right now; who has cried tears of sorrow, been divorced more than once, been an addict, been raped, abused, mistreated, felt defeated, lost control, had a miscarriage, had an abortion, been discouraged, or even spoken ungodly toward someone, and they could still help you get off that heartless course; maybe even prevent you from going down an even darker road.

Sisters in Christ, we need one another to get through the tough times. We might not all look the same, act the same, talk the same, not even think the same, but God created us all exactly the same way. How can we not treat one another exactly the same as Christ treated us: with love? Show the love of Christ because somebody somewhere desperately needs it!

Session Two

IX. Integrated Integrity

Does your reputation precede you?

I
Betrayer—Judas

What betrayals are still inhibiting you?

Do you remember when you were a child dealing with people who would tease and mock you? Kids can be so cruel. They laughed at how you looked, where you lived, or even at the clothes you wore. Do you remember just laughing along with them and giving off a happy appearance all while feeling extremely torn on the inside? No one ever asked if you were okay, so you never said that you weren't. I have some of those kinds of memories where my outward appearance didn't line up with my God-given inward appearance in the sight of others. Satan uses the people around us to make it appear that something is wrong with us and when we're not careful, we'll believe that lie!

In Genesis 2:23 (KJV) when God presented the woman to Adam, he said *"This is now bone of my bones, and flesh of my flesh: she shall be called Woman, because she was taken out of man."* Eve was the original design of who a woman was supposed to be, and there wasn't anything wrong with her natural state. From the very beginning she appeared to Adam perfectly! God gave her everything she needed in his eyes.

Satan is a deceiver, the one trying to make women believe that they are not complete unless they change something about themselves! You are a vision of beauty created to be loved and adored, just as you were presented by God to man! Satan attempts to keep us gagged and bound by placing barriers in our lives that distract us from our purpose. He's in hope that if he halts you, he's halting God's divine plan for you too.

He starts doing it while we are still children. As children we don't know how to defend ourselves against spiritual attacks, which is the perfect starting point for him to manifest his attacks against us. It's at that level where, as a child, you will believe the lies and hopefully carry them into your adulthood. As children we are absent-minded, vulnerable, and lack the intellect necessary to fight in warfare, so we are abused, mistreated, even neglected and Satan uses these things against us as adults to hold us bound to our child-like tendencies! That's why some adults find themselves still carrying the weight of their childhood abuses as if they had happened to them yesterday. They can't let go, because they haven't forgiven being a victim to a deceiver themselves.

The answer to your problems wasn't in the methods you chose to forget with; it wasn't in the alcohol, the drugs, the men, the addictions, the complaining, the cursing, the shame, the smoking, or anything else; but getting to Jesus was the answer to your deliverance from your problems! Satan used these things to keep you from getting the understanding that Jesus is a healer. He can heal you from all things no matter what method you choose first! Psalm 107 says, *"Then they cried to the LORD in their trouble, and he saved them from their distress. / He sent out his word and healed them; he rescued them from the grave. / Let them give thanks to the LORD for his unfailing love and his wonderful deeds for mankind"* (Ps. 107:19–21 NIV).

God never planned nor intended for any of us to live our lives alone, divorced, raped, abused or mentally, emotionally, or physically distorted! He never meant for anyone to lose their minds, for any of our children to be abused in unimaginable ways, nor for our men to be falsely accused, nor people killing one another in the streets, women with women, men with men, even priests have been neglectful and abusive. We went from bone of bone and flesh of flesh to being cursed by man in the fall of Adam! No one but God is the judge and jury, inhibited is just a form of our true nature being displayed as a result of how we've consciously handled life as we have lived it!

This fall in the garden of Eden affected and led to the reversal of how we are to be treated as women of God and how we have allowed ourselves to be treated and to many horrific acts against who we are as women. We must start to take back our power by shutting it down, gathering all the broken pieces, and putting them back together according to the way they were originally designed to be—perfect! Then, close the door and evict anything and anyone who doesn't place value in you. Have faith in God to heal you and free you from all the suffering this life has placed in your hands. Mark 5:34 (NIV) says *"He said to her, 'Daughter, your faith has healed you. Go in peace and be freed from your suffering.'"* Don't sleep on your worth. You are too valuable to the kingdom of God!

Joel Osteen said on his radio station "You have already been equipped and empowered with everything you need. You don't have to struggle and try to make things happen. It's already in you." William Murphy released an album in 2013 titled God chaser which contained a song called "It's Working". "This is my season for grace, for favor . . . this is my season, to reap what I have sown. It's working for my good!" And Pastor Rick Warren said on a YouTube message, "If you are that important to God, and he considers you valuable enough to keep with him for eternity, what greater significance could you have?"

God never intended for our lives to be lived in shackles, I thank Him that He had other plans for you and I to be touched by His internal love. Even when those around us don't know how to love and treat us, God placed value in us to have a harvest of His love! He has placed His heart to our hearts, His spirit in us, His love around us, and given us His power that strengthens us, so that we will speak life and not death into His people. When you're able to speak through the power of Christ and understand His plan is one that has rectified you and I, then all we will need to do is believe in the plan. The plan is in the Bible, the Word of God!

If you read the plan until you get it on the inside, and study it to show yourself approved (be able to answer when asked about God), then all things are working for your good. Yeah—easier said than done—but ask yourself "Why do I believe in everything else and study it, place more emphasis on that, but I can't commit to the one thing that can set me free from the inside out?" You deserve better, so you must do better!

Inhibited is a plan of action, not just a source, but a necessary resource. The Holy Bible is the ultimate means God has given to us as the true infallible Word of God, yet He also allows us to be able to use other means, other avenues, in getting some much-needed understanding of our divine calling, for we are all called to do something! 1 Peter 2:9 (KJV) states *"But ye are a chosen generation, a royal priesthood, a holy nation, a peculiar people; that ye should shew forth the praises of him who hath called you out of darkness into his marvellous light:"* Now let us begin to show forth or proclaim who we are in Christ by our actions!

Getting past your inhibited form will allow you to tap into an area of hopefulness and help you to understand that God expects you to make changes in your life for good, even when it appears that everything is going bad. Your divine path is finding out what's the purpose of your personal kingdom agenda: "Where do I fit into it?" "How does God's kingdom apply to my life?" "What must I do to walk the road of righteousness as God sees fit for my life?" These are honest questions everyone should ask themselves for many really don't always know how, when, or where to begin. One thing's for certain, edifying the body of Christ starts with reading and studying the Bible daily. It prepares you in gaining a closer relationship with God and the plan He has for a more rewarding life.

Inhibited is intended to help you to gain an even closer relationship with each other by teaching you how to make your lives change righteously toward one another and helping women to recognize that it takes a gradual course of action to remove layers of build-up. Nothing happens instantaneously; it's a faith walk! Put your war clothes on and your righteous shoes and get ready to run this race together.

It took time for me to get there, but once I understood my calling, I gained my purpose. That's when I was able to pen my first sermon for the Lord. It was a blessing to know God had greater in store for me and I'm finally operating in it!

Here's my first sermon:

My Scripture reference: 1 Corinthians 9:19–27 (NIV)
Paul's Use of His Freedom:

> Though I am free and belong to no one, I have made myself a slave to everyone, to win as many as possible. To the Jews I became like a Jew, to win the Jews. To those under the law I became like one under the law (though I myself am not under the law), so as to win those under the law. To those not having the law I became like one not having the law (though I am not free from God's law but am under Christ's law), so as to win those not having the law. To the weak I became weak, to win the weak. I have become all things to all people so that by all possible means I might save some. I do all this for the sake of the gospel, that I may share in its blessings.

The Need for Self-Discipline:

> Do you not know that in a race all the runners run, but only one gets the prize? Run in such a way as to get the prize. Everyone who competes in the games goes into strict training. They do it to get a crown that will not last, but we do it to get a crown that will last forever.

Therefore, I do not run like someone running aimlessly; I do not fight like a boxer beating the air. No, I strike a blow to my body and make it my slave so that after I have preached to others, I myself will not be disqualified for the prize.

The Amplified (AMP) version reads: But [like a boxer] I buffet my body [handle it roughly, discipline it by hardships] and subdue it, for fear that after proclaiming to others the gospel and things pertaining to it, I myself should become unfit [not stand the test, be unapproved and rejected as a counterfeit].

Sermon Title: **Running This Race to the Finish Line Without Getting Disqualified!**

I asked this question: "How far are you willing to run or go to share the gospel, the good news of Jesus?

—Do you get tired before the race start, before it's over, or even during?

—Do you get exhausted and just give up? Or start and go sit back down?

—Maybe you're someone who doesn't feel that you have to run this race!

—Your actions, your situations, your positions, your flesh, or your life choices should not determine whether or not you win or lose.

You should decide to win! You should decide to run this Jesus race because of who He is to you! If you're going to go the distance in this race for souls, you have to be willing to reach out to people and talk to somebody about Jesus, you have to be willing to get a little dirty—cute is out of season—you might even have to run this race in the rain, sleet, or snow. So, get up and run your race.

Ask yourself "Am I even qualified to run?" Getting qualified takes time and effort on your part. See, when you start a race you head for the starting block, you kneel and get ready to go, but somehow, we start running in different directions. Because we're not sure where we need to go or what we need to do. We are not qualified yet! But don't sit down, find out what you need to do.

We start off together and somewhere along the way some of us go by the wayside, some of us get stuck in the mud, some of us even stop for breaks and lose sight of the goal. Others forgot to stretch and never left the starting block. They showed up for the race and became an observer of the race, not a participant, because they didn't meet the necessary standards it took to be a runner for life. You have requirements that have to be met.

We have to be the ones who run this race to the finish without getting distracted, without giving up, without losing sight of our duties, without letting our way of thinking hinder our walk, our attitudes, our biased opinions, our anger, our rejection of God's people or His Word delay us in our race of ushering souls back to Christ. Do not sit down on the job; those that do are the ones who will be disqualified.

Everyone doesn't start off the same at the starting block. Some people start by crawling, others power walk, some jog, but the runners who learn how to pace themselves and correctly breath as they press on recognize early on in the race that they have opponents who are likely to reject them, taunt them, even mock them—not all Christians act Christlike—but they go on anyhow hoping to win them over from their Jewish ways.

I'm referring to the ways built on particulars and participators! Victory is reached in a particular way, and only righteous participators are qualified to attend. Paul said in verse 20 of 1 Corinthians (NIV) that he became like a Jew, meaning we have to step outside our comfort zones knowing that sometimes people reject us because we're different, we're not as educated as they are, we live in a particular area of town, we look a certain way, or we don't participate in the same things they do! We're not supposed to be like everyone else that's what makes us peculiar.

We're even rejected for our own way of thinking, our individuality, the one thing that makes us each unique! The apostle Paul knew he had to learn how to adapt because Jews have ways that are guided by stringent customs and traditions. It's particularly hard to uphold to their strict diets. You can't just eat whatever you want or act however you like in this race, so he adapted to fit in, only he made every effort to reach them and introduce them to Christ Jesus our Lord! He respected that they didn't have to be like him in order for him to speak life into them!

Although Jews mean well, they're not always great at being understanding and merciful when you fall short in your race. They're in it to win it, so you better come ready for the race. Be prepared to have Bible study, prayer service, and anything else it takes to keep you running at full force. You'd better be a good sport; not everyone will accept you in this race! Just keep going, and don't let differences stop you from advancing God's kingdom!

Running a race is a sport. Its reviving, rejuvenating, and rewarding, but when you're out for a run there's some familiarities, good and bad, keep alert, especially to the unfamiliar people running alongside you on the track; not all the people you encounter have the same passion and intentions for the race that you do. Some people just come with the territory. They have a motive, and helping you win isn't one of them.

Paul said *"To those under the law I became like one under the law (though I myself am not under the law), so as to win those under the law."* (1 Corthians 9:20 NIV)

He knew we would encounter some people who are on the track (under the law), you know, the kind of people who always watch your every move, ensuring you do no wrong or they will have you disqualified immediately. They are hypocritical, for no one is perfect, except Christ! They can't wait to broadcast your mistakes. They can't wait for you to fumble or fall short. They live for it! Paul didn't do as they did by judging people for their mistakes, he merely entertained them to get close enough to win them to Christ. So, tell your enemies that you're running for the Lord, not for them.

People who are under the law with their no tolerance rules and their no exceptions to the rules attitudes will be unbearable at times in this race, so don't backslide in your race. They're only here to observe the laws of the race, so you'd better know all the rules of the game if you plan to run this race. Remember participants—Satan will be in this race whether you like it or not—he is an opponent who will be watching and waiting to trip you up. Make sure you have excellent balancing skills and you won't trip.

The longer you hang in there, you'll soon realize that there can be trouble in the line-up and sometimes this is not good, especially when the people who can "care less about the law" or are "without the law" line up on their starting blocks. They can cause you a little concern about what their real agenda is in this race. Keep your eyes on the prize or you might find yourself acting like you're above the law.

In verse 21 Paul says, *"To those not having the law I became like one not having the law (though I am not free from God's law but am under Christ's law), so as to win those not having the law."(1 Corth 9:21)* These are the group that calls themselves the unbelievers and sinning against the other runners gives them such satisfaction. They don't care about who you represent; their goal is winning at any cost, *not* getting an eternal prize but a temporary fix. They fix their eyes on causing a whole lot of trouble in your life to keep you from getting ahead of them. They need you to continue in a sinful lifestyle, so they can feel good about their own shortcomings. This is that team of runners who feel like they're undefeated, they're the majority, and they call themselves the ones who are without the law.

When you have no law, you don't know about the grace and mercy of God that's truly the winning force behind this game. They don't know Jesus is running with us, and they can't stand hearing you talk about church or a man named Jesus! There's definitely more of them than there is of us, so keep up your pace don't lag behind!

The men without the law will cut you off, throw down obstacles in your way, say things against you, and do anything to distract you from the real prize, which is Jesus. These runners make it harder on everyone else, because they're always making the road look easier than it really is, it's a trap. Booby traps are set up everywhere, and a lot of us get caught in their traps. Don't allow the people and things of this world to take you off course. Do whatever it takes not to backslide in this race!

"To the weak I became weak, to win the weak. I have become all things to all people so that by all possible means I might save some." (I Corthians 9:22 NIV)

Of course, at every meet you have someone who's weaker than the rest, unable to discern the right way from the wrong, and they start to lag behind in their spirits. Some call them the weakest link, others cling to them to appear stronger. It's our job to make sure we work at the proper pace and that we catch them up spiritually to help them get properly prepared and equipped by getting them in Sunday school and Bible study for proper training. Paul became weak to win those who are weaker to Christ.

Being partnered with someone who's weak or immature in spirit might weigh you down if you're not strong in your own faith. This can cause them to be considered a slacker when you're paired with them in this race for souls, especially if they get in your way. They have to learn that God wants us all to minister to His people and help them get stronger in the Lord, but be careful for in their weakness they tend to always find themselves in everybody else's lane.

They don't have the Christian maturity needed to win in this race just yet, don't give up on them because God didn't give up on you. Our job is to help them to do better so they can do better. At some point in our live this was all of us, we haven't always been mature Christians!

This is why it's so important that you get yourself spiritually strong before you try leading someone else and that you make sure weaker vessels are spiritually sound and properly schooled before they take to the starting line-up or work in ministry. It's the strong who survive, so we must empower all God's people to do their absolute best.

The apostle Paul was trying to teach the Corinthians a lesson about giving up your rights, your ways, your wants, and your expectations for the sake of Jesus to gain the best freedom ever, the freedom in the good news of Jesus Christ. He said *"I do all this for the sake of the gospel, that I may share in its blessings."(I Corinthians 9:23 NIV)*

He wants everyone to know that God came as a man and lived a perfect life and died on a cross for all people regardless of who they are, what they have done, or their color or race. God wants us to tell everyone about Him! Get in this race and finish it! I hope there's no one reading these words who thinks this isn't your calling, because we are all called to do this for the sake of the gospel in order to share in its blessings.

Paul teaches us that obtaining this kind of freedom is like no other experience you'll ever have—gaining such a prize as this is priceless—just by becoming a physical slave for Christ to everyone you encounter, everyone you meet, regardless of who they were, or what they believed. We have to care about all people and try to reach them all. Their salvation depends on us running in this race until we finish it.

Paul taught in his public ministry that by physically winning all people to Christ and by being a servant of all people and having a spirit open to instruction for all we may come to have faith in Christ. This is the reward we will receive. Do you want it?

The apostle Paul also demonstrates the power of love for all God's people by meeting them right where they are. In whatever state of mind they have, we still had to show them the love of God—a great example of godly love. He never said anything about only the ones of this color, this age, or this nationality. He wanted us to follow His example and to offer Christ to everyone!

That means everyone: Blacks, Whites, Hispanics, Asians, Jews, atheists, Jehovah's Witnesses, Mormons, etc. *Everyone* means "everyone." We must do it even knowing that they all won't be willing vessels to listen but while running in this Christian race we'll do it anyhow. We still have to be available to them all.

This is what God expects of us all. Don't be biased or prejudiced in your race! Be loving, kind, and an example to others who are watching!

Philippians 3:17 (ISV) says, "Join together in imitating me, brothers, and pay close attention to those who live by the example we have set for you.."

God doesn't want us treating him like he's not in charge of our lives.

1) God is in charge of our lives

2) God is the head of our lives

3) And God is the Alpha and the Omega of our lives.

    A) God just wants you to stay on course.

    B) Get yourself ready for the race.

    C) Pace yourself.

    D) Be disciplined, and

E) Endure your training.

F) And be available to everyone while you're running this race.

We're running toward the prize which is eternal life, it never fades away!

In order to receive a prize, you first have to run the race!

God wants to reach us, to direct us, and to talk to us! But we take off running our own race without getting prepared. When you prepare and you take steps, even if they're baby steps, you're moving toward the starting block.

Our starting block has to begin with Jesus and when you run this race, He'll run with you. We don't wait on God to show us His plan, we're too busy with our own plans, but the moment things get tough, we're out of the race ready to give up; back to our old ways!

We become suicidal, start getting drunk again, doing drugs, depressed, defensive, promiscuous, disrespectful, angry, lonely, and desperate when all you had to do was run in the way God says run, stay encouraged, and just wait until He shows you the plan He has for your life, and then run it to the finish line with everything you have in you.

Psalms 27 says wait on the Lord and be of good courage.

It takes courage to

1) stay on route!

2) stay on the course.

3) stay aligned with God's will.

4) keep your eyes on the prize which is Jesus Christ!

So, stay in the race!

Inhibited

What does it take to get you to the starting block and not get penalized because of a false start? Jumping out there too soon causing someone to fumble!

When you are running this race, you have to wait until God says Go!

Sometimes you have to just stand at the starting block and assess the distance, evaluate the track, consider where you want to go, but most important wait on God!

Maybe then you,

1) might not stop.

2) won't get tired of running in the race for winning souls to Christ

3) won't get discouraged or get sidetracked so easily.

4) understand the seriousness of this race!

Running is an exhausting sport. We have to muster up some faith and rebuke the discouragements, stay on course, and not take shortcuts.

You need to know what God requires of you by pressing on, even when you're in your trials and burdens, you got to press!

Paul says in Philippians 3:14 (KJV) *"I press toward the mark for the prize of the high calling of God in Christ Jesus."*

I'm staying aligned with His will. This will help you press toward the mark of the high calling which is in Jesus Christ, so keep your eyes on Him! He already knows our shortcomings! Don't focus on your flaws, just run the race.

You will have to sometimes push your way through and endure to the end to finish your race, just stay on course and recognize that all you need is God to get though.

When you run in a marathon some preparations are required—you don't just go to the starting line, look at your opponents, and just take off running.

First you have to decide that you want to be a runner!

Then you take the necessary tools or steps to learn how to properly make your body work for you by getting training! Get spiritually trained as well as physically trained!

God doesn't want us to foul out, give up, nor get disqualified, because we broke the rules and went back to our old ways, so get your flesh under control; then get yourself ready so you can properly get to your marks!

All athletes know when you're in training a coach's job is to work out the muscles, teach you how to endure the pain, show you the necessary safety methods so that you won't get an injury, and warn you when you're doing something wrong. They know how to get you prepared, but if you go to a bad coach, you could get seriously hurt and never run again in the race. This is a spiritual principal as well.

We hear about people getting wounded in churches all the time and leaving with open wounds never wanting to return again because they didn't like something said or done to them. In Matthew 7:15 (HCSB) Paul warns us against false teachers and not being prepared. *"Beware of false prophets who come to you in sheep's clothing but inwardly are ravaging wolves. You'll recognize them by their fruit."*

You get wounded or hurt in church because you're not properly trained to handle the growing pains and uncomfortable aches of being cut open by the Word and then and once you've heard something you didn't like your race was over. We can't expect to hear what we want but what we need to help us grow, even if it hurts!

Hebrews 4:12–13 (NIV) *"For the word of God is alive and active. Sharper than any double-edged sword, it penetrates even to dividing soul and spirit, joints and marrow; it judges the thoughts and attitudes of the heart. Nothing in all creation is hidden from God's sight. Everything is uncovered and laid bare before the eyes of him to whom we must give account."* It's the Word of God that hurts, not me!

Don't believe everything you hear. Get yourself spiritually developed so that you're ready and prepared to run in this Christian race and won't be easily wounded. If there's no winner on the team, then you need a new coach. Even if you've been injured you can still recover and be healed! There's healing in the blood! In order to run this race properly, you have to get to know Jesus for you! Don't just take somebody's word, get your own understanding.

When you get to know who Jesus is for yourself, you're winning because you're getting spiritual nutrients and necessary ingredients needed to run as long-distance runners and to hang in there for the long haul. Your preparation is molding you into mature Christians who can't do anything but win with Christ.

As distance runners you have to prepare your bodies: body building, push-ups, aerobics, cardio, cycling, mind training, a balanced diet, weight lifting, and proper rest. But when you run in this Christian race it has its own principals and requirements and it takes preparation, discipline, and practice. You prepare by daily prayer. You have to read your Bible daily. Study to show yourself approved. Lift up holy hands in the sanctuary. Make a joyful noise unto the Lord. Tell somebody about a forgiving God. Prepare a table for a needy heart. Love thy neighbor. Train your sister how to walk the walk and talk the talk. Exercise your mind and body to strengthen your spirit.

Then you must believe and have faith in what you're doing and discipline yourself for the race. Practice it daily!

Believing is having enough faith that you'll cross the finish line otherwise it's just wasted efforts and lost time, blocking you from accomplishing the goal.

Faith is believing even when you can't see what's ahead.

Once you've made preparations and you're better equipped to stay in the race, excise your God-given abilities and gifts by getting on your marks.

Once you're equipped to handle life then you can get ready for the race, you have to get in the kneeling position for kneeling shows humility. You're leaning and depending on God. The power of the Holy Spirit has tested and stretched you spiritually and physically. It has exercised your strengths and weaknesses. You've achieved ample power to withstand the pain and hardship. Your dependency and assurance validate the spirit just as your jumping jacks, stretching, lifting, and healthy eating enhances you physically.

Both are necessary tools in learning how to lean and depend on our training so we can withstand the marathon.

Depending totally on God isn't as easy as it sounds. It's a tough road, and some people get disqualified for lack of preparation. Once you learn how to depend on and rely on God for everything, you learn how to hold up under pressure, so you don't give up before you get though a lap.

Now that we're on our marks and we're ready for the race, we have to believe in Him by getting set! Get your minds set on the task ahead!

Set your mind on belief mode. Ask yourself what do you believe in. Is it belief in a corrupt world, belief in people, belief in false gods, belief in your job and money, even believing in yourself as the source of everything you've achieved? What do you believe or do you believe in the Father, the Son, and the Holy Ghost?

In 1 John 3:23–24 (AMP) we read,

> *And this is His order (His command, His injunction): that we should believe in (put our faith and trust in and adhere to and rely on) the name of His son Jesus Christ (the Messiah), and that we should love one another, just as He has commanded us. All who keep His commandments [who obey His orders and follow His plan, live and continue to live, to stay and] abide in Him, and He in them. [They let Christ be a home to them and they are the home of Christ.] And by this we know and understand and have the proof that He [really] lives and makes His home in us: by the [Holy] Spirit Whom He has given us.*

How can you get set for the prize if you don't believe in God or love all God's people? This is why Paul said (I Corthians 9:22 NIV) *"I have become all things to all people, so that I may by every possible means save some."*

Believing is staying focused on the task at hand and believing in a higher power than yourself and staying committed, keeping your eye on the prize that you keep running your race.

Believing is making it over the hurdles, withstanding the cramps and pain, the discomfort that comes with running, breathing steadily when you feel like you're running out of air, then pushing yourself past your opponents.

Believing is having faith in God and having enough substance to stand firm.

Believing is also being in love with God and His Word!

You're on your marks, you're ready now, you're finally set, so how do you go? Now how do you cross the finish line and receive your reward?

When the starting gun sounds and it's time to go, before you go, you have to have confessed with your mouth that you believe in a righteous God, a loving God, a redeeming God, a forgiving God, and you have accepted Him as your Lord your Savior and now you can go with all power!

John 1:12 (AMP) says, *"But to as many as did receive and welcome Him, He gave the authority (power, privilege, right) to become the children of God, that is, to those who believe in (adhere to, trust in, and rely on) His name."*

In order to finish and cross over we have to walk with him, have faith in Him, receive Him, trust Him, depend totally on Him. God wants to say "well done my good and faithful servant," but will you remain faithful and hold on to cross over the finish line?

Our training pays off when we are dedicated and put in the work. Dedication doesn't mean you won't get tired or frustrated it simply means you won't stop, you'll keep going, you'll hold on just a little while longer, you'll have faith, ample power, self-determination and belief in knowing that God is the prize, you'll know He's worth running for, leaping for, hurdling for, you have gained control over your flesh so you won't be eliminated, and you now know what it takes to get there.

Joyce Meyers said on The Word Network, "if you know what to do—do it... if you don't know what to do and firm abiding in Christ Jesus knowing he won't let you down,"

So, keep your eyes on the prize, stay focused on the prize that awaits you, press your way through, and continue on your course. Never give up and you will cross over the finish line into the heavenly gates.

Through all your hard trials, through all your temptations, you've made it. You're on your mark, you're ready for the race, your mind is set on Jesus; now you're ready to *go*! At the very moment you cross over the finish line, your name is called and your crown is presented, the ultimate rewarder awaits you with His outstretched arms. Jesus is telling you job well done—you have finished your race—enter in! All God's people enter in!

But for the ones who become disqualified, it's because you failed to meet the basic training requirements and could not participate in the race at all, therefore get your flesh under submission that your sins don't disqualify you. And you are left behind!

As Paul said to Timothy in 1 Timothy 2:7–8 (KJV), *"Whereunto I am ordained a preacher, and an apostle, (I speak the truth in Christ, and lie not a teacher of the Gentiles in faith and verity. I will therefore that men pray everywhere, lifting up holy hands, without wrath and doubting."*

Prayer and supplication are the keys to understanding God's Word and required in running your race to the finish-line without getting disqualified! Get on your marks, get ready, get set, and now *go*! Amen!

I pray this message helped you go further in Christ Jesus in your race to the finish line. I could not have written this sermon, without Christ Jesus!

Inhibited

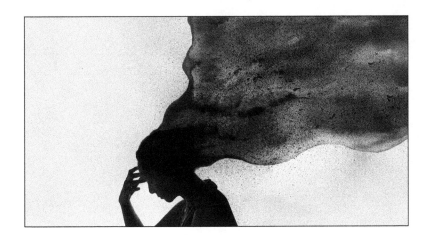

II

Negative—Esau

Is a negative response ever applicable?

I bet if I asked, many of you could tell me stories about negative people, probably more of them than positive ones. Negative doing, acting, and speaking occasions are more common responses for people who are feeling attacked or emotionally or verbally abused by others and these stories are more memorable to people who witness them.

The Bible tells us that Jacob and Esau were twin sons of Isaac and Rebecca and the grandsons of Abraham. Esau and Jacob characterize two different attitudes people can take toward life; they represent two different categories of people who will always be in a struggle against one another due to how they handle their differences. Although twin brothers, Esau and Jacob were two people who showed jealousy and negativity toward one another, and as a result the first murder was committed.

Can you imagine being a pregnant woman as Rebecca was and grasp a vision that disturbs you, because you realized that there was a struggle going on within your womb; the twin lives you're carrying don't have love for one another and as their mother you can feel it in your spirit!

Have you ever felt that there was something negative going on—on the inside—that you weren't sure of; that you sensed was disruptive to your peace of mind? Imagine if your spirit sensed that there was an internal war against your peace of mind hindering what should have been a happy occasion, because the birth of your boys was about to take place.

Rebecca was told by God that she has two nations growing within her womb; in other words, they were warring with one another to see who would have the dominance and they would always be at war. Have you ever dealt with a sibling rivalry? Well, can you imagine it starting inside the womb?

Rebecca knew there would never be peace within her home with her twins! Twins usually bond immediately, look out for one another, dress alike, feel each other's pain, but never war against each other for power! This had to be a sad revelation for a mother to be to deal with! Even today we find ways to continue the war against one another every time we say something to one another that's negative or causes contention!

Here's the story as they grew up: Esau was the oldest, and was set to inherit the spiritual and physical inheritance through his birthright as the first born; Esau came in from hunting and he asked his twin, Jacob, for something to eat and Jacob said, "I won't feed you unless you give me your birthright" and Esau took him up on the offer. What a horrific, tragic mistake that was. He gave up a considerable amount for something so minute!

Now, God's divine order was changed over a bowl of soup. In other words, His natural characteristics that are described for us are also descriptive of His spiritual attitudes. What you do in the natural will also affect you spiritually. Jacob's name meant trickster! Sometimes, when we're hungry or tired the enemy will use the one we know hates us to destroy what's rightfully ours! No mother ever wants to endure watching her children at war against one another, tricking each other, being negative toward the other, but this is what Rebecca had to deal with even before her children were born!

What Esau represents is that mindset, that lifestyle that would be willing to give away things that are sacred, of eternal value, or holy. In this case he traded his birthright for a bowl of soup. It is sad, but this is the behavior of some of the people in our society. They are willing to compromise the importance of what their ancestors worked so hard to pass down to them.

Esau, literally for a "quick fix" sold his whole family and destiny out from the plan and purposes of God After realizing that you've been tricked in a negative yet major way, I'm sure your response would have been as Esau must have felt, furious at Jacob. This level of deceit caused Jacob to flee his home for nearly 20 years still afraid of his brother's reactions. Once Jacob returns home, he's still worried about his destructive behavior and how Esau is going to receive him back home. When you betray the trust of your family, you have gone to a level that only God can mend and fix what's broken in you that you allowed yourself to be labeled as a trader!

Although he was so troubled, Jacob finally meets Esau and they hug and embrace and everything appears okay.

And Jacob tries to give Esau a gift, Esau said, "I have enough." I want you to know that this Esau spirit has killed many a revival, many a service, many a church, and many potential moves of God.

Because so many are like Esau when they say I have enough. God's glory doesn't just come automatically, Ricky Nelms wrote a message titled Avoiding The Esau Spirit in 2010 and posted it on Sermon Central he said that Gods glory doesn't just come "we must search for it, long for it, ask for it, seek for it, and knock for it; it takes believing for it.

What behavior shows your character? So many people are following an Esau pattern of behavior: no morality, no fear of God, no respect for correction, giving into their carnal ways, pursuing materialism, selfishness, and abandoning their liberties and their values just to fulfill their immediate desires within this world. You can't have what you want and not be concerned about who fought for your right to make a choice.

We cannot allow the negative spirit of Esau to rise up against us in our homes, on our jobs, in our minds, or anywhere else that we partake of, that we find ourselves using trickery and deceit against one another for things that aren't rightfully ours!

God gave us all our own divine purposes and if we waste our time chasing what belong to others we are underachieving in this walk. You can't gain from anything taken out of greed! Be careful how you treat one another. God sees and knows everything and we are held accountable for our actions, even the ones we just think of! Your reputation is what people think about you, but your character is who you are! Who are you?

III

Judgmental—The Pharisees

Do you care about what is said about you?

What is my reputation? Can I stand firm, knowing I have a good reputation? What do you really think of me; am I the only one who sees me as a good, respectable person? Seriously, does it really matter what others think about me?

Reputation: One's standing; the way in which one is regarded by others.

Are you a trustworthy, reliable good Christian friend? Are you supportive, encouraging, a great listener or do you tell people's business, gossip behind their back, betray their trust, or even stab them in the back? Are you the kind of person who considers what you say about others? What would others say about your reputation as their friend?

The Holy Bible says,

> *We know that the law is good if one uses it properly. We also know that law is made not for the righteous but for lawbreakers and rebels, the ungodly and sinful, the unholy and irreligious; for those who kill their fathers or mothers, for murderers, for adulterers and perverts, for slave traders and liars and perjurers-and for whatever else is contrary to the sound doctrine that conforms to the glorious gospel of the blessed God, which he entrusted to me.* (1 Timothy 1:8–11 KJV)

A reputable Christian friend should never be concerned about properly displaying their righteousness.

When you consider the time that the law was established it was being mishandled by many, but Paul stresses that if we must use it for good as it was originally intended, it has great benefits to us, but false teachers are mishandling it and using what was given to us for good illegally and causing chaos within the church. When you are bickering over anything that God had appointed, you are lacking the knowledge of who He is. When you reject correction, you are rejecting God's Word. Sometimes, we need to be reminded that we are acting like lawbreakers and rebels, the ungodly and sinful, the unholy and irreligious, contrary to scripture, and we're sinning against God. We need to become aware of our sin so that we can correct our mistakes by repentance.

When we are defiant are we just as our accusers, the people who do not know the truth, or like the atheist who just refuses to believe the truth? When we run around with people of the world, hanging in clubs for reasons unbecoming of Christians, strip joints, bars, on street corners prostituting ourselves, sleeping with someone else's husband (adulterous affairs), having our bodies violated again and again before marriage (fornication), helping ourselves to things that do not belong to us (stealing), stretching the truth to suit us (lying), doing anything and everything with no regard for ourselves (selfishness); we get caught up in hiding our sins so that we can keep living them out without consequence. This is nor righteous living and your reputation can be tainted by the display you portray.

Remember, God is preparing you for more. The more sin you commit and hide the more chaotic and less concerned you are about what others think about your actions. You can become so involved in your ungodly choices that you may never consider how your actions affect the people around you, your families, and even your friends. You even might not have ever considered how it will affect your future! Never forget how other people's reaction will be to your situations, everyone won't always be in agreement with a messy lifestyle, or is it that you just gave up caring as long as you can continue to live how you choose?

Although we are no longer under the law, this is a good example of how we should seek sound doctrine that conforms to the glorious gospel of the blessed God, which He entrusted to us. But we have become just like the non-Christians, the ones we are supposed to be trying to help change their lives and live as we all should be living for Christ Jesus. It is a bad thing to have a non-Christian see you in an ungodly place doing ungodly things and expect anything more from them than what they see you doing.

You are now discredited in your faith walk! You are not seen as a spiritual resource any longer in their eyes, because they now see you living just like them. You have just lost your credibility, and when you say "God can do anything, but fail" why would they listen to you when you are acting and doing the same things they do? The message you speak is truth, but your actions make it hard for a person trying to change to believe that it's better being like you, when you act just like them!

Are the things being said about you when you enter a room positive or negative? It is not always jealousy that causes people not to want to be in your presence, it just might be your attitude, murmuring, or your unapproachable demeanor. Do you run around with your friends' man; lie to your sisters in Christ telling them that something doesn't look well on them when you really know it looks fine? Do you say you are too busy when you are asked to do something for someone, knowing you just don't want to do it? Say what you mean and mean what you say, even if it is the truth. I would rather you told the truth and hurt my feelings than have to stand on judgment day with nothing being said that was good about your life. Is this you?

When we want to be blessed, we must be a blessing. We have to be there to serve when needed or asked; it is not a choice we should make or take lightly. Godly love outweighs all, that's what people need more than your fake attitudes and disruptive behaviors. They need to be loved!

Don't be one of the people who have become a part of a judgmental society. We need people who have godly reputations in our court, not people judging each other's differences, sizes, color, styles, beauty, or religion. I would only hope that God is pleased with our actions and not displeased with our decisions toward His people. He is a God of love, peace, and happiness. *"Who are you to judge someone else's servant"* (Rom. 14:4 NIV).

"Therefore, let us stop passing judgment on one another. Instead, make up your mind not to put any stumbling block or obstacle in the way of a brother or sister" (Rom. 14:13 NIV). In living out the Christian walk, weak or immature believers can cling to relatively unimportant details about the faith. We must treat immature Christians with dignity and exhort them not to argue about things that, ultimately, are not of eternal significance.

Everything is not a big deal. You are not always right! We have got to stop arguing among ourselves about frivolous things. *"Let us therefore make every effort to do what leads to peace and to mutual edification"* (Rom. 14:19 NIV). We must learn how to talk to one another in love, peacefully, concerning, and learn how to properly channel our emotions. *"Let the Lord fight your battles and stop worrying about His business. For the kingdom of God is not a matter of eating or drinking, but of righteousness, peace and joy in the Holy Spirit, because anyone who serves Christ in this way is pleasing to God and receives human approval"* (Rom. 14:17–18 NIV). God gets the glory when we speak love into one another's spirits. They cannot help but to see Christ in us when we find ways to properly filter our feeling for one another by beginning to show nothing but the love of God in everything we do.

I used to feel like everything I did and said was on display to be judged whether or not it was acceptable! I was a small frame young woman with a large tush and small top. I never carried myself provocatively or inappropriately, but I was always judged because my shape showed and it was my fault that it drew attention. I found myself dressing twenty years older than I was just to fit the stereotype for Christian women.

For years, I felt like I had to dress way older than I actually was just to please other women. I was twenty-five-years-old dressing like I was over forty—covered up head to toe—because I thought that I had done something wrong by having such a large tush. My husband was the one who finally said "If you're with me, my opinion and God's is the only one that matters." And that was so reassuring to me because I was being treated horribly by women who said they were Christians.

We can't make people feel diminished because of how they look or because we feel threatened by their gifts. As a young woman I felt how a lot of young women feel today, like the senior saints are always judging them based on how they look, not by the content of their characters. Now in some cases, there are women who know they have gone way too far with how they dress today, but that's not what we're speaking about in this segment. I'll save that for the next book!

My judgment wasn't based on my inability to be a witness for Christ, but some folks chose to single me out because I had so many children that they assumed I was loose. I raised six kids, and they only saw the kids and never took the time to learn my story, so the insults begun. We are designed to be whom God created us to be no matter what judgments are cast at us, be able to showcase God regardless!

Once God showed me that my season was up at the place I was in fellowship with, I moved on and upon leaving I had fear of telling anyone about being called to preach the Word of God for several years, because I felt inadequate from hearing so much negativity toward me and my family. No matter how much we've blessed others, we are still put under the fire!

I found myself becoming more concerned about being liked, instead of being obedient to the call upon my life. I didn't know how to say I was called to preach because during the entire eighteen years of my fellowship at this church we never had a female preacher speak, unless it was for Mother's Day or a women's retreat and she was only addressed as a guest speaker, not as a minister, and definitely not as a pastor! God was calling me, and I didn't know how to answer!

I knew God was moving me, so I could utilize what He'd put inside of me to give Him glory. I am in no way mocking God's house nor my former pastor. I loved my church family and friends; I was just reluctant to tell my story for my own lack of self-assurance as a minister. I didn't even mention it until God moved my husband and me from the church. Then, I was content and assured in my faith that I was being obedient, although I still needed ample training!

During my transitional phase my husband went through sickness, so we temporarily joined another church and I thought it was safe to share my testimony with my new pastor after being there six months, especially since he was my professor at the Christian college I attended. So, I shared with him what God was calling me to and he immediately started to preach from the pulpit that no woman will ever set foot in his pulpit, nor teach in his church. He went on to say, that women are only designed to teach children until they reach the age of twelve and looked me straight in the eye as he made his statements, knowing of course the negativity had an influence on how I received his teachings in my classes and his reputation was tarnished in my eyes, but I never judged his opinions. I took my apprehensions to the Lord for myself.

These were major setbacks to my spiritual self-esteem and these could have caused me to spiritually fall had I been an immature Christian, but I knew God had called me and I wasn't going to be judged by old-school thinking that a woman's place is only in the kitchen or the bedroom! We must know for ourselves whether we are hearing from God, so that we don't get the opinions of man crossed up with our spiritual assignment!

I was forty years old and still fighting off spiritual attacks against my calling, so I went into deep prayer and study and that's when God confirmed who He said that I was in my spirit. He confirmed that I was called by Him to preach and to teach His Word. I cried out to God for direction and He answered my cries by allowing me to preach a powerful sermon to Him at that moment. I knew then that I had been called to ministry as a preacher, and from that day forward I began to walk unashamed in my calling! *"Therefore do not be ashamed of the testimony about our Lord, nor of me his prisoner, but share in suffering for the gospel by the power of God"* (2 Tim. 1:8 ESV).

Opening my mind up to receive godly instruction allowed for the Holy Spirit to remind me of how I was letting God down every time I did something against His will. And this calling was in the will of God. I couldn't abort it. It was like Jeremiah said, *"A burning fire shut up in my bones."* (Jeremiah 20:9 KJV) I was also reminded that my spiritual maturity mattered for the sake of my personal growth, my obedience to God, and overcoming my old-school mentality. I had to grow up in Christ, get past the delays, and let go of the doubts that I'd allowed people to put on me. I was now leading and how can I lead lest I be led of the Holy Spirit?

By listening to the voice of God and not listening to what others had to say about the gift(s) God placed in me, it was revealed to me that this kind of hindrance, these judgments, could halt other people's gifts from flourishing as well, or cause them to go astray, or even set them back spiritually. We have to be careful how we make people feel when they share their testimony. I thought about the places I could have wound up, or got caught up in at any moment, that could have led me astray all because of a few hurtful words. I almost let go and lost my way based on the words of people who shared their negative opinions that hindered who God said that I am. Knowing who you are in Christ is so vital!

Hearing and listening to the voice of God will keep you aligned within your training toward leadership and ministry. You'll see your life differently! You won't be focused on who thought you were adequate for the job as long as God sees fit to use you. So, every time you feel the desire to go back and revisit your old habits, you can't! Something inside of you will remind you that it's all about Jesus, and by the grace of God you will be able to turn and walk the other way.

The Spirit of God that dwells within you will give you a glimpse of what your future was doomed toward if you had continued down that dead-end road. The road of life has many detours, so stop trying to appear stronger than you are and start trusting and believing in God for everything! It's His strength that we lean and depend on! It took some time, but I found out that the person in the mirror looking back at me was beautiful, outgoing, smart, and wonderful in every way, with all her flaws and deficiencies. With that revelation I had no choice but to surrender to God's plan and not my own.

We should willingly give up our will to God's will. When we have surrendered it all over to the Lord, He can take over and give us the guidance we require! Not until that moment will we learn how to encourage ourselves in the Lord and have faith that He'll work it out for our good! God gives us permissive will to choose Him, although He already chose us, before we were formed in our mother's womb. *"Before I formed thee in the belly, I knew thee; and before thou camest forth out of the womb I sanctified thee, and I ordained thee a prophet unto the nations"* (Jeremiah 1:5 KJV).

Because we have already chosen to be whom we are before our mothers ever conceived us in their wombs, the need to be affirmed by others no longer matters. Encouraging yourself in the Lord gives you the ability to also encourage others! Once you have accepted the Lord, you will learn how to love you just as you are and just as He created you to be.

Tell yourself, "If God loves me just as I am, why not love me just as I am!" Being true to you, and true to who God said you are, will lead you to a truly happy, responsible, and more rewarding life. That's where I found joy, direction, and my calling to ministry! Where I found the Lord, who was just waiting on me to say yes to His will and, yes, to His way!

Then, I had no choice but to change my ways, and it started by trusting the God in me and the plans He had for me. I started believing there was a better path! Up until that moment in time, I was happy in my selfish ways; at least that's what I thought! I was selfish, because I had it all: good health, financially okay, family, love, and career savvy. Yet I still thought I needed more! I truly thought my happiness was in gaining the stuff, the education, and the titles; not realizing that God had so much more for my life than I could have ever imagined. God has more in store for you as well!

All we really need is Him and His direction, and all that other stuff will be the icing on the cake. I realized at that moment that, even if I lived in a box or had nothing at all, He would still love me the same and that should be enough. He would still have called me for He knew me before my own mother ever did. He has always been there; I just wasn't looking for Him, how selfish of me! I had unimaginable joy in knowing that His love was enough. Can you imagine a life that fills you with love beyond words? Well, now I can!

Ladies, if you want to be different, look different, or be like others that you're willing to turn toward altering the woman you were created to be, consider the fact that it could only be a temporary fix. I'm not referring to alterations that must or cannot be helped, but some of the ones we sometimes choose unnecessarily! They can sometimes still leave us feeling empty inside. I'm not saying you shouldn't want to improve yourself, but only do changes that will please God and you! Don't do it for any other reason or for anybody else! No one deserves to tell you you're somehow better because you are now pleasing to their eyes. Maybe they just need to close their eyes or look another way when they're in your presence! If they don't like you now, as you are, then they don't deserve you when you're new and enhanced—I'm just saying!

Some of you seek these self-enhancements to feel adequate; don't make life-changing choices because of a lost dark world's expectation of *you*! God created you perfectly! Alterations should be a personal choice made by you alone. Don't make them because of society's expectations of who you are, but know it's only temporary! Nothing cosmetic will ever define your self-worth. Your value comes from God. Once we know our worth, we don't focus our attention on mediocrity as much anymore!

Nothing external will ever change what's internal! If you're depressed, that's the issue you need to deal with. If you're suicidal, that's what you deal with; lonely, deal with that; afraid, deal with that; death of a loved one, deal with that; but do it knowing that nothing external will fix your internal lack unless you address it. Take the appropriate action for the situation. First, start by taking it to the Lord! Then seek professional advice!

Be assured by telling yourself, "If I don't like me, then changing the outside won't fix what's going on inside of me. I have to let Jesus fix it for me, not methods and tools." Not only can He, but He will! Some wounds cut us so deep that we need Jesus and we might even need a psychiatrist's couch to lay on and work through our feelings, and believe me when I say that's okay too!

Remember that you are made in the image of God, so embrace the person looking back at you in the mirror with a satisfactory salute to the maker of it, with a bold, *Oh, yeah*, attitude! Tell yourself, "I'm outstanding just as I am" and walk in it! Accept everything about yourself, so you can come to grips with your perfections and learn how to embrace your imperfections as well! We are already made as a perfect image of God, so what changes do we really need to make? God loves us just as He made us. If you make a change, do it from the inside out! And fall in love with who that woman is! Just as she is!

One change that I can simply say did me some good was to change the people around me who weren't satisfied with me! Everybody doesn't have your best interests at heart, so why are we trying to please them anyway! Focus on pleasing God! He loves you just as He created you and He only wants changes in you that lead to an everlasting (eternal) life, peace of mind, joy, and goodness. His pleasing power doesn't include anything that will ever physically or emotionally hurt you or feel like an attack against you! Although God allows things to happen that might not feel good or may hurt, He's allowed those things to build our faith and draw us closer to Him. When we learn how to trust God through it all, that's when we are building our faith and trust in Him.

When you make internal changes toward God's love, it has a sweet savoring aroma, peace within, fruit of the spirit filling. God doesn't break the heart He caused to beat to His rhythm. He doesn't hurt the ones He loves. He doesn't turn His back on us because we messed up or made bad choices. Get in sync with God, because when you're out of sync you start to blame God for your circumstances or get mad at Him for the things that happened in your life that you don't agree with. Instead of becoming bitter, pray about it without ceasing, knowing in your heart that God chose you and He knows what you're going through. No one can change it or do anything about it, but God.

The apostle Paul told his son in the ministry, Timothy, this in 1 Thessalonians,

> *We always thank God for all of you when we mention you in our prayers. In the presence of our God and Father, we constantly remember how your faith is active, your love is hard at work, and your hope in our Lord Jesus the Messiah is enduring. Brothers whom God loves; we know that he has chosen you.* (1 Thessalonians 1:2–4 ISV)

In all your circumstances, keep the faith, stay on the righteous path, and never lose hope; God loves the ones He has chosen. Pray that you continue to endure until the end and for one another to have the same hopes.

Sometimes, it's necessary to look your best when you don't feel your best. Put on whatever makes you feel alive, rejuvenates you, uplifts your spirit, especially when you are experiencing hard times. It's hard motivating yourself to put on a smile and press on when you're in the midst of a bad or uncomfortable situation or depending on your environment, this might be a stretch, but, if at all possible, look your best as you work your way through your stress!

The best way to endure is to not mask the pain, but rather live your best life while going through the pain! I truly believe that if you look good on the outside, you temporarily feel better on the inside. Keep making attempts until the good feeling gets into the inside permanently. If your situation is a danger zone, get immediate help and don't stay in a hostile environment. I am not advising anyone to continue to endure pain at the hands of others! I'm referring to the fact that there are many

Inhibited

other painful situations that can feel irresolvable, but please know that with Christ we can overcome!

God never expected us to let ourselves go and become like dead men, so don't let your spirit die within a bad situation. If you're in an uncomfortable place in your life, don't wallow in it day after day. Take a stroll, call some friends, dance, turn on some uplifting music; do anything you can to get yourself motivated to move forward and beyond your current situation if at all possible. Even if the situation doesn't change immediately, you'll feel better about it for the moment.

When unforeseen stuff happens, speak life into your spirit—words that encourage you, confirm you—keep telling yourself, "I am amazing, I deserve the best, I am worth it, I can do all things through Christ who strengthens me," and eventually you'll start to believe it and walk in it. And the messy stuff will not consume you when it comes.

Repetition, repetition, repetition gets results! If ever it's more than you can bear or makes you depressed, suicidal, or want to harm yourself, you must seek professional help immediately. God knows when we need additional help; that's why He made doctors and counselors along with everything and everyone else for us to utilize. Use your resources when necessary! Don't wait until it's too late, seek help if needed!

IV

Bitterness—Saul

Has life made you bitter?

For some people reality is like sucking on a lemon, it's bitter! When you see them, they're never smiling, looking mean or angry all the time, unapproachable! If you have a bitter attitude, you're walking about this world weighing down your shoulders and limiting others.

The Holy Bible says that bitterness is one having anger and disappointment at being treated unfairly. It's resentment and envy. We already described Esau and Jacob, one brother feeling unjustly treated by the other, so he murders his brother out of hatred and pity for himself. You must take ownership of your emotions, your situations, and give God control of what is out of control for you. *"For I see that you are full of bitterness and captive to sin. (NIV) For I see that thou art in the gall of bitterness and in the bond of iniquity. (ESV) For I see that you are poisoned by bitterness and captive to iniquity"(BSB)* (Acts 8:23). This is the type of man King Saul became as a result of being so consumed with himself. He became jealous of others and his true character were revealed.

Saul was Israel's first king. Here's a summary of his story: when we lack obedience, we get jealous and bitter because we weren't willing to listen nor humble ourselves to God's command.

Now the LORD had told Samuel in his ear a day before Saul came, saying, To morrow about this time I will send thee a man out of the land of Benjamin, and thou shalt anoint him [to be] captain over my people Israel, that he may save my people out of the hand of the Philistines: for I have looked upon my people, because their cry is come unto me. And when Samuel saw Saul, the LORD said unto him, Behold the man whom I spake to thee of! this same shall reign over my people. (1 Samuel 9:15–17 KJV)

The Lord had always intended to give Israel a king (Deut. 17), but Israel's sin was in demanding a king from the wrong motives, in looking for that king in the wrong tribe, and in demanding a king before it was God's time to give them one. A man named Saul, from the tribe of Benjamin, was chosen, a man of impressive stature who embodied the basic ideals Israel had at the time, being much more concerned with his appearance than his heart. It's sad how Saul's character turned out to be a reflection of Israel as a whole.

Now there was a man of Benjamin, whose name *was* Kish, the son of Abiel, the son of Zeror, the son of Bechorath, the son of Aphiah, a Benjamite, a mighty man of power. **And he had a son, whose name *was*** Saul, a choice young man, and a goodly: and ***there was*** not among the children of Israel a goodlier person than he: from his shoulders and upward **he *was*** higher than any of the people. (1 Samuel 9:1–2 KJV)

Although Saul was a handsome man himself, he was also a weak and ineffective king who didn't do much with his life except try to murder his son-in-law, David. He was bitter toward knew David was destined to take his place one day on the throne and he also knew that he was loyal so he had no reason to treat him badly. Saul's hatred and insane jealousy for David made him fail as a king and Samuel regretted anointing him. Saul's reign ended in disaster. He received no answer for his prayers, and even sought the help of a witch.

When you become so bitter for no apparent reason, you are choosing your bitter avenues that could destroy everything you were designed to be. Saul went to the next level in breaking God's commandments and as a result **And Samuel said to Saul, Thou hast done foolishly: thou hast not kept the commandment of the LORD thy God, which he commanded thee: for now would the LORD have established thy kingdom upon Israel for ever. But now thy kingdom shall not continue: the LORD hath sought him a man after his own heart, and the LORD hath commanded him *to be* captain over his people, because thou hast not kept *that* which the LORD commanded thee." I Samuel 13-:13-14**

When we defy the Lord, we bring damnation upon ourselves. We must wait for the things God has for us. His plans are always better than the ones we plan for ourselves. When we don't listen to correction—why are you angry and bitter—repercussions arise.

Have you heard people say to you "Why are you looking so mean," or "What's the matter with you," or "You look upset, what's wrong?" Our facial expressions are not supposed to be expressions of doubt and despair, but expressions of love, kindness, peace, and joy. Take a good look at yourself—what do we see written on your face?

The Women of Faith Bible study defines for us what a heart filled with bitterness is and what it is derived from:

> It is slow and subtle, growing undetected until you find yourself drowning in it. It taints your body, your soul and your spirit. It saturates your heart. It overflows and infects those around you. It colors every part of your life until you recognize the darkness, you're living in. It is an ancient enemy called bitterness. Bitterness can be caused by circumstances: the death of a child or other loved one injustice,

the overwhelming troubles of life, foolish children, or your own sin and rebellion against God. Yet the circumstance doesn't produce your bitterness; your reaction to it does. Refusing to forgive a sin or a hurt committed against you gives bitterness fertile ground in which to grow. Refusing to repent will give bitterness a foothold and will result in a scarred relationship with God. But you can have freedom from bitterness; you can enjoy God and life again.

We are sometimes bitter because we are living in a dry routine place in our lives and we are having trouble becoming effective! God can't get the glory when we are stuck in a routine. We get up, go to work, hang out with friends, pick up our kids at the same time, dinner at the same time, and go to bed at the same time . . . our ineffective routines.

Some of us look at our routines as planning ahead, organized, justified; but it's still a routine!

When the enemy knows your habits, your every minute, how you function daily it allows him time to throw a monkey wrench in your program. What happens after complacency? Boredom! Dryness! Then you are allowing unwelcomed people within your circles, getting mixed up with bad friendships and bad relationships because life has gotten dry and boring! People who mean you no good are suddenly being allowed into the most intimate parts of your lives. Bitterness doesn't just happen; situations arise to cause us to become bitter! When we've been betrayed, when we have allowed the devil to entice our thoughts because we're drying out from our daily practices.

Sometimes we find ourselves wearing our feeling on our faces like frown lines. We are so uncomfortably that God isn't getting the glory from your lives any longer. While we were sitting comfortably, our focus got out of alignment, and we couldn't see the war going on right in front of our faces! You can't become so complacent that you are not willing to relinquish your routines for God's. He has a plan and everyday has to start by asking what would you have me to do for you today.

Lord!

Whatever you do is not about you, the devil will put you on a platform, make you look great, feel important, get confident in your routine, and then God has to let something or someone come alone to break you out of what's comfortable just to get your attention. Some of you even sometimes have the nerve to get bitter, or mad, at God for allowing things to happen to break you, so you can see that the enemy is at hand. The devil takes your love for attention, your welcoming of accolades, your weaknesses, your people pleasing mentalities, your vanities and use them to blind you to the fact that you are at war within your spirit.

You are not in this alone. It's a set up to be at war with the enemy and not be aware! He has spent countless hours studying your routines, where you go, what you like, who you are attracted to, how you think, and so on just so he can send exactly what you desire—instead of what you need. Once you grab the bait; test the waters, why not: your eyes are shut and you are wide open for mess at this point! The sad part is that you don't even see it coming or know it is happening, until it's too late. Now you are in so deep, and you're drowning in the mess you created for him!

We gain knowledge when we lose possessions, get fired, injured, abused verbally or physically; then we realize that it a warfare going on! Attacks are coming, betrayals are visible, friends are few, life is weighed down with disappointments, and we are mad and bitter because this is not what we expected! When you get steered wrong and find yourself going in a different direction than the one God has for you, don't become ashamed, start calling out those spiritual attacks for what they are. Call the enemy out of your situation with your words of wisdom, start rebuking him for who he is: a liar, a thief, a deceiver, and an enemy who must be exposed for who he really is. If you don't expose him, he will only become the way to death and destruction in your weakness.

Speak and declare it as dead: declare that the bitterness, the disappointment, the setbacks, the attacks are dead to your spirit and take back what God said is yours. Your growth comes with being accountable to God. We can't stand back knowing that there's a war going on and continue in our routines, continue in our dryness, continue in our resentment. Sometimes, God has to get our attention so He can reveal the enemy to us through our trials.

Saul was so convinced that his looks, power, and position were the source of his power instead of God; therefore, he went ahead of God and paid the price for his vain decisions. This was his own warfare that he didn't know how to get over, how to walk through it, overcome it or get through it, so he blew it instead and became a very bitter dead man! God is still the way, the truth and the life. We have to refocus ourselves back to Christ and allow Him to lead and to be the head of our lives.

Stop sleeping with the enemy and allowing him to be entertainment in your life's desires. Nothing shall inhabit your space but God! Put your spiritual eyes back in alignment with God so that you won't be blinded by the deceit of your enemy, because you seek after recognition, position, and power, instead of God.

A bitter heart lies within a lost soul! Turn your focus back to God or He will allow things to happen that you caused and wait for you to ask Him for help. Don't allow distractions, things, or people to cause discord, to feed your flesh, or to exalt you above God. It's not worth having bitterness of a bleeding heart, when you can have the heart of God instead!

Session Three
Pleasingly Powerful—The Fruit of the Spirit

If the fruit of the spirt is love, joy, peace, longsuffering, gentleness, faith, meekness, and temperance, are you using what you have with all your might to be fruitful?

I
LOVE—LOVE OURSELVES AS CHRIST LOVES US

Is all that you do in love?

If I could give anyone advice, it would be to embrace yourself and gain as much love for yourself as possible! We are extraordinarily and wonderfully created, perfected from the very beginning; therefore, why are we forever varying? We have many variations of multiple adoptions, the action or fact of adopting or being adopted, of giving up something we love or do not love to another, even to ourselves!

Christ adopted us as His own children, yet we don't always seek His love. Acceptance of the love for ourselves as we are has to become our first positive decision. This decision to love myself above all else has to be a determining factor in order to embrace the God in myself. God chose and loved us first, now we have to learn how to love everything about ourselves too, with all our imperfections and flaws! When you are the perfection of your Father, know that He took the time to perfectly make you with perfect qualities and of perfect ingredients. And the recipe came out impeccably! We are made of God-given components and that is our defining worth! We are worth more than rubies and gold!

Don't you wish you had understood this sooner? If only someone would have only told me when I was younger that I was already picture-perfect; that I was worth so much more than I allowed others to treat me as! If I had only been advised and shown who I truly was, then maybe my life would have been built on more than just my looks, my body, and my accomplishments!

I don't believe that I am alone here. I just know that I spent so much time focusing my energy on all the wrong things, eagerly chasing my brokenness trying to fill the void in my life with possessions and accomplishments that still didn't fulfill me. I thought this was who I needed to be in order to be who they thought I should be. This was reckless, thoughtless, and worthless to my significance as God saw me. Can you relate to having this type of a character as well?

When you start loving you, your realty will start gaining more clarity! One of my friends in Ministry, Minister Kyla Williams said, "God is calling people out of shadows and caves, anointing them with fresh oil and trumpeting his voice over their voice. If you listen, you can hear him speaking and dealing with your heart."

Although my mien, physique, academic credentials, or expertise each reflected a part of me, they were not all that I am! They did not set the value on the person that I am! Neither my achievements nor my looks will ever identify me or give me my self-worth. This came from my creator. God is the best in me! What He placed within me was the best part of me.

I am proud to have achieved things beyond my wildest imagination and of having lived life to the fullest and having been able to explore and enjoy so many beautiful places in the world, but none of that has outweighed the satisfaction I've received in gaining a closer relationship with God. These experiences and achievements have just confirmed the glory of God and His entire splendor in this world! His creation in heaven and on earth is magnificent! But my self-worth was given to me by Jesus.

God has placed his value of me, His assurances of us, His reflection of us, and His purpose for us in our hearts as guides for us to follow. He knew we would need something more satisfying than fleshly accolades from any earthly being! He knew our divine importance was greater than our outer core, for greater is He that is in us than He that is in the world! (I John 4:4 KJV)

God doesn't want our self-worth distorted by jealousies, corruptions, lies, betrayals, abuses, or any other ungodly remedies set up by Satan. That's why He gave us Himself and our values first, before any other thing we received. Learn for yourself who you are in Christ in order to receive the fullness of Christ.

We shouldn't need anyone except Jesus to place significance in our lives! The rest of our worth given by man should be icing on the cake, it covers what's already good and enhances it to make what's good even better! Tell yourself "I am a picture of perfection in the sight of God who made me just as I am and I'm not only good, but God said 'it was very good' when He created me!" Before we ever allow anyone to define us, let us first ask God to show us who we are to Him! Everyone else will reap the benefits of our godly excellence once we have been validated first by Christ.

In fact, when I was growing up, my self-image wasn't always this way. It hasn't always been a clear picture. There were imperfections, pimples, red eye, fuzz, glares, and so many other distortions in my self-portrait. No matter what, I never saw a clear picture worthy of my own looking glass. Getting to my picture of perfection was a day to day, spirit against flesh war. I kept finding myself having to retake picture after picture; not realizing that the distortion was going on inside my head. And my spirit-man was losing for so many years, until I became spiritually aware, gained spiritual maturity, and changed how I was using my lenses.

I was looking in my spiritual glasses backwards until I took control of my life choices and changed how I viewed myself in them. I cleared up my thinking pattern and started using the light inside of me to give me a better-looking picture. My pictures were looking better, but I still had some imperfections and massive flaws. So, I turned it over to Jesus and decided to trust in the Lord and let Him shine on me and through me. Then the glares started to become perfected, the distortions started to improve, and the portrait took on a whole new dimension. The reflection of myself was looking better and better every day. I started my healing process from that self-destructive behavior and began moving into my own. I was finally seeing a picture of perfection through my flaws.

I saw beauty in my imperfections and I realized that I had to ask for His forgiveness and let Him guide me through my process of security, because I had drastically gone astray. It wasn't easy for me to accept that I had so many imperfections and flaws, but I realized that God loved me with every one of them. He loved me past my early denial stages into my recovery. He was teaching me how to love myself within all my mess, as He did. I had begun to see a bigger, brighter picture. Things had finally become clearer for me, and if He can do it for me, He can do the same for you. All you have to do is trust Him at His word.

It wasn't an overnight process but with consistency I can now say that today, in this present time, I know who I am in the Lord. This wasn't always my reflection. I reflected some very unstable traits that I can't identify with any longer. In my quest for spiritual maturity, I had decided that enough was enough and that allowed me to ask myself some serious personal life-changing questions:

- Why did you want to change or alter yourself to the point you were willing to go to such extremes to satisfy society's vision of who or what you should or should not be?

- Why did it matter to you what others said about how you appeared to them?

- What will you accomplish by changing the way you think about your situation?

- Will changing the way you think about your situation be for the greater good?

- Where and how do I start?

These questions were the basis of me freeing myself from destructive ideas and habits in my life. I had to ask myself some other tough questions like

- Will you be any happier or more satisfied, internally, if you changed for anyone but you?

- Why don't you love the skin you're in?

- Are the things that happened in your life still hovering over your future?

Then I had to process each one of these questions and take time to answer myself, honestly! I really didn't know the answers at first, so I had to pray and ask God to show me who I really am and who He wanted me to be. I didn't receive immediate revelation, so I just kept praying daily. When He finally answered, I was still sitting in denial. So, I kept praying for another answer, but the moment I got sick of things failing and backfiring and going wrong, I decided to try it another way—God's way! I followed the instructions I had already received in my spirit, but this time I didn't do it grudgingly but in obedience.

This was the start of my life's lesson on spiritual maturity and self-assurance co-existing. These were great and necessary questions in my self-development as a young Christian, and I've had so many more lessons to learn and questions that needed answering over the years. My questions came faster than I was ready to receive the answers, but I asked God to help me deal with the tough ones, although I felt that they were all tough ones for me in the beginning.

Growing spiritually led me into further studies, bountiful questions, and evaluation of them all were necessary in getting a spiritual revelation. I sought after and needed to hear godly truth. I didn't want to live through the eyes of the people who said I wasn't good enough for them any longer. I was ready to live the life Jesus had for me. Jesus called me out and saved my broken spirit! That's why I had to hear His divine ripostes; mine weren't working!

Even, as I tried to improve my Christian lifestyle, grow spiritually mature, and develop new life choices, my spirit was at war with my flesh every day! This war led me to begin a study on who I am and who I intended to become, which allowed me to personally speak life over the dead corporeal situations that were still holding me bound in more areas of my life than I cared to realize. Speaking the truth about my depraved choices gave the opportunity for growth. I began to work at overcoming my own personal dilemmas of self-destructive behaviors. On the surface I wanted to indulge and I welcomed worldly affairs, which had to be tamed and removed, but learning how was the real dilemma because this was what I had fed upon for many years?

The spirit of God within me (my spirit-man) kept reminding me of everything that I had already allowed to go wrong when I had negatively partaken and given in to my own desire. The Holy Spirit impelled me to want to become better! This was the new life I now wanted to live, and finally feeling the Lord working on the inside an internal conviction was taking form, a conviction that actually felt bad when I did wrong! I was a nice person, did good deeds, helped people, but I was filled with ulterior motives internally that didn't bother me until I desired to change spiritually. So many of us will not give this confession, but God knows our hearts.

It's time out for getting hungry, but not being fueled on the goodness of God. What are you expecting to manifest once your spirit is full? Are you ready to eat the fruit of your spirit's expectations and love what you eat in God?

II

Joy—Happiness Within Ourselves

Can joy be found in everything you choose to do?

In my pursuit of truth, I found myself starting to speak out loud when tempted to go against the natural Christian grain and indulge outside God's will. I would find myself saying things my grandmother said, like "not today, Satan," "get thee behind me Satan," "no weapon formed against me shall prosper," and "I rebuke you, Satan, in the name of Jesus." As I spoke out against such wickedness it became easier to say no and truthfully mean what I said! Even thinking in a negative manner was a conviction to my new life. I thanked God for saving me and for keeping me, even when I fell short of His glory. He's a loving and forgiving God, and He'll do the same for you, if you ask!

Once you've tapped into this level of spiritual maturity, you can clearly hear from God and respond to the beckoning of the Holy Spirit. You will begin to feel bad about doing wrong, feel guilty about acting ungodly, and become very uncomfortable around people who have made the world their top priority. You won't desire to turn back to those types of people and you will stay as far away from anything and anyone who would tempt you to go back to your old behaviors. When you're maturing you will still have desires to return to your old ways, so until you do all you can to become strong enough to withstand this group of people, stay miles away!

Eventually you will learn how to befriend like-minded people and let the old ones go forever. Giving over to your own wants and desires will no longer be an aspiration. The ability to go to the Lord and hear His voice of conviction whenever you want to partake outside His will; it will be amazing and frightening at the same time.

Hearing the voice of God allows you to hear from the Holy Spirit and know what God expects of you.

The Holy Spirit will prompt your spirit multiple times on how you might be lying to yourself or hiding your true feelings; you must surrender to Him. When you are afraid that people will find out you are not all that you portray, you will continue being a liar; like being a wolf in sheep clothing not aware that we all have weaknesses and are in need of the Holy Spirit's indwelling!

In our weakness not once did we realize that we are in need of a Savior, and until that realization comes, we will remain connected to our sinful past. Some of us don't want to appear vulnerable, needy, or spiritually immature, so we keep everything to ourselves, hiding behind our lack of self-worth. I myself was always in church, seven days a week, as a child; I went to church, but I had to get the Word in me! I had to become the church, experience God for myself, and learn to quit hiding behind my faults. God allows us a test to have a testimony. We can't testify to His goodness if we're hiding our test! Some of you have to say, "Jesus helped me through this process of my testimony." Even my leadership qualities were nonexistent, until Jesus showed me how to lead His people. I didn't have the ability to do it on my own. I had tremendous obstacles to overcome just to get to this testimony.

Becoming a minister was one of the toughest battles I've ever endured. I had been told women can't be ministers my entire adult life! Women shouldn't preach! Women should be unpretentious and quiet! I was already a quiet and shy little girl who had finally learned how to spread her wings, and then Satan tried to shut my mouth again. God knew I needed a Savior to get me aligned properly. This was my greatest reward here on earth and how I finished this test would dictate my spiritual walk for life. It affected other people's lives! I just couldn't fail my test again!

When I was told women can't preach, it hurt me because I had a grandmother who pastored a church with my grandfather for more than fifty years until she succumbed to cancer in her nineties! So, are you telling me she wasn't called to preach and teach God's Word her entire adult life? She was the person who introduced me to the Lord and set the basic foundation for my spiritual growth. She taught me right from wrong, how to play the piano in service, how to read my Bible, and how to pray, was all that in vain because she was a preacher who was a woman?

Not at all! God can use anyone He chooses to spread His word! It was confusing for me for years, especially after I was called to ministry to preach! I was afraid to share the good news of Jesus, afraid of what people would say! I knew that people can be harsh when they're trusting in their own beliefs! That's why I began to study the Word to show myself approved and get my own understanding from God and not from man's opinion. God is the source of who we are in Him. And my value to Him was all the confirmation I needed! The spirit that is in you is greater than the storms around you! Gain the joy of the Lord by gaining happiness within yourself!

III

Peace—Mind and Body, Spirit and Soul

Peace is our gift to each other
Have you blessed someone with yours?

If you are ever finding yourself at a place where you can't reach out, just reach up and know that there is a wheel in the middle of the wheel. Jesus is that wheel; He's all around us, in every direction, on every road. He is our driver, and we go wherever He goes as we are being driven and directed by Him. When you reach up Jesus will reach into your situation and begin the healing and restoration process. He'll surround you with Himself and become the center of your situation so that it doesn't overcome you!

When you need a hopeful solution, Jesus will fill the void. He'll be the source of your decisions and help you deal with your internal destruction accordingly.

Allowing the Lord to speak life into yourself and creating a self-love is crucial to your spiritual growth. It detoxifies your mind, body, spirit, and soul. We must learn to love ourselves, so we can get stability over our decisions. The Bible said *"For God so loved the world that he gave his only begotten Son, that whosoever believeth in him should not perish, but have everlasting life"* (John 3:16 KJV). God already loved us enough to die for us.

When you're spiritually and motivationally stable, get proactive! This walk is not only about you, so don't waste all your time pleasing only you! Be happy with who God created you to be, but get yourself prepared for kingdom work as well. Start the process by studying the Word of God, and let your walk be pleasing to God, not man! Have self-love, but don't be vain or selfish. You have to be a beautiful and loving servant of God by staying committed as His servant. And loving yourself and His people is part of the kingdom assignment!

Embrace your true inner beauty from the inside out, then you'll be less likely to do something thoughtless, embarrassing, or regretful to yourself or others! Love that you are in Christ and be satisfied with all your imperfections; He gave them to you to be a positive influence and that's why He still said "it is very good" when He made you! Negativity is a backward spiral, too much and you can start to deflate that which is good in you!

To be proactive means you've decided to get involved in your own spiritual growth and the spiritual growth of others! When you make God the center of your thoughts, you are utilizing the goodness of God's Word to build up yourself while you are on this spiritual journey.

What should you treasure more than yourself, just God! Then the love of God and the love for yourself will becomes easier and easier. The more you think about Him through love, the more you're able to love your family, friends, and others unconditionally, even when they're unlovable! Love has no boundaries at this level because you're focused on the one who is love!

When you struggle to love, find where the heavenly treasures lie; they lie within the building-up of your love! Your treasures are built within your heart; *"For where your treasure is there your heart will be also."* (Luke 12:34 KJV) Find yourself some places you treasure, people you treasure, things you treasure, and rely on those things to help you manage the difficult things you face in life. First, treasure yourself in whatever state you're in! Our hearts can be carnal (worldly), but if our treasures are heavenly focused, our hearts will be sincere in this world.

Show us a woman who has a warm loving spirit filled with love and with a beautiful heart, instead of madness, anger, malice, indecencies, drunkenness, trickery, jealousies, betrayal, rudeness, negativity, or any other form of ungodliness! Be a treasure!

The Lord God made women beautiful inside and out, that's when God brought the woman to her man and the man married her based on what God put inside of her. The outer appearance was just an added plus! God even knew that someday man and woman would have a visionary problem, a relationship problem, and a humanity problem and they would forget His original plan (the plans for man and woman). Society as we see it today is no surprise to God! We must not adjust our vision to fit someone else's!

If we seek obedience and growth in the Lord, we have to treasure what's in our hearts from God before anything else. Don't fear the unknown! Seek God for your answers. Bind His word in your hearts. Ask Him for direction and follow His instructions.

Satan has man focusing on first seeing our outer appearances before ever embracing our inner beauty, which wasn't in God's plan for us! This is a distraction to take us off focus as to why we are really here and what we are created for. Ladies, change is coming! God will put things back in its original order—internal before external—live your lives as if it's heaven on earth and not hell!

As a result of you and I collaborating on this journey and placing a barricade up against Satan, we are a part of the change. We've started the process of change outwardly (externally) but there's more to learn in how to be effective as we change. Society shows us this every day. We see one another with a view of the exterior first; we see what we see meets the eye, and if it feels a certain way and if over a certain amount of time it still appeals to us, then just maybe we might stay planted there.

It has gotten so bad that we're afraid to trust anything and anyone we see with the naked eyes. Women wanting women, men wanting men, women dressing like men, and men dressing like women; we should be afraid of just trusting our own natural eyes. In most cases, we don't even know what we need, we only know what we see and what we want! Isaiah 41 says, *"So do not fear, for I am with you; do not be dismayed, for I am your God. I will strengthen you and help you; I will uphold you with my righteous right hand"* (Isa. 41:10 NIV)).

Internal reconstruction (love for one's self) is a learned value that comes as a result of having internal peace of mind! Outward reconstruction is more easily accomplished with money and a little healing time. You can change almost anything society places in front of you. It's the internal reconstruction that takes time, practice, and patience! Taking it one day at a time is what leads to real progress!

No one ever tells us how to be what my pastor and husband calls "converted internally." We hear about being changed on the inside, but how? Internal reconstruction starts with knowing and receiving Jesus Christ and allowing God to be our converter! Conversion is "the process of changing or causing something to change from one form to another." When it comes to religion or beliefs or the action of persuading someone else to change their beliefs," is conversion. And we don't have that power alone. We don't have the power to change ourselves! It's easily said, but hard to live by! That's why we need the help of the Holy Spirit's correction and direction.

The act of a spiritual mature conversion is taking that which we're trying to make outwardly perfect and tuning it inwardly in order to be internally converted and not just changed! You can change your name, change your clothes, change your hair, change your eye color, even change your appearance and look great outwardly, but nothings ever happened on the inside. Was the change effective? I'll let you answer that for yourself! This is why we wear such great masks. It's not really the look we were going for, but it covers so well we're able to stay hidden behind it and we rarely ever become converted or freed! We just keep us a variation of disguises! Cover-ups are great, but it's time to be converted!

It is like being internal slaves; we've forbidden ourselves to be exposed to the truth! That's why we must never judge others for we don't know the internal battle that could be taking place. Just because you're beautiful outwardly doesn't mean you're okay! It doesn't mean you're not hurting; it's just that we don't want to be exposed of our truths. Let me help you uncover the truth and get spiritually healed! Let me introduce you to a man who can covert and change anybody! Jesus said, *"Come to me, all you who are weary and burdened, and I will give you rest"* (Matt. 11:28 NIV). It takes time for you to rest too!

IV

LONGSUFFERING—HEALTH AND WELLNESS

Your longsuffering is your love enduring.

When someone is masquerading, they are in a costume, wearing a mask, and pretending to be someone else. They are putting on an image to the world and hiding their true identities. Even with all that covering, God still knows who you are and sees what's real beneath all the disguises you've put on. We can't hide from our truths! God wants us to be true to Him as well as to ourselves.

"For I rejoiced greatly when the brethren came and testified of the truth that is in thee, even as thou walkest in the truth. I have no greater joy than to hear that my children walk in truth" (3 John 3–4 KJV). Over time, everyone learns their truth and eventually makes up their mind to take the initiative to think about their situations differently and try to step outside their norm. A vain lifestyle will have you believing that, although life wasn't perfect, it was good for you just as it was and you're doing great with the blemishes. If the life you've been living didn't need attention, then why can't you get past its failures?

Flawed images may have felt good in the making; they may even start to look so great to the naked eye that they will have you pressing and failing and pressing and failing again with no substantial gain in the end, leaving just you sitting in a whirlwind of your life's mess. The bigger the mess, the greater the destruction! Some people call it persevering, because it hasn't limited them. Your flawed image is your new norm. Vanities can tell you lies, which you could believe as your truths, because you are too perfect for imperfections to be accurately displayed!

The Bible is the milk of God's Word. It will put our images in check and the more we feed ourselves on it the stronger we'll become, and over time we will become more susceptible to what we are able to eat. We'll be able to chew on the meat of the Word, and that's the level at which we should be seeking. Being a baby in the Word of God was where we were, but if we seek after more of God in desperation, wanting to know Him at a deeper level and to grow stronger, then we can chew on His Word with a better understanding, and all the flaws in our own imagine will correct themselves over time.

Some of us think with our ungodly realities, "It's my reality!" Some of us see life through our own lenses, "It's my view." Some of us only hear what we want and what we deem necessary, "It's my right." Has the bulb gone on? You are not thinking, seeing, or hearing what God is ordering in your steps. Until you view life through your spiritual eyes as designed by Christ, you will always be a blemished vessel! Christ diminishes the blemishes when we are obedient to God.

We're walking through our inhibited lifestyles to get to our new days where we can now realize God was and has always been just waiting for us. God never left us in the midst of our mess; He's waiting on us to make a decision to choose Him over our mess!

Your power is a gained through your repositioning. You're no longer controlled by your way of analyzing your flaws, and now that there's no weaknesses, confinements, disobedience, or anything else keeping you restricted from God, you can endure your reality.

Living a life free of correction, reproof, and training have initially developed a sense of tiredness for you. Being tired of doing things on your own, you may have felt like things were going very well when it really could have worked out a whole lot better for you sooner if you would have allowed God to lead you from the beginning. Turn it all over to the Lord and see what transpires.

A great scripture to begin studying is Paul's Final Charge to Timothy:

> *You, however, know all about my teaching, my way of life, my purpose, faith, patience, love, endurance, persecutions, sufferings—what kinds of things happened to me in Antioch, Iconium and Lystra, the persecutions I endured. Yet the Lord rescued me from all of them. In fact, everyone who wants to live a godly life in Christ Jesus will be persecuted, while evildoers and impostors will go from bad to worse, deceiving and being deceived. But as for you, continue in what you have learned and have become convinced of, because you know those from whom you learned it, and how from infancy you have known the Holy Scriptures, which are able to make you wise for salvation through faith in Christ Jesus. All Scripture is God-breathed and is useful for teaching, rebuking, correcting and training in righteousness, so that the servant of God[a] may be thoroughly equipped for every good work.* (2 Timothy 3:10–17 NIV)

This scripture has that wow effect one might never have anticipated could have ever materialized spiritual change. Up until this point, you may have never had any major life concerns; especially if you're young, carefree, liberated, and content. Life is still transpiring so you haven't lived long enough to feel its effect! When you're older, more seasoned you still may have felt that there wasn't anything about yourself that needed to change, but change means growth in some aspects of living life righteously! As Christians or people wanting to gain a better understanding of who Christ is, we must make a decision to give our lives to Christ or surrender our will to His will; that's how God fixes the pieces that are broken, more like shattered, in our lives! That is the value of growth!

Don't spend so much time focused on how you personally think life should work out for you without caring about what others think or what they have to say about anything pertaining to your life; everyone needs correction. Gaining love for another is a part of your purpose, it cannot be all about your own life, your own way, what you think, and of course what you say, the way you say it; this way of thinking is not Biblical. God can't uplift you if you don't think about how you exhibit His love.

God is love and exhibits such an amazing act of love that everyone should jump at the opportunity to share their love toward one another, but instead there are many people just looking for love in all the wrong places. Can you see what's wrong with this picture? The way we make people feel is very important to God, so it has to become important to us as well!

There are countless people still thinking and believing they don't owe you anything! *"The thief cometh not, but for to steal, and to kill, and to destroy: I am come that they might have life, and that they might have it more abundantly"* (John 10:10 KJV). The thief came to kill our blessings, steal our joy, and destroy our destiny. If we do not change our way of thinking he might just take our souls straight to hell and steal our entire existence and the divine purpose God intended for us to have. The devil is a liar! If we're not careful the devil will even try to steal our children and our grandchildren's inheritance! We cannot allow Satan to have anything that God has promised to us all! Love is the key and Jesus is the answer! The advantage is yours!

Satan thinks he has you. If you don't take advantage of what's intended for you, if you don't see that the advantage is yours, you may never realize how close of a neighbor he has become in trying to destroy your life. You are partaking in your own demise when you can't see the enemy watching your every move. Satan has no reason to mess with anyone; he already has lots of people going in the wrong direction. No one should continue to allow him any power over their destiny! God's grace and mercy allow us time to get things right. *"If we confess our sins, he is faithful and just to forgive us our sins, and to cleanse us from all unrighteousness"* (1 John 1:9 KJV). If you repent and confess that you were wrong, accept Jesus, and trust in His plan, start believing that He is your Lord, the King of Kings, the Alpha and the Omega, the Prince of Peace, the great I Am, and He's *your* Savior and *your* Redeemer, and so much more. If you repent and confess that you were wrong, He is able to save you and change your destiny and change what you believe about the destiny of your beneficiaries when we accept Him and believe that He is the son of God with all our heart.

A bleeding heart is a heart ready to tell your story; God knows, it's written in your heart! We can remove the wounds by professing that "in the name of our Lord and Savior, Christ Jesus, is the only name that saves us from our sins and puts us in a rightful relationship with God the Father," and leads us toward a state of enablement. Christ is the necessary means to unifying our lives and the bleeding is healed upon our profession of our sins unto Christ!

We must align our lives within His will in order to gain access to everything that's of Him! Confess your sins and be renewed (reborn again)! Your spirit-man will become a new creature with a new identity! Over time your thought pattern will begin seeking additional spiritual information to process. Thinking of others and not just yourself becomes relevant! You will thank God for enhancing your vision and restoring your view! There will be no more morally paralyzed visions. You will not be spiritually dead anymore. You will witness your new identity transformation take place now that you are alive. You will no longer see things contrarily to the Word of God, for you are on a path toward virtue. You will love the feeling of stepping into your spiritual renewal! This revelation is ours to have! It's totally free!

V

GENTLENESS—PATIENCE (FAMILY TIME)

Are you gentle and kind all the time?

When I meet people, they usually say "you don't look like you gave birth to six kids," and I always follow up with "I raised six, birthed three!" Still, it never mattered if I gave birth to six, I'm still the mother of six: four boys and two girls. When I met my husband, he was a single father of three young children and I was a new mom to a two-year-old, yet we fell into deep lust right away—well our right away was within three months! There wasn't any godly concern of fornication rules, biblical concerns, or churchy convictions, although we both went to church. At twenty-one it didn't have any apprehensions for me. I was not convicted; I only saw a good man with great potential to be in my future.

We continued the pursuit and were married two years later. A year after we married, we gave birth to our first son together. Although he was the fifth child in our home, he was our first child together! Over the next three years, we—meaning my five kids and me—lived a fun, loving, happy life and our second child was born, making our household a family of eight now! I had patience, but my husband often ran short and the family structure was cracking!

When our family size expanded, we found ourselves stressing over bills: childcare, food, money, transportation issues, medical bills, sports fees, school fees, clothing, shoes, phone payments, school lunch expenses, rent, water, electric, and on and on and on! Now that lust to love to frustration mode has kicked in and we were faced with the question, "What have I gotten myself into?" We were contemplating divorce, separation, or staying in the struggle and making the ends meet! Although we felt like we were sinking in our mess, we chose to stay! We both knew the Lord, we attended church, we prayed, and we were trying our best to do what was necessary to keep the family structure from crumbling.

Staying united as one meant we had to change how we did things and going to church was fundamental, Bible study was prioritized, Sunday school was necessary, and getting rooted in the Word of God was the thing that started the change in how we functioned as a Christian family unit! It didn't happen overnight, but we saw how it was blending us as one through our faith in Christ Jesus! Every year got better and we grew stronger in our faith! Our children saw how we changed and that gave them an outline to follow as they grew!

When your family structure starts to crumble, you have to truly trust God and lean on and depend on Him to meet everyone's needs. You can't only expect to always get what you want, but you should welcome the needs God satisfies as He sees fit. The time you dedicate to your family, the time you spend together, is important and worthwhile for everyone. It allows you to come together with a support system in place. The care, concern, love, and protection you share; there's nothing more valuable than what you impart among each other.

Families might not always see eye to eye, and as a result there will be disagreements that can separate the family bond; that's where your faith is tested and strengthened in the closeness you have in God. How you depend on His direction to see you through as life throws darts at you will develop His presence in your family. Your family must stand their ground together, knowing it's only a temporary interference! The more you withstand together, the stronger your family structure develops.

Have patience with one another. Patience is a virtue and talked about throughout the Bible in the Old and New Testaments. According to 1 Samuel 13:8-14 (KJV), *"lack of patience can cause you to miss blessings."* In Romans 5:2–4 (KJV), Paul says, *"By whom also we have access by faith into this grace wherein we stand, and rejoice in hope of the glory of God. And not only so, but we glory in tribulations also: knowing that tribulation worketh patience; And patience, experience; and experience, hope."*

My children taught me patience and my tribulations built up my faith!

Patience is the level of your meekness being in alignment with God. How do you interact within your life, with your family, your friends and co-workers, even your enemies when they try to take you out of character, when they touch a nerve and push your buttons; how patient are you in your moments of testing, or how impatient do you become toward your accusers? To what capacity do you accept, tolerate, suffer your way through without getting angry or upset? Do you endure your difficulties well?

When we struggle to delay our responses to negative circumstances; persevering over them comes with a straining. It's hard not to become disrespectful and get angry and want to retaliate when we didn't foresee the thorn awaiting us. Patience is an essential virtue that we all should be striving for in order to survive the attacks. We can't wait to fall into the thorns, by then the pain will be too unbearable to tolerate. We must work on building our endurance, so the effect of the sting won't crumble our spirit. Practice waiting, listening, getting understanding, watching your words, and knowing when to react instead of losing your patience and overreacting!

Your patience is important to building trust with your loved ones, your children, your friends; when we part this world no one wants to be remembered as unloving, impatient, unfriendly, or unsociable. We want our families to remember how much love we shared with everybody, remember how soft our voices were, how kind and giving we were. Take time for one another and build on each other's strengths. The time you share together will be remembered. The smiles you exhibited are priceless, the you love you speak is unforgettable, the joy of your laughter will be cherished! They will remember the good times, but being patient with family must be practiced in order for our loved ones to have the proper memories associated with us. How you exhibit how much you care is found in having a gentle spirit toward our family and friends.

VI

Goodness—Reach Out and Lean On One Another

The goodness of a person spreads in all directions

Having a Christlike fruit-bearing image filled with joy, hope, love, longsuffering, meekness, goodness, and peace gives us spiritual security that all our expectations shall be met exceedingly. What am I saying? We are designed to bear fruit in the image of God! God said when we make a decision to give our lives over to Christ, we are changers in the making, but we need to do more to remain on that path. We have to become Christian educators for life—pray and study daily, read our Bibles, live righteously, teach others about Jesus—and practice what we preach!

Education is very important. From the time we are born, our parents start immediately teaching us to say "ma-ma" and "da-da," to say "yes" and "no," to say our ABCs, to play Peek-a-Boo, then they start teaching us our numbers—counting from 1 to 100—and eventually learning our colors. Their consistency eventually pays off once we've learned these elementary tools that will be for our good someday.

In the beginning of your Christian walk, it will be the same process of starting as a spiritual infant, advancing to toddle stage, to elementary, to adolescent, and on to spiritual adulthood. But you have to keep progressing from level to level until you reach maturity or adulthood. That's where milk or being bottle fed progresses to chewing on meat. (Hebrews 6:1–2 BSB) says *"Therefore let us leave the elementary teachings about Christ and go on to maturity, not laying again the foundation of repentance from dead works , and of faith in God, instruction about baptisms, the laying on of hands, the resurrection of the dead, and eternal judgment."* These are basic doctrines, the fundamentals, that must be learned.

We must know and believe that Jesus is God in the flesh (John 1:1, 14 KJV) who bore our sins in His body on the cross (1 Peter 2:24 NIV), who died, was buried, and rose from the dead (1 Cor. 15:1–4 KJV), and that we are justified by faith (Rom. 5:1 KJV). Doctrine is very important, without it we cannot be saved, it defines who we believe in, what we believe concerning God, and what He requires of us. Our faith is essential and non-negotiable to the deity of Christ, the resurrection, and salvation by grace. Maturity comes when your understanding of truth and your actions are one and the same. God want us to mature in Christ; He wants us to have perfect faith. (Hebrew 6:1) "The only way to perfect your relationship with God and improve your walk in holiness is do it by faith and obedience to His Word." —Radio Host Matt Slick spoke these words in one of his online sermons.

People who fail in their learning curve are considered illiterate, and if you can't read or write, eventually you might drop out or have trouble advancing to a higher level. The same principles apply when studying God's Word, you must take it bit by bit and piece by piece. Eventually your study gives you some understanding and advances you to the next level. You have to start to chew on a small piece of the Word a little bit at a time in order to gain ground in it. The more bites you take, the better it starts to taste to you and eventually you start to crave more and more. This is when you find yourself hungering and thirsting for righteousness and getting filled.

As you drink the milk of God, at some point you'll begin to move up a grade and over time your spiritual growth moves past the elementary level and ultimately moves you into a higher educational level. This helps to build a personal relationship between you and God as you learn more and more about who He is to you. This is a very important educational tool to your spiritual growth and it's crucial to learning who you are in Christ and who Christ is. It all starts with first learning the fundamentals. The growing point of chewing on the meat of the Word comes over a period of time, and when you do you become more and more like the Word you've been fed.

What happens if you only learn enough to get through first grade then quit or only go so far or only put in a little effort? You would have started the process without having done enough to move to the next level. You are what we call "left back," "detained," "flunked," which means you have to redo the same level all over again. You can't go straight to graduate school without college or to college without high school, or to high school without elementary school or even get to any of the next educational levels without first learning the basics.

That's sort of how Christianity works. It's constantly educating yourself in Christ, gaining a better understanding and knowledge of who God is but never fully knowing enough yet always seeking to find out more. We have to continue to train our minds to receive God's Word so that we can learn all we can about Him and what His plan is for our lives. We'll never know or fully understand everything, but the more you know the more you grow your faith! It's a lifetime certification.

We are blessed to have a mind's eye glimpse of God's free will. Our dedicated commitment and determination to better ourselves help develop our ambitions and it must never be effortless. Although the impossible is a possibility, gaining ample possession is your goal. You are ever-changing! Everything that you know and everything you learn is changing you day by day. And changing for the better is growth in Jesus and the Word of God.

VII

Faith—Trusting One Another

Faith is unquestioning belief.

God wants to bless you. He wants goodness for all of His children, but He also knows He can only give us what we can handle. If you are fed food too fast, you might choke on what you're eating. If you drink water too quickly, you might cause swelling in your cells because it was too much way too fast and your system isn't designed to handle it at a rapid pace. If God gave us everything we needed at a rapid pace and we couldn't handle it, it could cause someone to choke and possibly spiritually die, because they weren't mentally ready for what He was trying to feed them.

If God made us all rich today, we would forget about Him, because a lot of us would be out shopping for something we don't need. If He allowed us to have everything we wanted right away, some of us would become selfish and greedy and totally forget about Him! If He let us do and be whatever we wanted, the way we wanted, we would think we did it ourselves and become needless of Him; we would start acting like we are all that and it was because of something we had done. That's why He gives us what we need at His pace.

Everyone just cannot be successful, rich, or even poor. What would become of our testimonies if we all had everything or we all had nothing? We would say "there is no God" or "God is not a just

God" or I would not be living like this." Sometimes we are not ready for a blessing, but in the perfect place to just be a blessing to someone.

No one wants to become their own worst enemy, hindering their own blessings by just being out of the will of God when they can just choose Him by faith. Do you resent someone else for being blessed before you, wishing it could have been you? Wishing ill-will on someone else's good fortune is not of God's will for any of us. We should not say or even think negative thoughts toward another's blessing but instead encourage them and be glad with them. When you're fumbling, be grateful that you haven't falling beyond the point of getting back up; then get back up! "We fall down, but we get up" means don't stay down too long when you fall, don't get upset, don't get disappointed with yourself, don't feel bad about what didn't work out; just start again, for with Christ all things are possible.

The Bible tells us that "We are saved by grace" and "His grace is sufficient" these are enough reasons for us to want to try again to make a change in our lives. We have to establish a proper attitude, one that says to ourselves that "I got it going on" with an outward biblical attitude and not one of inner arrogance. Our faith should be like having the application of an ointment that when it's properly applied it develops a natural Christlike healing that glows outwardly. The harsh chemical application of our long time "fake facial scrubs" starts to slowly peel away. We start reflecting the truth now to ourselves as well as to others. We don't have to put on airs any longer, for we are the real deal!

The extent of how we allow Christ to use us will help define who we are for Christ on the inside as well as out, flourishing our God-given gifts. When we begin to seek after the desired change of our nature and realize that life is working for our good, then we'll find ourselves thinking about how our lives were designed by faith through all the things we've endured.

The course we're on to find the proper use of our actions will then be fitting for ourselves to ask the question, "What about me?" It helps start the mending process of our foolish pride that has seeped in. Asking yourself the question, "What about me?" leads us to a moment of self-reflection and an opportunity to meet the person who we have learned to love, that special someone inside of us! You deserve to be pampered, catered to, made to feel important, valued; you're not selfish because you have become self-conscience and aware that if you're caring for everybody else who's caring for you? Ask then, "Who's seeing about me?"

What's God's purpose for [your name] me? As you start to understand that it is okay to ask "What about me?" then you can remove some of your daily stress, alleviate some of the heavy burdens, filter out the junk in your life, turn toward the direction of God and what He has for you, especially now that you know your worth.

We are uniquely made by Christ who loves us, and He recognizes that you're new in Him. God is preparing you for greater works and greater wonders beyond your comprehension, it's a very important life lesson! Reconnect with "thus saith the Lord," and reevaluate your direction; you will then recognize and know for yourself the voice (truth) of God. The Psalmist says *"Be still, and know that I am God"* (Ps. 46:10 KJV). When you allow the flesh to guide your movements, when you are jumping out there too soon without godly counsel first, you're not going to be properly prepared for the service. God has to go ahead of us in order for us to be effective in His ministry and for us to be properly prepared for it.

God really is watching over you. He wants nothing but good things for you; isn't that enough reason to get right with Christ? Isn't it enough for you to want to make a change for nobody else but you? We are the ecclesia of Christ, the church (the called-out body of believers), therefore we should walk worthy of our calling. God called us, He's still calling us, and He will continue to call us. All we need to do is answer the call!

Your call requires reading and studying our Bibles, praying for one another, daily devotion, and going to church for us to truly reap the benefits promised to us; good works alone isn't enough! When we just study, read, go to church, or pray without actions, we are not doing as Christ instructed us to do. He said *"Go ye therefore and teach"* (Matt. 28:19–20 KJV). When we act on the message of God, He receives the glory from our works. It benefits us when we reach out to others gracefully in love, and when we support one another that enforces our growth.

We are family, all God's children, and we need to work together in this fight against evil destruction (Satan). We should teach one another what we know; together we are a stronger unit. In other words, whatever God reveals to you in the understanding of His Word, show it to me and whatever I receive I'll do the same. Working together will help us both grow in the Lord but recognizing our differences (gifts and talents) does as well. In times of struggles read, pray, or study, don't get distracted, take time to step back reevaluate, and ask yourself why it is hard to find a way to a peaceful reassuring mindset.

Once you recognize that Satan is on the battlefield fighting for your life. When these sorts of distractions come, keep pressing on, start recognizing who's causing the disruption. Pray for intervention from Christ daily that Satan cannot get the upper hand in your prayer life. You have to learn how to pray your way through your circumstances, especially during moments like this. And then show someone else how to get through and trust God for themselves, that's putting their faith into action with yours.

Due to the seriousness of the attacks against God's people we have to get ourselves yoked up in the spirit realm with other Christlike people to support one another through the difficult times so that we all endure. Our desire for change in ourselves can begin within the realm of just having a daily faith-based fellowship; you have my back and I have yours. We will survive our mistrusts of one another by stepping up and reaching out, holding on to one another until we can become more accountable to one another. Be sisters and brothers in Christ!

Many of us always question the loyalty of other women, but how much can you love Jesus and He can't trust you to have someone's back in this faith walk! Our loyalty to Him is what truly counts, but we need each other too. We need someone who's willing to walk the walk, not just talk the talk with us to help us stay focused. Don't just go through the motions, become my sisterhood. Are we truly, faithfully, with conviction attempting to do the right things that we know we should be doing: honestly seeking "His face," walking by faith, and believing in the truth, which is the Word of God? Can your reflection of Christ make my reflection of Him greater? as the song writer sang, "I need you; you need me!"

The way we connect together will give us a deeper connection to the blood, by the way we walk together, in the love of Christ Jesus, and by believing that He was born as a child to His virgin mother Mary to fulfill the prophesy, that He died for our sins, He rose on the third day for us, and He's sitting in heaven on the right hand of God waiting to return for us. It's about you and I loving each other as He loved us. It's how you live for Christ. Teach about His love, so you can show others how to love and they too can do the same toward someone else, but it all starts with how we share our love first!

VIII
Meekness—Power Under Control

Meekness is calm confidence, settled assurance, and rest of the soul.

My power is nothing alone, no matter how strong I am physically!

There was a girl I knew many years ago in junior high who would do just about anything to get attention from boys to the degree that she was willing to be untrustworthy to anyone just for her selfish desires. Being so young, it appeared to be a taught act or some unknown force of action she lacked control of; no one really knew!

All people saw was a person willing to give in to whatever was asked, submit to anything that was presentable to the eye gates, someone who was of easy persuasion and had a lack of self-control for all worldly pleasures. It was hard watching the willingness she publicly displayed for everyone see!

Some people might not see a problem while others see recklessness and no home training, yet God sees love for His daughter who hasn't figured out that He has a plan for her life. He sees her as anointed, called, and His chosen vessel, and although she had no power over what was controlling her at that time, she eventually learned that pleasing others was causing her life hurt, harm, and danger and separating her from what God saw in her.

Some of you have judged people sometimes based on what you have finally achieved over the years. You have overcome yours, but there were times you were lacking self-control as well. Our preexisting conditions doesn't disqualify us from God's grace and mercy! Jesus Christ accepted us all in the conditions we were in when He died for our sins. None of us are without sin!

The scripture says, *"the meek . . . shall inherit the earth"* (Matt. 5:5 KJV) author's paraphrase), which means once you become meek, then you will have self-control. Once you achieve self-control you are then humble in heart, teachable, forgiving, confident in spirit, and you will gain your inheritance here on earth; not before! It's a process! Forgive yourself so that you may find the cleansing of your spirits, the detoxification of your minds, and the healing within your hearts!

Meek people doesn't mean weak people; it means patient people, mild-mannered people, kind people who have gained because they are without resentment. My old schoolmate may have been promiscuous and thought the way to be accepted was by being abusive to her body and by negatively mismanaging her worth! Even when the rumors are true and you are privately, publicly, or personally slandered, you can still recover and gain the meekness God desires for you. No level of disrespect or violation can make you useless in the eyes of God!

We are only as useful to one another as we are to ourselves. Treat yourself well and you can treat others as yourself. When you have power of influence use it wisely to help reach people who need reaching. When you have less desires to be only concerned about your plans, your ways, your own ideas, and become concerned about someone else, then your quietness, gentleness, softness, kindness, and calming spirit will be revealed through others.

They'll be able to see your heart of thanksgiving, the peaceful mindset you impart around others, the humility you carry in your words; God will radiate through your spirit of meekness! This is where all your pre-existing conditions, your inadequacies, and your lack is received up and forgiven so that you can rest in the storms of your life without feeling ashamed!

Your quiet spirit is what someone who's living in a life of despair might need to survive the turbulence of their storms. The stillness of your heart being at peace and rest could be the thing that settles the raging fires within someone else's spirit. Your assurances, your confidence just might be the tool for their soul to find rest in a weary land. Your selflessness could deflate the anger, bitterness, and loneliness that sparks within one of your sisters in Christ.

You cannot assume that because someone appears to demonstrate strength, you elude them, because they might not have their power under control, they could be weak in spirit or in need of words that can tame or help to defuse their inappropriate actions. Your words of wisdom, acts of kindness, or showing of love beyond measure will help them to lift up their eyes unto the hills whence cometh their help from the Lord. It enables us to control ourselves, not in having to control others when we are content within our own meekness.

Humility is power under control, your ability to be content must be shown by God's direction, ask Him how to display it to others that you don't come off cocky and arrogant! Consulting with the Lord for guidance is essential, so you don't hurt others who are still getting their power under control.

Inhibited

When you are content it is expressed in your satisfactory display of how God has taken control of the situations that used to cause restlessness within your life. You are able to keep this God-given power in check, subdued, restrained. You are not a wimp; you are not passive; your God-given strength is under submission and you have gained your peace as a result of the strength you are content therewithin.

Once your inner beauty becomes satisfied with what you are expressing outwardly, you'll be less restless, happier, more controlled! The character of the person within you has strength, dignity, and peace that it is now quiet and reserved, not selfish and controlling! It is evident that God is in control of your life.

When we operate from a standpoint of pride, that is foolishness on the part of the person exhibiting it for it only shows that you are concerned for yourself and no one else and you lack contentment, authority over yourself, and harbor a foolish pride. You cannot find delight in the Lord if you have no self-control, and you need to be restored to a rightful position in Christ Jesus! If you are carrying pride, arrogance, weakness and a lack of strength being under control in your flesh, it could cost you everything! Remember, the meek will inherit the earth because they have governed their own spirit accordingly!

IX

Temperance—Self-Restraint... Forgiveness

Temperance in everything is requisite for happiness.

Temperance to be a virtue must be free, and not forced.

Change is a very good thing for it allows you time to transition and refocus, regroup your thoughts, and gain restraint of those things that have occupied your attention! How you act, your thoughts, or how you feel affects your appetites, your passions, and what you desire, for what you chew on and whether or not you can remain abstinent from its use starts with your ability to restrain yourself. Your abstinence from such attractions gives you time to restrain yourself!

Wouldn't you agree that God could have chosen a different course and just decided to leave the world as it was: dark, cold, unpeaceful, and void, and without you and I? Any place without the knowledge of the existence of Christ is a place in deep darkness and a doomed place for in such a place only lost souls reside.

We were so lost in our sinful natures, had taken off all restraints, broken every promise we made, yet the Bible tells us that, *"For the Son of man is come to save that which was lost."* (Matt. 18:11 KJV) In spite of our temperance, God sent forth the light of the gospels to enlighten us and bring forth life and hope that we may be transformed by it.

Though we were lost in sin and in need of change when change isn't an easy thing to do, He still gave us life. Knowing you struggle at being decent, being kind, affectionate, generous, giving, and are filled with various addictions, a lustful nature, adultery, fornication, gossip, hatred, envy, greed, lying, stealing, rape, molestation, bigamy, deceptions, and the list goes on and on, He still signed on the forgiveness line with His blood as Holy, Sanctified, and Saved on our behalf.

We all have something within us preventing us from reaching our fullest potential in God and keeping us from reaching out to one another in spite of our differences. Denial is one of our greatest enemies. It leaves us wondering, *Why didn't I do something sooner that I'm still carrying this unforgiveness within my heart?* The happiness in your lives will depend upon the quality of our thoughts, our joy will only come from God, so refocus your relationship toward Him.

Jesus taught His disciples the Beatitudes because He wanted them to know a guaranteed standard of judgment comes to the fortunate people who were privileged, sanctified, and common people like you and I shall be well-off and blessed immaculately. He said,

> *"Blessed are the poor in spirit, for theirs is the kingdom of heaven. Blessed are those who mourn, for they shall be comforted. Blessed are the meek, for they shall inherit the earth. Blessed are those who hunger and thirst for righteousness, for they shall be filled. Blessed are the merciful, for they shall obtain mercy. Blessed are the pure in heart, for they shall see God. Blessed are the peacemakers, for they shall be called children of God. Blessed are they which are persecuted for righteousness' sake, for theirs is the kingdom of heaven. Blessed are you when they revile and persecute you, and say all kinds of evil against you falsely for My sake. Rejoice and be exceedingly glad, for great is your reward in heaven, for so they persecuted the prophets who were before you."* (Matthew 5:3–12 NIV)

Jesus wanted us to see that it's a blessing when we change our behaviors to His behaviors. We are given assurances that He will take care of us in whatever state we are in as long as we do it all to the glory of God and for His name's sake. Align your life to His will and speak the truth about the Word of God and get your blessed rewards in your existing state. Just how you are right now you will be blessed when you have a beatitude mindset!

"But he said unto them, give ye them to eat. And they said, we have no more but five loaves and two fishes; except we should go and buy meat for all this people" (Luke 9:13 KJV). Jesus is speaking with the disciples and all they could see was a lack; but Jesus was present and He was all the provisions they needed. He had all power, but their mindset impaired their vision.

A Beatitude mindset comes when you're "poor in spirit;" when you show forth a humbling spirit, one without lack, you are content, blessed in this present spiritual kingdom while waiting on the physical kingdom of God to come into existence someday. Poor doesn't mean people who lack material gain, poor in spirit means people who are willing to give of themselves without bragging about it or being arrogant, because they realize that they are in want of God's kingdom more than being unsatisfied with where they are here on earth right now! You are indebted to God for your everything!

"Those who mourn," are those with a sinful nature seeking to find joy for their grievances that only comes from the Holy Spirit who can remove all our lack when we allow Him to examine our inadequacies. Consider how your nature affects how the Holy Spirit grieves over your sins and wants to comfort you. Your mourning can become a good thing when you are mourning as a result of losing your old habits for new righteous ideas, new ways to handle your desires to do wrong. We're crying now because we have been delivered out of the sin that so easily entrapped us! Even knowing that the Holy Spirit grieves should point us to Him for our chastising. He has to correct our bad habits so that we may find comfort in Him; now our mourning can flow toward the joyfulness of Him!

God doesn't take away His grace based on how you should feel from within, what was toxic, but He has given us His grace and mercy freely. God wants us to be Christlike, knowing we are greatly blessed in whatever state we are in. We are "the "Bomb" for and in Christ. Meaning we are great in Him! If we look at Christ being our balm, meaning our healer, then it doesn't matter if we're the bomb or not. What we look like on the outside really doesn't matter. It's our internal spirit that matters to God! How we treat and care for one another is worth more than gold. Jeremiah 8:21–22 (NKJV) says, *"For the hurt of the daughter of my people I am hurt. I am mourning; Astonishment has taken hold of me. Is there no balm in Gilead? Is there no physician there? Why then is there no recovery for the health of the daughter of my people?"* Let Jesus heal you and be a blessing in your mourning.

"Blessed are the Meek," blessed are you when you live righteously, when you show that you are under control in your character! Blessed are the meek when they are not acting self-righteously nor acting out! The inheritance of God comes as a result of your living righteously here on earth, until He returns. You won't see your inheritance in a discombobulated and perplexed state of mind. When your life is confusing, complicated, disconnected from what's right, it's hard maintaining a sense of control. Living frustrated, disoriented, always upset, blabbering off obscenities, talking nonsense, and being out of order isn't displaying inheritance qualities. God wants blessings to flow upon His righteous children who are quiet, reserved—upon you who are soft-spoken, loving, forgiving, kind-hearted, accepting, and gentle in your tone.

What kind of people are "hungering and thirsting for righteousness?" This is a person who has made a life-long commitment of faith, love, peace, and hope; one who has a strong desire to do right by God. They have made a commitment to doing what's righteous, working for God exactly as He commands and have emptied themselves of all unrighteousness.

They have worked diligently at overcoming the desires of their hearts to get right with God, realizing that in order to be filled they must empty themselves of self-assurances, selfishness, and recognize that God has replaced their lack with His righteousness alone. These are people whose so hungry and thirsty and filled with the right motives that they long for Jesus morning, noon, and night, because they want what's right and fulfilling in Him.

The way to show mercy is to obtain it by being merciful toward one another. Someone who is blessed in God, is someone who is "Merciful" in Him as well, for they have shown forth the necessary qualities of mercy in order to receive the mercy of God in return. It is being a forgiving, caring, empathetic, appreciative, kind, generous person who exhibits the same qualities they want God to show toward them.

When you are left wounded by people who have betrayed you, stabbed you in the back by breaking trust barriers, dishonoring your friendship, being disloyal in your relationship, your heart struggles to remain pure. "Being pure in heart" is a beatitude that comes with a heart issue attached to it! One that must be accomplished in order to see God!

It requires that you deal with the effects of your trust issues, the doubts, the pain, the insecurities, and the hurt that has infested your heart that God said He can see in you! *"The Lord does not see as mortals see; they look on the outward appearance, but the Lord looks on the heart."* (1 Samuel 16:7 NRSV) What guilt has hardened your heart and stolen your peace as a result that the manifestation of God has trouble reaching you? To be pure in heart requires regeneration within your heart. Let go and let God restore your heart back to Him.

It's hard to find peace when you've never been peaceful; when you're the person causing the commotion. There are life lessons that we were taught, but to someone else's advantage, we were deprived of our peace as a result of someone's pleasure. How can you find peace or become a peacemaker when you're struggling with you own insecurities? Verse 9 in Matthew says, *"Blessed are the peacemakers: for they shall be called the children of God."*

Being a child of God doesn't mean someone else has to make peace with you, but that you must make peace with all the stuff you've endured that was unpeaceful to you! Your lack of gaining peace is letting someone have your power! You control what has power over your spirit. God wants you to reconcile your differences with your relationships, so that you can help others reconcile their broken relationship with Him. Becoming at peace comes solely from God, and being in harmony with Him will allow you to bring someone else to becoming a child of God and also come into the divine peace of God!

"I was once lost, but now I'm found" is a statement of reverse psychology, especially when you have flipped from a negative thing to another for the better! One side of you wants to continue being unrighteous and the other wants a righteous way of living right. When you are being "persecuted for righteousness' sake" it asks, "What side of the coin are you on?" "Which way of living have you chosen to follow, the self or the right?" "Who are you standing with, the unrighteous or the righteous?" You're being persecuted, but is it for the sake of the Lord?

When I was growing up, I remember seeing things that were very unsettling. Vengeance taken out on people who were innocent, violent acts against people, acts of rage, disrespect, unforgiveness lingering; people casting off all restraints just as they do today. Today it has gotten even worse in our society. *"Where there is no revelation, people cast off restraint".* (Prov. 29:18 NIV) *"Where there is no vision, the people perish"* (Prov. 29:18 KJV).

In order to be blessed you must endure persecution. Persecution should not cause you to take off all restraints to the point that you lose vision and perish. Evildoers are among us and though it may be unsettling, God is our vindicator! *"Blessed are you when they revile and persecute you, and say all kinds of evil against you falsely for My sake"* (Matt. 5:12 KJV).

Everything we speak about that is good and righteous is all for the sake of God and for Him alone. Don't be afraid of being persecuted for speaking out against injustices: for speaking up about the resurrection of Jesus Christ; for speaking for what God has done for you; for speaking up for the one who justified you with His blood! Speak up every opportunity you get, no matter what anyone has to say about it.

Your level of temperance is choosing to have self-restraint, having self-control, being emotionally connected to a healthy life choice. Analyze how you're living. Is it for the glory of God! Your accountability should be to Him and when you are being persecuted for His sake you will have all restraints intact. That's when the rejoicing will take place and you can genuinely rejoice because you are joyful and blessed "and be exceedingly glad for great is your reward in heaven." You are fulfilled with the joy of the Lord when rejoicing takes place as a result of being persecuted for being justifiably righteous.

Get into heaven and rejoice because there's nothing anything nor anybody living here on earth can do about, say about, nor had anything to do with your well-done heavenly reward. You are rejoicing because you were in control of your responses, your actions, your nature; you didn't forget about the limits or who made the decision to remain on the battlefield for the Lord. The test of your patience wasn't compromised, you had control over the harmful forces that tried to restrict you, you remained committed to the relationship you had with Christ, and you prevailed. You remained righteous for the sake of our Lord and Savior and heaven is your reward.

You will see those who have gone on before you someday. Your mothers, fathers, sisters, cousins, grandparents, aunts, uncles, friends, and all those who are in heaven suffered persecution for Christ; therefore, you should expect to go through it as well. *"For so persecuted they the prophets which were before you"* (Matt. 5:12 KJV). You should expect people to betray you, treat you unkind, lie on you for what you do and say for Christ's sake.

Dedicated to: My friends, my sisters, my daughters, myself, and to all women.

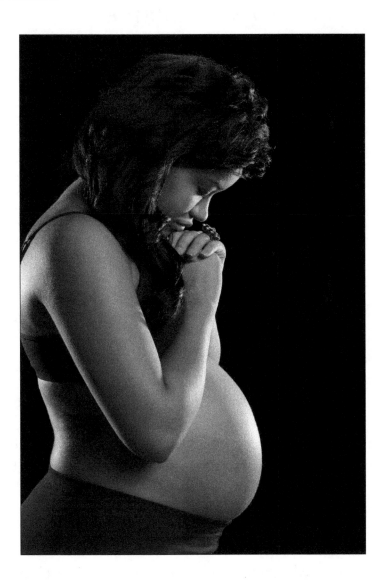

Lord, Deliver Me, So I Can Conceive

(My Droughts and Doubts)

Genesis 1:28 (KJV) *"And God blessed them, and God said unto them, be fruitful, and multiply, and replenish the earth, and subdue it: and have dominion over the fish of the sea, and over the fowl of the air, and over every living thing that moveth upon the earth."*

People who were fruitful and multiplying occurred throughout the entire Bible, in fact some of the most powerful conceptions took place because they believed in their expansion, their multiplication, their fruit. Some even produced although they were barren—God has the power to produce fruit through us, even while you're barren.

What are you carrying spiritually that wants to be delivered?
—You can't get in the birthing position without bring forth Life!

What are you in position to birth that you haven't conceived yet?
—You can't give birth if there's no conception!

God has placed something inside of us all that we must bring forth and give it life.

Were you ever mentally barren, feeling hopeless, yet birth took place in spite of what was said?

What was done to try to prevent it from living?

—God is the one who gives us life!

No one can kill what He has produced, but with a barren mindset we will halt our ability to harvest what we are carrying!

If you don't believe it can happen, then it won't! You can still produce life if you believe that with Christ you can! Your belief system can change your trajectory just by changing how you think about your situations, your circumstances, your course, even how you view your life! When you give birth whatever has been growing inside of you will eventually want you to push so that it can survive.

Here are some examples of barren women in the Bible who conceived when their circumstances didn't look favorable.

Look at Elisabeth and Zachariah she was barren but gave birth to her son John the Baptist, who grew up and baptized Jesus.

—Design appointment!

Abraham and Sarah were both old in age, but they still conceived their son Isaac in their nineties.

—Faithfulness!

Isaac's wife Rebekah was barren, yet he prayed fervently to God and she brought forth life through their twins Esau and Jacob twenty years after Isaac prayed.

—Trustworthy!

Jacob and Rachel—God kept her womb closed, but her love for her husband released her blessing and her womb was open to birth not only one, but two sons: Joseph and Benjamin for the man she loved.

—Loyalty!

And we can't forget Manoah and his wife. The angel of the Lord appeared to her and told her she will have a son although she was known to be a barren woman, but she gave birth to her son Samson, who became a mighty warrior.
—Devotion.

Earthly Conception is to carry life, the joining and fertilizing of what is to be conceived, being pregnant with a promise of life, until it's time to deliver or birth what we are carrying.

Spiritual Conception is to carry life in our spirit, the joining and fertilizing of what is to be conceived, being spiritually pregnant with a promise (the gift of life) from God, until it's time to deliver or birth the gift of the Holy Spirit, which we are carrying.

Don't allow anyone to convince you to give up on being able to be delivered from a barren situation. They can't see what lives inside of you; no one knows what God has purposed to live through you! It's your spiritual baby waiting to be delivered! It's between you and God! It can sometimes appear that you won't produce when you are not in the rightful position for conception. How you live determines how your seed grows. Seek the direction of the Holy Spirit for your rightful positioning. You might not be positioned correctly today, but that doesn't mean tomorrow you won't see your delivery taking place.

Realign yourself—stop doubting yourself, because of what hasn't happened yet, it's on the way! We are carrying what God has produced—conceived—promised us! We will either birth it out or abort it by being stagnant in our believing that it will not come to pass. Our unbelief is how we lose way to its conception! If we have uncertainties about utilizing our gifts then they will die inside of us! And we will miscarry the life God has placed within us!

Millions of women have experienced miscarriages and it's painful. You never forget the hurt, yet you try again to conceive! God wants to help us not to have to go through delivering life that died before we gave birth by putting us in the right environment for our spirits to grab hold of the life we want to someday witness growing up and maturing.

Everyone has their own level of power to conceive, but not everyone will give birth, because some of us have too many doubts holding back our blessings. When you live with fears and regrets, uncertainties block what you are trying to bring forth. You drain the life out of your gifts because you don't believe that you are worthy of the gift, or you fear using them and that hinders the power you have to soar in them.

God wants to deliver us. He wants to set us free from the sin that so easily entangles us up in it! He wants to give us power, strength, and deliver us from the schemes that bind us, the strongholds that have us entangled to them, the emotional roller coaster we ride so freely, so eager to just throw in the towel in our relationships, the financial failures that have filled us with hopelessness. He's trying to prevent us from allowing Satan to kill our seeds before they're fertilized!

We allow the strongholds to pile up on us and attack our spirits, but God says He still wants to deliver us from the things that has us entwined to them, so we can give birth to what He has ordained for our lives. God has a plan and a purpose that must come to pass! No attack can defeat you; no addiction can win against you; no sadness can overthrow you; no death can overtake you; no promise will ever forsake you when you submit yourself to God. Scripture says when you resist the devil, he will flee you. You have to resist the temptations and bring about that gift of life you're carrying.

The Lord wants us to know that He is our hiding place, our refuge, He will protect us from trouble and surround us with songs of deliverance. Just say Lord, Deliver Me! Psalm 34:4 (NIV) says, *"I sought the Lord, and he answered me; he delivered me from all my Fears."* The spiritual attacks that come and the schemes Satan uses to put us in a drought and cause us to have doubts have been cast out; we are blessed, for we have put our trust in the Lord! No drought will cause us to tremble when Jesus has already set us free!

Fulfilling our promise and producing its growth has moments of droughts and doubts, but developing that which is to grow cannot come to full maturity if there are contradictions as to whether or not we allow the promises of God to live or die. Scripture says whoever hears the word of God and believes Him will have eternal life and will not be condemned; he has crossed over from death to life.

Romans 14:8 (NIV) says, *"If we live, we live for the Lord; and if we die, we Die for the Lord. so, whether we live or die, we belong to the Lord."* So, stop focusing on your birthing pain; instead, focus on your process. You are ready to deliver, so concentrate your attention on God! He needs you to be in position to push!

Do what is required to get through your delivery process. Speak life not death, stay encouraged in His word, meditate on the goodness of His majesty, bathe in the splendor of His glory, and appreciate His wonders. Your miracle is ready to be birthed out of you! Profess, "I know the Lord is always with me. I will not be shaken, for He is right beside me. Oh Lord, deliver me!"

Sometimes, it's best to be silent. When we are pregnant with a promise, we have to protect what we are carrying. Don't allow your actions to affect your aura! Don't let your voice overshadow God's illumination!

When we are out of sync, it shows in our actions. Words don't always get interpreted the way we meant for them to be received. Pregnancy brings sensitivity, weariness, irritability, weight that weighs, hunger that lasts, and words that strike! But when you're carry the seed of the Holy Spirit, you have to be in control, display that you have been blessed and you will have dominion over everything God has placed in your hands.

God's promised that He will always be with us, He is always in control, He is always good, He is always watching, and He is always going to be victorious! Don't let your character display anything that delays His promise. When you are expecting, when you are waiting for your territory to enlarge, when you have surrendered your silence, you surrender to God your lack, your doubts, your worries, your uncertainty, your fears, for you are in alignment with your faith!

Believe what you see in your spirit and not what you see in your natural sight; you are on display to be an expansion of Christ! Your delivery should only upset the devil! Satan wants you to believe that you can't bring forth anything productive, nothing more than a wavering attitude, un-settled spirit, un-sureties, doubtful intentions, un-deciding faith, un-believing lack of confidence, and an un-certain road to redemption just one to death and destruction.

Satan doesn't want life to grow from your loins, promises to be fulfilled, barriers to be broken, fences to be mended, brokenness to be rectified, pain to be forgiven. But Scripture teaches us *"Now this is the confidence that we have in him, that if we ask anything according to his will, he hears us,"* (1 John 5:14 NKJV) so start professing that he is Lord, your Father, your Redeemer. You are fearfully and wonderfully made, you are bold in Christ for He is your protector, your provider! Profess that, *"He who dwells in the secret place of the Most-High shall abide under the shadow of the Almighty."* (Psalm 91:1 KJV) You are anointed, stand firm in your faith! Let nothing move you from your birthing position for your laboring in the Lord is not in vain.

If Satan can keep you believing that you are a skeptic, un-worthy, un-loved, un-wanted, un-appreciated, then you might miss the blessings in store for the fruit of your labor. God will keep in perfect peace those of us whose minds are steadfast and whose thoughts stayed on Him! In order for birth to take place you must deal with your pain! Press forward and propel over all limitations in your way! Overcome your obstacles by facing up to them!

Stand firm in the faith! Stand on the Word of God without doubting! Be courageous. Be strong! Never quit believing that you will produce! Live as if your life depends on you delivering what you are carrying! Choose life over death! What's beating on the inside and living within you wants to come to pass, to survive the droughts and the doubts your flesh is undergoing. It wants to be delivered, to survive! Don't give up on you!

So many of our natural eyes have seen things that are against what is true in the spirit, and we have convinced ourselves as a result of what we have seen and experienced that our fruit must be rotten, because we're only seeing the negative side of things when in fact it's ripe and ready to be plucked. The fruit represents all the good inside of you, but somehow, we focus more on our mistakes and mishaps instead of the conquests we've overcome. So, let us not become weary in doing good, for at the proper time we will reap a harvest if we do not give up on ourselves!

Remember that you are who God says that you are, you shall live and not die, your seed shall produce and bring forth good fruit in its season. Our God is the way, the truth, and the life, and His Word cannot return to Him void (unfulfilled). Therefore, what He shows you can only change if you allow what you negatively believe to interfere with what He has already shown you. What He has already ordered in your steps can only be altered by you!

Most of us have doubts about some things and when droughts come, it feels as if we're not going anywhere, that we're not accomplishing nor producing anything. God knows we are struggling with the things that cross our minds and try to lead us astray, that's why He has given us a voice to speak up against such things that come with the intent to cause us bodily harm, spiritual turmoil, or the people, places, or things that are trying to hinder us in any way that causes us to believe we shall fail because we had partaken in them. Claim that you will be an overcomer; that this will not be your storyline.

Open up your mouth and proclaim your liberties, never become captive to anything! Take to heart this scripture, *"The spirit of the Lord God [is] upon me; because the Lord hath anointed me to preach good tidings unto the meek; he hath sent me to bind up the brokenhearted, to proclaim liberty to the captives, and the opening of the prison to [them that are] bound"* (Isa. 61:1 KJV).

Have faith knowing that you can do all things through Christ who strengthens you. Being fruitful and multiplying can come to pass once we recognize the image, and your image is one of the most beautiful sights anyone could imagine seeing. We are created in the image of God and remaining like the image of Christ is how we bear our fruitfulness.

Take the time to abide in Christ Jesus through the created image He has made us to glorify Himself in. Rid yourself of anything or anybody that's a distraction; no matter what you do you cannot please everyone! Sometimes your deliverance is only between you and God. If He is well pleased, carry on! You might have to leave some people behind when you step into your birthing chamber! They might not like what they see radiating from you and dear that their ugly spirits will dim yours and prolong you giving life to your gifts from God.

Don't let anyone stop you from conceiving God's spirit. Remember while you're pushing forward, pressing on, professing what's inside will be great, everyone won't appreciate your elevation! They won't always celebrate the fact that you're pregnant and your visions and dreams are about to birth out greatness! Don't skip a beat by looking back, keep pushing!

When God says push, just push without doubting what's coming forth; then, He will help you to deliver the gifts He has placed inside of you: all your dreams, your fruit, your inspirations, your talents, your unbelievable wonders, even your strongholds will be broken, and you will birth or bring forth life and everything He has for you will be manifested and multiplied out of you, because you believed and you were faithful!

Now that you have started to multiply the image of God and remained faithful in every area of your life, spreading His good fruit all over the world and subduing it, there's no longer any doubt about why you were intended to conceive or why God choose you! You are obedient, grateful, loving, kind, meek, humble in heart, and very caring. Your faithfulness in spreading the glory of God is why you were born to give life and not die! To reproduce God's seed for your womb is blessed!

Be comforted in the hope of God's promises and remember that you must produce, multiply, and give life, for our children will inherit the land and none of them shall be barren in the land. They shall produce more of God's images everywhere they go, and their seed shall continue to multiply as well. Believe in Him for the fruit of your womb, for your producing is of good fruit that keeps on reproducing! When you begin to live according to God's Word, recreating His image is a powerful tool to conceive! Are you in your birthing position?

My Testimony

The unknown life endeavors!

What shakes us up can cause us to stumble, fall, or stand depending on how we handle ourselves in the midst of all the chaos. Do you feel like you're about to fall apart and crumble? Do we have enough faith to weather the storm? Is life a roller coaster that never ends and just keeps going round and round making you dizzier and dizzier? Sometimes the mess we bit on before getting on the ride has us hurtling over the side rail because we weren't as prepared as we had thought. Well, this is us when we don't eat enough spiritual food before getting into a situation that overwhelms us. We have to feed our minds, bodies, and spirits, not just our flesh. We have to be prepared spiritually before the storm comes or we might not find our way through the rumbling of the rain or the howling of the wind raging in our lives.

I remember a time of reading my Bible, singing a gospel song, and laughing with my husband as we walked into the hospital doors. He was having severe backaches just after joining the gym, and we were under the impression that he'd pulled a muscle. I was making unhealthy, "can you keep up with me" silly jokes about how he was out of shape. We were both so full of peace and joy, although he had some pain in his back. We never took time to consider that anything else could be going on. He'd always been very vibrant and outgoing; although we were not in the best shape we could have been in; we were content with who we were.

Inhibited

This is what led us to finally say one day "let's get a membership." We decided that we wanted to feel better, look better, and regain more of the energy we once shared. As we entered the hospital, the atmosphere was so welcoming. It was a new hospital only open about four months, and they were very attentive and immediately gave us a room and showed every concern for our present need.

We were very pleased with the attention we received. The doctors were very thorough and very attentive to my husband's needs. I spoke to my husband about all the attention as they prepared him for some tests just to make sure everything was fine. I remember thinking about how some years ago hospitals used to be a place everyone dreads visiting because it was time-consuming, wearisome, and a very prickly place. It felt like you'll never get out and back to your normal life, to whatever felt normal to you anyway, and yet this visit for us was not a waiting game but an immediate response. It was heaven sent. The immediate response came with direct attentiveness and favor as we patiently gave God praise for directing us to this particular hospital.

As we waited for the results of my husband's back and chest x-rays, we tolerantly collected our thoughts on, prepared for, and even prayed about everything being okay, but nothing could have prepared us for what came next! Immediately as the specialist and doctors approached us with distress covering their faces, we could since their disappointment. It showed though their eyes and silence filled the room as we heard the words "you have cancer." It was as if we had just traveled down an unknown road and fallen into a deep black hole. Not knowing what to expect next. this unfamiliar road had us trying to decide whether or not to hold on or let go of the desire to fear.

What? The shock was like having blurred vision or being in a burning house that just filled the room with a thick black smoke—a smothering, suffocating thick smoke that was rising higher and higher—and we just couldn't seem to find our way out of the nightmare. It came like a windstorm building up around our lungs and choking us out. I found myself thinking about what if . . . , how can this be true…, if only…, why us…, but I never let any of it leave my mouth, for Satan would never rejoice at our expense. We sat there for what seemed like hours, then we said, "Lets pray," so we had prayer together. I don't even remember praying, just speaking and feeling lost in my thoughts, but I believed with my whole heart that God heard every word that was said!

At that moment, being faced with this unfamiliar husband/wife experience that led me to feel like the smoke was choking the life out of me, calling on God helped me to find my way back out of that gloomy moment though it felt like years had passed. God knew that we needed Him and He gave us peace in the midst of our pain.

We were finally able to look at each other in the face all while trying not to alarm the other, then we were finally able to ask "What's next?" We were told possibly surgery, chemotherapy, radiation, EKGs, CAT scan, MRIs, port insertion, bone marrow, brain scan, total body scans, cancer staging, and so many other things I felt my head was back spinning on that roller coaster again. All I could find myself saying was "Jesus…Jesus…Jesus…Healer…Healer…Healer…Provider…Provider…Provider…. What's His name? Jesus!" That song wouldn't leave my head. I thank the song writer for helping me see just who was in control regardless of what man may say.

Although I had trust and belief that God will and already had healed my husband and this is just a faith walk, my life was not the same moving forward. Some days have still become what I call "the unknown." There was such a drastic change. Suddenly, we went from ordinary life into this unfamiliar cycle of life.

My life was hectic, but I could basically count my day's comings and goings like clockwork, because now it involved medications, doctor's appointments, and care giving. In no way am I complaining, for I know this was how God was developing my character into becoming a better person. I just didn't like watching my husband go through and weather this storm physically. It was hard to watch the person you love so dearly losing their hair, growing weary, losing weight, being unable to eat, and having memory loss, enduring all the things associated with sickness of this kind.

One thing I recognized is that it could have been any one of us; we have to support one another, you never know when you might need someone in your corner. *"My brethren, count it all joy when ye fall into divers temptations; Knowing this, that the trying of your faith worketh patience. But let patience have her perfect work, that ye may be perfect and entire, wanting nothing"* (James 1:2–4 KJV). My test was underway and I was working on growing my faith level in this new trial. No matter how great of a disturbance I felt they were, I had to continue to have joy within my trials that my faith may grow stronger in the Lord. We had to endure the test to receive our testimony. I had gone through this ordeal before with my sister who had died of cancer at the youthful age of seventeen and later, I lost my mother to cancer.

Even in knowing that the Bible tells us, *"But of that day and hour knoweth no man, no, not the angels of heaven, but my Father only"* (Matt. 24:36 KJV), we don't know when we will leave this place nor when our Savior will return. But one thing I am assured of is that Jesus knows the plans He has for us and His plan for me was to be by my husband's side in that season. God made a way for us to enter into a brighter day regardless of our current situation. As I sat at my husband's bedside, I began to think about just yesterday. The moments before we ever walked into the hospital, we were sitting in class at divinity school, without a concern . . . and worry free!

I had a moment of recollection, a premonition of my past, of the old person I used to desire to be.

You see, I once was somewhat selfish and self-centered. It was all about Pam living her life in this world anyway she felt. I felt like I had to become again that liberated kind of a woman. I had to learn how to do things for myself that I had become used to my husband doing, and I felt a little selfish about going back to being the woman that I once was many years ago.

Then I remembered that now I am a new creation, and God would never leave me nor forsake His daughter. I was no longer that woman and I knew God had truly changed me! He had given the one true love of my life who now depended on me for his well-being, and I found my strength to give him the best care any wife could give to her husband in his time of need. In my weaknesses I was made strong and became focused on trying to be the backbone and strength for us both.

I watched as he wearily tried to stay focused and be brave for me, but a shadow of fear had set up in his mind as Satan tried to enter into his heart, yet his love of our God savored in his soul and lifted his spirit higher than any disease could ever possibly travel. He assured me that all is well when my comforts were subsiding, yet we had learned together how to lean on and give total dependence to our Lord and Savior and that gave us all the hope, joy, faith, and trust we ever needed. Now this was the new God-centered me!

I became a woman who knew that she must speak life back into her own situation and remember that her source is always and has always been her faith in Jesus and the Word of God. So, I popped in a gospel CD, and began filling our spirits with songs of praise and rejoicing and changed our atmosphere from gloomy to gay!

This is how you defeat Satan at his game, by never allowing yourself to stay in a defeated position but retaining the power given to you in Jesus Christ. We must sing, shout unto the Lord, jump, and dance, continually praising Him and giving thanks in the midst of our circumstances, knowing that the Lord is God and He can get us through anything if we seek Him.

> *Make a joyful noise unto the LORD, all ye lands. /* **Serve the LORD with gladness: come before his presence with singing.** */ Know ye that the LORD he is God: it is he that hath made us, and not we ourselves; we are his people, and the sheep of his pasture. / ⁴Enter into his gates with thanksgiving, and into his courts with praise: be*

thankful unto him, and bless his name. / ⁵For the LORD is good; his mercy is everlasting; and his truth endureth to all generations. (Psalm 100 KJV)

If you're one of those people who doesn't handle bad news well, ask the Lord to give you peace and read scriptures relating to peace of mind. We all might not be faced with this sort of a reality but we all will someday be faced with something that's outside of our comfort zones. Will you be able to handle your persecutions? One day you awake to find yourself as happy as this life could ever bring you here on earth, only to be knocked out with a left hook that begins with the words "we found a large mass on your lungs," "another mass on your sixth rib," "and another mass under your left arm." "We need to do a biopsy; it looks like cancer." This was my reality!

What do you do when you don't know what to do? Where do you turn when it feels like you just hit a brick wall? How do you cope when your backbone has just been crippled? As the song writer said "you just stand," but stand on what? You must learn how to stand on the Word of God by speaking life back into your situation. Motivate the one you love even if that someone who needs motivation is you. The Word of God is such a powerful tool with the necessary force needed to get you out of that smoke-filled room, where you feel like you've taken your last breath and you look up and see a figure in the mist. It's that feeling of relief, of just knowing help is on the way.

When all else has failed and you've done all you can humanly do and now you recognize that you have somewhere you can lay this thing down—the burdens of your heart, the worries, the frustrations, the guilt—and now you can leave it at the cross, knowing the power of God's love is your refuge. When do we run to the city of refuge, for we have all been criminals to something, murderers to ourselves, pretenders instead of defenders, abusers of something or someone, trend-setters of selfishness, slackers, lazy-tasters, which basically means we've all fallen short of the glory of God, that's why we need to flee to the city of refuge where we can confess our sins and be protected by God's grace and mercy, and give Him our burdens.

The Bible tells us of six cities of refuge in Joshua 20:7–8; that as long as you flee to the city of refuge and state your case, you would dwell among the elders; and as long as you were there no harm would come to you. Although it's speaking of the manslayer, one who has killed, we can see it as Satan trying to steal, kill, and destroy us, and our refuge is in Jesus Christ where we can dwell in the midst of Him and have peace of mind, safety, and security in knowing the Word of God is a safe haven for us all. Zechariah 14:11(NASB 1995) says *"People will live in it, and there will no longer be a curse, for Jerusalem will dwell in security."* Deuteronomy 33: tells us"

> *"The eternal God is a dwelling place. And underneath are the everlasting arms, and He drove out the enemy from before you, and said, Destroy!*
>
> *So, Israel dwells in security, the fountain of Jacob secluded, in a land of grain and new wine; His heavens also drop-down dew.*
>
> *Blessed are you, O Israel; Who is like you, a people saved by the LORD, Who is the shield of your help And the sword of your majesty! So, your enemies will cringe before you, And you will tread upon their high places".*
> (Deuteronomy 33:27–29 NASB 1995)

We have a safety net, a secure, reliable, dependable place to turn to when we know we can come to Jesus with cancer, diabetes, leukemia, molestation, abuse, addictions, or anything that may come our way, knowing He cares for us and our safety. We are blessed not defeated.

When we recognize God's security, we can then see His love. The Bible tells us that He cares for us, He abides in us, He chose us, He even created us; how can you not love someone who's done so much for you? The ultimate love of God is shown in these words of scripture, *"For God so loved the world, that he gave his only begotten Son, that whosoever believeth in him should not perish, but have everlasting life"* (John 3:16 KJV).

If God gave us life through the death of His son Jesus and He wants nothing but the submission of our will to His will, then we can have everlasting life filled with peace, hope, joy, and love. We can be secure in the love of God while we go through our storms.

My husband spent his days in rest and peace with God knowing the love of God was his refuge; therefore, he had a safe haven, a secure place to lay his head. This goodwill helped us to get past the storms of our trials and tribulations. We can go through knowing God is with us without being filled with defeat or despair. I know God is keeping me because I haven't cracked, I haven't been committed, I haven't lost my strength, I haven't been discouraged, I haven't forgotten what He's already done for me. I can go on and on about what could have been, but why, for Jesus already paid the price for my sins and now I have such peace, even in knowing my husband had cancer. I can say *had* because, in the name of Jesus, there's healing; in the name of Jesus, there's power; in the name of Jesus, there's victory; in the name of Jesus, there's deliverance; in the name of Jesus, there's everything you need to claim that it's already done.

And today, my husband is a survivor because we had the ample faith to believe God would and could heal him, and God showed us favor over his life. I called on that great name of Jesus and found that was all that I needed to do and you can call on Him too and believe Him for your healing in whatever area of your life you need a touch over.

When your faith has been tried and tested and you've endured your training, then you can encourage someone else instead of them constantly having to encourage you. I found the more love I give the more love I'll receive and not everyone can be lovable but they're love-worthy, so it's not easy but when we think about John 3:16 don't you think that the least we could do is to love one another wholeheartedly. John 15 gives us the standard of what Christ love entails. Love should be a standard, *"This is my commandment, That ye love one another, as I have loved you"* (John 15:12 KJV).

Love should be fervent, show passionate enthusiasm, don't be fake or a pretender of your love, *"Seeing ye have purified your souls in obeying the truth through the Spirit unto unfeigned love of the brethren, see that ye love one another with pure heart fervently"* (1 Peter 1:22 KJV) or *"Beloved, let us love one another: for love is of God; and every one that loveth is born of God, and knoweth God* (1 John 4:7 KJV). This is the power and permanence of God's Word.

Love should also be sincere, be honest and open, mean what you say don't just say what you mean, *"Let love be without dissimulation, abhor that which is evil; cleave to that which is good"* (Rom. 12:9 KJV). Don't disguise or hide your true feelings, thoughts, or intentions let your love for one another be pure. *"For this, Thou shalt not commit adultery, Thou shalt not kill, Thou shalt not steal, Thou shalt not bear false witness, Thou shalt not covet; and if there be any other commandment, it is briefly comprehended in this saying, namely, Thou shalt love thy neighbor as thyself"* (Rom. 13:9 KJV). Be devoted, affectionate, and dedicated; don't be a hater, for hatred is not of God.

God gave us more than we deserve but He doesn't punish us by hurting us or placing sickness upon His children, but you have to be one of His children in order to reap the benefits of His love, power, grace, and mercy. Don't let the circumstances of your life rob you of living your life, loving your life, grabbing hold of your life but first you have to love yourself enough to know that love starts with first knowing Christ and having a personal relationship with him. Get to *know* Him for yourself!

One night I found myself in a place, and God gave me this poem to let me know He was there hearing my heart and carrying me through my circumstances. He loved me enough to put a poem in my heart to let me know He loved me even when I wasn't listening.

How Do I Love Thee?

There are times when we need someone who loves, knows love, and wants to love but won't always know how to love.

Life takes us in search of love from our first breath . . . we breath and cry out for that unknown . . . love.

Birth happened and our first reaction is . . . love!

Sometimes love fails!

Not all will find it in that initial moment; some are left alone longing for it, being rejected and not knowing the why!

Love lived within the surrounding, yet fell outside the limits of my love's space.

Only very few are lucky enough to see, to be, within His reach, His limits.

Love reached out then released, saying, "this wasn't supposed to be, not you, not me," and he left me without . . . without, just without!

I begged, I pleaded, I cried, I tried, then I said "you can't do this to me," "Cannot" He said, "I am not of the love you need, and I was only here for my moments please!"

I thought this was the love of my need. He just had to be!

Wait, I proclaimed, I have searched for my love among the good, the bad, even the ugly—still no reach, so I turned to the happy, the sad, and the beautiful, yet, you still see only me . . . alone . . . still unloved.

"Why me," I moaned? "Why not," he groaned?

Determined, frustrated, and weary I said "enough" . . . I surrender, this is my final request.

I had no more to give! There has to be something real, true, and worthy to live.

Right then I heard someone finally say, "Let me, let me be your love? Let me be what you need? Let me be your one and only?"

Stunned, I reached out, jumped up, looked around; even felt around for this amazing sound; from somewhere, anywhere, he had to be found! Had I found what was supposed to be . . . or was it just unbelief?

My eyes were wide open, mind ready to receive . . . oh love, I called, my heart rapidly beating, but I couldn't find anybody—no one was there to see!

So, in an anxious attempt to see, I said again just a little louder "Who's there speaking and where might you be, and are you sure you're speaking to me?'"

Unaware, unafraid, unsure, I heard once more Him say, "Yes, I've longed for you and your warm embrace. I knew someday we'd meet, your sweet, loving songs, you sang so gently, I hoped they were of me. I watched you and tried to get you to look up at me, but I was blind to thee.

"I even saw you cry and went to wipe your eyes, yet you never looked unto me. My heart was broken watching, the drinking and smoking . . . a broken hymen, shattered spirit, lonely heart, abuse of you is an abuse of me. I reached to you, but you said, he was to be. You told me stories, you showed me a glimpse of your smile, yet you walked right on by me.

"In the morning I waited, hoping you'd notice the breeze I sent your way, just hoping to properly meet you someday, but you just shut the window in my face and kicked up your feet.

"I loved when you danced; I tried to take your hand;

"Oh, how your twirls blew me away, then to my surprise to know who they truly were for, another man . . . instead of mine, you took his hand.

"In the midnight hour I whispered goodnight, but you cuddled your pillow instead, as if you couldn't stand for me to be in your sight or within your night, for you had other plans and he and I could not meet. Although I tried, you fed me your lies, until I said I'm the one who will not forsake thee. At that moment your eyes opened and you finally saw me, for me!

"I had asked you daily to take a stroll with me, to accompany you, just once, but you never spoke a single word to me. You wouldn't let me take your hand and guide us down the trail to comfort your spirit and unveil . . . unveil the internal love to be seen. I needed to just guide you through your grief!

"You preferred to be alone, on your own, surrounded in self-pity, so I left you to be . . . be alone! Alone in a loveless sea . . . without me, for you showed yet another your time, attention you gave, and he continued to fail you in every way . . . this is why you didn't see!

"When I heard you surrender, I knew and remembered the first words I'd ever heard you say, so I laid aside all your past transgressions and accepted your confession, for they were behind us to revisit no more. Our new love was a must, the two had become one. I knew it was real, sincere, forgiving, and true, so I accepted it immediately and we are together to be entrusted.

"Oh, your love is here, I confessed to you in your moans that I would never leave you nor forsake you once you gave me your life and adhered to the truth. You said you needed my love, wanted to be loved and was willing to be my lover forevermore, so I give it freely and your acceptance in return opens up so many new doors. Like a raging fire, shut up in my bones . . .. A roaring lion whose anger has been tamed am I, that mine, my love, has been spared.

"I stood, I waited, I followed you, elated; that I wanted to be your king . . . still there was no turn. I answered, I called, and I pleaded ever so patiently, for you to listen to me. I even became weary trying to be your one and only true love, but I never gave up on you. Did you not know that I am the way, I am the truth, I am the life . . . I am *in you*, and that I loved you for I am Love! Now we are eternally paired. We are joined together though the grace and mercies of my Father who sent me to bring you home. To love you, caress you, show you that He is everlasting to everlasting with only one requirement, that you confess Him as your Lord and Savior and change from your ways to His own! I am He and you are me, so we are forever destined to be . . . together! Heaven is home, so don't stand alone when it awaits . . . *you*!"

Sincerely,

Jesus Christ, Your Lord!

Inhibited